AN INTRODUCTION TO KACHCHAYANA'S GRAMMAR OF THE PALI LANGUAGE

AN INTRODUCTION TO KACHCHAYANA'S GRAMMAR OF THE PALI LANGUAGE;

WITH

AN INTRODUCTION, APPENDIX, NOTES, & C.

BY

JAMES D'ALWIS

GYAN

Published by

GYAN

Gyan Publishing House
5, Ansari Road
Daryaganj, New Delhi-110002
Phone: 011-47034999, 9811692060
E-mail: books@gyanbooks.com

Distribution Network
gyanbooks.com
India, USA, Canada, UK, Australia, France

ISBN: 978-81-212-8001-3 (PB)
First Published, 1863

2nd Impression 2023

Printed at: Gyan Press, Delhi.

AN INTRODUCTION TO KACHCHAYANA'S GRAMMAR OF THE PALI LANGUAGE
Author: JAMES D'ALWIS

KACHCHÀYANA'S PÀLI GRAMMAR.

AN

INTRODUCTION

TO

KACHCHAYANA'S GRAMMAR

OF THE

PÀLI LANGUAGE;

WITH

AN INTRODUCTION, APPENDIX, NOTES, &c.

BY

JAMES D'ALWIS,

MEMBER OF THE CEYLON BRANCH OF THE ROYAL ASIATIC SOCIETY; THE AUTHOR OF AN INTRODUCTION TO SINHALESE GRAMMAR, THE SIDATSANGARA, CONTRIBUTIONS TO ORIENTAL LITERATURE, THE ATTANAGALUVANSA, ETC., ETC.

COLOMBO.

1863.

WILLIAMS AND NORGATE, 14, HENRIETTA STREET, COVENT GARDEN, LONDON; AND 20, SOUTH FREDERICK STREET, EDINBURGH.

To Sir Charles Justin MacCarthy, Kt.
Governor and Commander-in-Chief.
&c., &c., &c.,

Sir,

The practice of inscribing a literary work to the Ruler of the land is very ancient, and very general. In the East it has been almost universal; and in Ceylon, while the Poets and Historians of old sought the patronage of the *King*, the translators and compilers of recent times have dedicated the result of their labours to the British *Governor*.

In inscribing, however, the present work to you, I do not merely follow a time-honored rule, nor seek to do homage to a Power which stands in no need of any evidence of our loyalty and attachment. But, remembering that it was your kind patronage which chiefly enabled me to publish a previous work; and knowing that to you, who are familiar with many of the questions discussed in the following pages, they will possess an interest which they do not possess to the general reader; I take the liberty of dedicating this work, as a token not only of my gratitude, but also of the high esteem which, in common with my countrymen, I entertain for your abilities as a Governor, and your attainments as a Scholar.

I have the honor to be,
Sir,
Your Excellency's
Most obedient and humble Servant,
James Alwis.

Hendala, 28th August, 1862.

THE

INTRODUCTION.

INTRODUCTION.

THERE is hardly a country on the face of the Globe which presents greater facilities for acquiring a knowledge of the *Pali*, than Ceylon; and, perhaps, no nation possesses greater advantages for its study than the Sinhalese. Pali, like the Sanskrit and the Sinhalese, forms a necessary part of the course of education pursued by the natives.* Our Alphabet is common to these several languages,† and the affinity which the Pali bears to the Sinhalese, both verbally and grammatically, renders its study far more easy to the people of this country than even to the Burmese.

Although the Sinhalese, as a language, has been latterly neglected; the Pali, from its being the dialect in which the Buddhist scriptures are recorded, has always been the principal study of the largest portion of the Ceylonese, who are followers of Buddha. From the period when it became the sacred language of the land, kings and princes have encouraged its study; nobles and statesmen have vied with each other to excel in its composition; and in it laymen and priests have produced some of our most elegant works. The names of Batuvantudàve, Hikkaduve, Lankàgoda, Dodanpahàla, Valàna, Bentota, Kahave, and Sumangala, amongst a host of others, are familiar to Pali scholars, as those of the learned who are even *now* able to produce compositions‡ by no means inferior to those of a Buddhagosa or a Paràkkrama, though, like the modern Sanskrit, certainly more artificial than some of the more ancient writings.

* See my Sidatsangarà, p. 222.
† Ib. p. xi., et seq.
‡ For a specimen, See Appendix.

The number of books, too, in the Pali language, is greater than in the Sinhalese; and, though those on Religion far exceed those upon other subjects, it is, nevertheless, a fact, that the Pali literature of the Sinhalese is not deficient in works upon other branches of Oriental Science. It presents indeed a proud array of extensive volumes on Prosody, Rhetoric, Medicine, and History. On Grammar alone there are no less than forty Pali works;* whilst in the Sinhalese there is but one, the solitary Sidat-Sangarà. From the constant study of Pali in the Buddhist monasteries of this island, the books in that language are found to be comparatively free from errors: and it is a well known fact, that the Buddhist priests, unlike the Brahmans, are willing to give Pali scholars, whether Buddhist or Christian, free access to their libraries.

Advantages like these, combined with others, enabled the Hon'ble George Turnour, late Colonial Secretary of Ceylon, to attract the attention of Orientalists to the high claims of the Pali language as existing in Ceylon. In the prosecution of his labours with such a praiseworthy object, he drew attention, in his elaborate Introduction to the Mahàvansa, to some of the Pali works formerly extant in Ceylon, and, amongst them, to Kachchàyana's Grammar, which he then regarded as extinct. This, in the very outset of my Pali studies, after many years' devotion to Sinhalese literature, I ascertained to be a mistake;† having added it to my library, in a purchase

---

* "The high state of cultivation to which the Pali language was carried, and the great attention that has been paid to it in Ceylon, may be inferred from the fact that a list of works in the possession of the Singhalese, that I found during my residence in that Island, includes thirty-five works on Pali Grammar, some of them being of considerable extent."—Rev. S. Hardy's *Eastern Monachism*, pp. 191-2.

† I find that this is also extant in Burmah. The Rev. F. Mason of the Baptist Union says:—'The grammar reputed to have been written by Kachchàyana, still exists. I had a copy made from the palm-leaf, on small quarto paper, and the Pali text occupies between two and three hundred pages, while the Burmese interpretation covers more than two thousand. I

of Pali books which I had then (1855) recently made from the collection of the late lamented F. D' Levera, Esq., District Judge of Colombo. Shortly afterwards I communicated the fact to some of my friends in Europe; and the repeated communications which I have received from them, especially from Dr. Rost of Canterbury, urging upon me the necessity for the publication of a Pali Grammar, and expressing a curiosity to examine Kachchàyana, have induced me to publish a Chapter from it, as an Introduction to a fuller translation.

In laying this before the public, I propose to give a brief account of some of the Pali Grammars known in this country, including a notice of the age and author of the work here presented; and also an Essay on the relations of the Pali to the Sanskrit.

The terms *Pali* and *Màgadhì* are at the present day indifferently employed in Ceylon, Ava, Siam, and even China, to express the sacred language of the Buddhists; and, being confined to those countries, the term *Pali* is not met with in any of the Indian writings.

Màgadhì is the correct and original name for the Pali. It was not so called in consequence, as some suppose, of the mission of Asoka, the king of Magadha, to introduce Buddhism into Ceylon.* It had received that name before the age of that monarch,† and was so called after the ancient name of Behar. It was the appellation for the ancient vernacular language of Magadha. It was the designation for the dialect of the Magadhas.—*Magadhanan bhàsà Màgadhì.*‡

made a compendium of the whole Pali and English, a few years ago, on the model of European Grammars, which might be printed in one or two hundred pages, and convey all the information contained in the two or three thousand in manuscript.'—*Am. Or. Journal*, iv. p. 107.

* *Professor Spiegel's Kammavachà*, p. vii.

† See *Sanyut Sangiya.*

‡ *Pràkrit Prakàsa*, p. 179.

Pàli is comparatively a modern name for the *Màgadhi*. It has not originated from 'the region called *Pallistan* the (supposed) land of the *Pali*,—our *Palestine*.' It does not come from *Palitur* in Tyre—the so-called 'Pali tower or Fort.' It has no historical connection with 'the Palatine hills of Rome.'* It was not called after the Pehlve, the dialect of the Sessanian dynasty, nor is it derived from "*Palli* a village, as we should now-a-days distinguish *gunavàri* 'village,' 'boorish,' from *Urdu*, the language of the Court."† Nor does it indeed *mean* "root" or "original."‡

Like *àli* the word *pàli* originally signified a 'line,' 'row,' 'range,'§ and was gradually extended to mean 'suttan,' from its being like a line;‖ and to signify edicts,¶ or the strings of rules in Buddha's discourses or doctrines, which are taken from the Suttans.** From thence it became an appellation for the *text* of the Buddhist Scriptures, as in the following passages:—

---

* See the Friend, vi. p. 236.

† Prinsep, Bengal As. J., vii. p. 282.

‡ Turnour's Mahàvansa, p. xxii., where he merely gives the opinion of the Buddhists; and this is no more correct than the Brahmanical opinion, that Pràkrita means 'the derived.'—Vide post, p. xxxix.

§ See Abhidhànapadipikà, p. 71. It is indeed not a little curious that Mohammedans, between whom and the Buddhists there was no intercourse at the period when their sacred books were written, call the larger portions of the Koran "Sowar," ('Sura,' Sing.) signifying precisely as the word *Pàli* does, 'a row, order, or regular series.' The Arabic Sùra, whether immediately derived from the Sanskrit 'Sreni' or not,—is the same in use and import as the *Sura* or *Tora* of the Jews, who also call the fifty-three Sections of the Pentateuch, *Sidàrim*, a word of the same signification.

‖ Itaran pana; Atthànan sùchanato; sùvattato savana totha sùdanato Suttànato sutta sabhà gatocha suttan suttanti akkhàtan.

'The other (which is) the *Suttan*, is called '*Suttan*' from its illustrating the properties (of duties); from its exquisite tenor; from its being productive (of much sense); and from its overflowing (tendency) the protection (which it affords); and *from its being like a string*.'—*Buddhagosa's Atthakathà*.

¶ Hevan cha hevan cha me pàliyo vadetha: 'Thus, thus shall ye cause to be read my *pàliyo* or edicts.'—*Prinsep's Asoka Inscrip.*

** Yattàcha suttena sangahitàni pupphàni navi kiriyanti naviddhan siyanti eva me thena sangahìta atthà. 'As flowers strung together with a string are not scattered, so likewise the *doctrines* which are taken from this (Suttan) are not lost.'—*Sumangala Vilàsini.*

Thereyàchariyà sabbe Pàlin viya Tamaggahun:—'All the three preceptors held this compilation in the same estimation as the *text* (of the Pitakattàya).'* Thera vàdehi pàlehi padehi vyanjanehicha. 'In the *Thera discourses* as in the *text* (of the Pitakattàya); and in an expression as in a letter.'† From thence again *Pàli* has become the name of the Màgadhì language in which Buddha delivered his doctrines.

The Pali has also received the designation of *Tanti*, 'the string of a lute,'‡ its Sanskrit cognate being *tantri*. From that signification it seems to have been originally applied by the Brahmans to *tantra*, 'a religious treatise teaching peculiar and mystical formula and rites for the worship of their deities, or the attainment of super-human power,' or, 'that which is comprized of five subjects, the creation and destruction of the world, the worship of the gods, the attainment of all objects, magical rites for the acquirement of six super-human faculties, and four modes of union with the spirit by meditation.'§ The Magadhas, before their secession from the Brahman religion, probably used the Màgadhì term, *tanti* in this sense; but when they embraced the Buddhist faith, they used it to signify the *doctrines* of Gotama, as in the following passages:— (i) Sammà Sambuddho pi te pitakan Buddha vachanan *Tantin* àropento Màgadhì bàsàyeva aropesi—'Buddha who rendered his *tepitaka* words into Tanti (or tantra or *doctrines*) did so by means of the Màgadhì language'—*Vibhanga Atuvà.* (ii) Tivagga sangahan chatuttinsa suttanta patimanditan chatu satthi bhànavàra parimànan tantin sangàyetvà ayan dìgha nikàyo nàmà'ti—'Having rehearsed the *Tanti* (the doctrines) which contain 64 *banavàra* embracing 34 *Suttans* composed of 3 classes, (this was) named Dìghanikàya'—*Bodhivansa.*

---

* Mahavansa, p. 253.
† Ib. p. 252.
‡ Abhidhànapadìpikà, p. 16.
§ Wilson's Sanskrit Dictionary.

From its application to the Buddhist doctrines, *Tanti* has become a name for the sacred language itself of the Buddhists—viz., the *Màgadhì* or *Pàli.* Thus in Buddhagosa's Atthakathà:—'Why was the first convocation held? In order that the *nidànan* of the *Vinaya pitaka*, the merits of which are conveyed in the *Tanti* (Pàli) language, might be illustrated.'* Thus also, in the *Bàlavatàra*, in a part of the passage which answers to §58 in the Rev. B. Clough's version, where it is left untranslated:—

Eva maññà pi viññeyyà
Sanhità tanti yà hità;
Sanhità chita vannànan
Sannidha'byava dhànato.

That is to say, 'In this wise know the rest of the combinations which are susceptible in the *Tanti* (language.)—*Sanhita* is the combination of letters without a hiatus.'

For the elucidation of the grammar of this language there are three schools; or, in other words, all Pali Grammars extant in Ceylon may be divided into three classes, viz., (1) Saddanìti; (2) Moggallàyana; and (3) Kachchàyana.

1. There are but few treatises which come under the first.

2. Under the second head there are several, all which have been written upon the principles laid down by Moggallàyana, the writer of Abhidhànapadìpikà. Owing to the omission of the *Introduction* and *Conclusion* of that work in the edition published by the Rev. B. Clough, oriental scholars have expressed various conjectures as to its date. As a help, however, to those who may be engaged in antiquarian researches, and with a view to fix the date of Moggallàyana, the omissions are here supplied.

* B. A. J., vol. vi. p. 511.—Pathama mahà sangìti nàma esà kinchà-pi vinaya pitake *Tanti*'n àrulhà. 'This first great rehearsal was moreover rendered into *tanti*, (the original discourses or the text) on the Vinaya Pitaka,'—*Sumangala Vilàsinì.*

Abhidhanapadipika.

1. Tathàgato yo karunà karo karo
'Payàtamossajja sukhap padan padan
Akà paratthan kalisam bhave bhave
Namàmi tan kevala duk-karan karan

2. Apùjayun yam muni kunjarà jarà
'Rujàdimuttà yahimuttare tare
*T*hità tiva*tt*ambu nidhin narà'narà
Tarinsu tan dhamama' maghà pahan' pahan

3. Gatan munindo' rasasûnutan nutan
Supuññakhettan bhuvane'sutan sutan
Ganampi pànì kata sanvaran varan
Sadà guno' ghena nirantaran taran

4. Nàma lingesu kossallam
'Attha nichchhaya kàranam
Yato mahabbalan Buddha
Vachane pà*t*a vatthinam.

5. Nàmalingàn' yato Buddha
Bhàsitassà' rahà n'aham
Dassayanto pakàsissam
Abhidhàna' padìpikan.

6. Bhìyo rùpan tarà sàha
'Chariyena cha katthachi
Kvachà' hachcha vidhànena
*N*eyyan thìpun napunsakan.

7. Abhinna lingìnan yeva
Dvando cha linga vàchakà
Gàthà pàdanta majjha*tth*à
Pubban yantya'pare parán.

8. Pumitthiyan padan dvìsu
Sabba linge cha tìsviti
Abhidhànan tarà rambhe
*N*eyyan tvanta mathàdi cha.

9. Bhìyo payoga màgamma
Sogate àgame kvachi
Nighandu yuttin chànìya
Nàma lingan kathìyati.

'I adore *Tathàgata*, who is a mine of compassion, and who, having renounced the beatific *nibban* within his reach, conferred happiness on others, performing all the difficult-to-be-accomplished acts in metempsychosis, the fountain of sin.

'I (adore) the sin-scaring *Dhamma*, to which holy sages, devoid of decrepitude and disease, have paid reverence; and by conformance to which the high and the mean, both (amongst) men and other beings,* have crossed the tri-annular† ocean (of metempsychosis.)

'And ever (do I adore) the supreme *priesthood*, (like unto) a merit-(producing) field, who have become the legitimate sons‡ of Buddha; and who receive reverence—are illustrious in the (three) worlds—preserve the *sanvara* § like life itself—and ever practise an abundance of virtues.

'Since an intimate acquaintance with *nouns*, and (their) *genders*, is essential to the (ascertainment of) the correct significations (of words), and is a powerful help to those desirous of mastering the word of Buddha;

---

* "*Nara* and *ànara* 'human and non-human.'

† The "*tivattambunidi*." 'The ocean, encompassed with three circles, is here used for "metempsychosis;" and the three barriers are *Kamma*, action which begets merit and demerit; *Klesa* evil, trouble, pain or sorrow; and "*Vipàka*" the rewards of merit and demerit.'

‡ *Sons*—a term applied to disciples.

§ That is, 'Preserve the *Sila* or precepts.'

'I shall publish the Abhidhànapadìpiká,* illustrating *nouns* and (their) *genders*, according to their application in the language of (the discourses of) Buddha.

'The masculine, feminine, and neuter are to be distinguished, chiefly, from their different forms; sometimes from the association of words (context); and sometimes by specific rule.

'[In this work] *dvanda* compounds will consist (of nouns) of the same genders. When words which denote the genders occur at the end or the middle of a line in a verse, (such words) refer to the (names at the) beginning (of that line); (but where they are placed at) the commencement, (they refer to) the remaining words (of the same line.)

'Know that the term *dvìsu* denotes both masculine and feminine; that *tísu* signifies all the genders; and that words ending in *tu* or (preceded by) *atha* &c., are given to express the commencement of a series of names.

'Nouns and (their) genders are (here) illustrated, according to their application, chiefly in the Buddhist works, and sometimes after the usage adopted in Lexicons.'

The above is the Introduction to the *Abhidhànapadìpikà*; and I cannot conceive why it was omitted in the translation of that work by Mr. Tolfrey, and was left out by his publisher, the Revd. B. Clough. At the conclusion of the same book are also nine stanzas, which are likewise left out in the publication above mentioned; and which, since they enable us to fix the date of the work, are here subjoined :—

1 Sagga kan*d*o cha bhù kan*d*o
Tathà sàmañña kan*d*akan
Kan*d*attayanvità esà
Abhidhàna padìpiká.

2 Tidive mahiyan bhujagá vasathe
Sakalattha samavhaya dípani'yam
Iha yo kusalo matimá sanaro
Pa*t*u hoti mahámunino vachane.

* Lit.—" Lamp of Nouns."

3 Parakkama bhujo nàma
Bhùpàlo guna bhùsano
Lankàya' mási tejassì
Jayì kesari vikkamo.
4 Vibhinnan chiran bhikkhu sanghan nikàya
Tayasmin cha kàresi sammà sammagge
Sadehanva nichchà 'daro dìgha kàlan
Mahagghehi rakkhesi yo pachchayehi.
5 Yena Lankà vihàrehi
Gàmà'ràma purìhicha
Kittiyáviya sambodhi
Katá khettehi vápihì.
6 Yassà' sàdhàranan patvà
'Nuggaham sabba kàmadam
Ahampi gandha kàrattam
Patto vibudha gocharam.
7 Kàrite tena pàssàda
Gopuràdi vibhùsite
Sagga kan*d*eva tattoyà
Sayasmin pa*t*ibimbite
8 Mahà Jetavanà khyamhi
Vihàre sàdhu sammate
Sarogàma samùhamhi
Vasatà santa vuttinà.
9 Saddhamma*tth*iti kámena
Moggallànena dhìmatà
Therena rachitá yesà
Abhidhànapadìpikà.

'The Abhidhànapadípikà consists of three sections—on Heavenly, Earthly, and General subjects.

'It interprets the names of all objects in Heaven, Earth, and the Nága regions. A sensible person who excels in this, will master the words of the great sage.

'There was in Lankà a Monarch named *Parakkamabáhu* —celebrated, successful, endowed with virtues, and valorous as a lion.

'He in the right manner (in the legitimate mode) reconciled* the *bhikkhus* and *Sanghas* of the three *Nikàyas*;† and, with unceasing love, long extended his protection to (them) as to his own body, with valuable objects of maintenance.‡

'He established to profusion in Lankà, in the same manner that it was filled with his renown,§ monasteries,¶ villages,|| parks,** cities,†† fields‡‡ and tanks.§§

'Being the special object of his wish-conferring patronage, I too, have acquired the privilege of authorship peculiar to the learned.

'Desirous of perpetuating the *Saddhamma*, the Abhidhánapadìpiká was composed by the erudite Moggallána *thera*,

'Of mild deportment, dwelling amongst the *Sarogàma*¶¶ fraternity (who were) received by the virtuous with approbation; and (residing) in the Vohára called the *Mahà Jetavana*;—

'[A monastic Establishment] adorned with the temples, ornamented porches, &c., which were built by him (the aforesaid king) as it were a portion of Heaven reflected in his Tank.'

Here we have sufficient data to fix the date of the *Abhidhánapadípikà*. It was composed by a *thera* named Moggallàna, who had been patronized by king *Parakkama*. His

---

* "He reformed the religion."—Upham Vol. I. p. 299.

† "Association or Congregation performing the same duties."

‡ *Pachchaya*—"Objects of maintenance" which are four, viz., *chivara* 'garments'; *pindapata* 'food'; *Senasana* 'sleeping objects'; *gilana pachchaya* 'that which is necessary for the sick—medicines."

§ See Ceylon Almanac for 1834.

¶ "He built the Viharas in the City of Anuradhapura"—*ib.* at p. 190.

|| "The King also made several hundreds of houses and many streets arranged with shops."—*Mahawansa.*

** "He formed many pleasant and delightful gardens."—*Mah.* C. B. A. S. J. p. 148.

†† "He built three more Cities."—*Upham's Mahawansa*, p. 277.

‡‡ "He formed Paddy fields."—*Mah.* C. B. A. S. J., Vol. VII., p. 141.

§§ "The King also repaired many ancient Tanks."—*Mahawansa, ib.* p. 149.

¶¶ This is a Pali translation of the Sinhalese proper name *Velgam.*

acts, which are here related, can only be identified with those of "the heroic and invincible royal warrior, gloriously endowed with might, majesty, and wisdom; and radient with benignant virtues,"* "the most martial, enterprising and glorious of the Sinhalese Sovereigns,"† who, according to history, was Parakkamabàhu of Polonnoruva. He ascended the throne in 1153 A. D.; and when we notice that that sovereign, who reigned for thirty-three years, turned his attention to the internal improvements which are here mentioned, in the latter part of his reign, and after he had brought his local and foreign wars to a termination; we may assign to the Abhidhánapadípikà a date at the latter end of the second half of the twelfth century. This, therefore, is posterior to the Amarakosa, which is much after the fashion of the Abhidhànapadípikà. To show their correspondence we need only present the three following introductory stanzas from the first named work.

'The masculine, feminine, and neuter (genders) are to be known chiefly by their different forms; sometimes by the association of words; and sometimes by specific rule.

'Here, with a view to distinct elucidation (nouns of) different unspecified genders are not rendered into *dvanda* compounds. Neither are they, without order, jumbled together; nor indeed expressed by *eka sesha*.‡

'The term *tríshu* (denotes) the three genders; and *dvayoh* the male and female. (Where a certain) gender is expressly negatived, the remaining ones (are meant); and, where words ending in *tu* (occur or) *atha*, &c., they do not refer to the preceding (words).'

---

* Inscription in Ceylon Almanac for 1831.

† Mahawansa, p. lxvi.

‡ *Eka seshah*: "one left out" *i. e.*, the omission of one to designate the same by another, which has been mentioned; or, conversely, the expression of one name to designate another omitted name of the same genus or family; as Asvinau "the two Asvin," in the dual, designate 'the Physicians of heaven, and twin sons of the sun, or children of the constellation *Asvini*,' who are separately named Nasatya and Dasra.

Moggallàyana's Grammar, to which we may assign the same date that was given to the Abhidhànapadípiká, is written in imitation of Kachchāna's style; and contains rules, supplementary notes or *Vutti;* and examples. The same writer has left behind a large commentary on this work. It has been further illustrated by Totagamuva* in his *Panchikà-pradìpa*, a Sinhalese work, held in high esteem among the learned. Piyadassi, a pupil of Moggaláyana has, moreover, written an abridgment of his master's work, called the *Pada-Sádana,* from which the following is extracted:—

Satthànam karunà vatà gatavatà
Pàram param dhìmatà
There nà 'tuma pàdapanjara gato
Yo sadda satthà disù.
Moggallàyana vissute niha suvach
'Chàpo viníto yathà
So' kàsip Piyadassi nàma yati 'dam
Byattan Sukhappattiyà.

'With a view to facilitate (study) this specific (work) has been composed by the ascetic named Piyadassi, who, like a paroquet which was taken into the cage of his (feet) tuition, was trained in the science of grammar &c., by the wise, generous, and erudite† Moggalláyana *thera* of (world-wide) renown.'

There is also a Commentary on the above by *Ananda,* a pupil of Medankara; from which we select the following introductory remarks:—

1. **Yassà tulan samadhi gamya parappasàdan**
Sampàditam parahitan vipulan mayedam
So sangha rakkhita itìrita nàma dheyyo
Bhànùva bhàtu suchiràya mahàdisàmi.

2, **Saddhà dhanassa patipatti paràyanassa**
Sallekhiyena likhità khila kibbisassa
Odumbarà bhi hita pabbata vàsi kassa
Medankaravhaya mahà yati pungavassa.

---

* See my Sidatsangara p. li.

† Lit. 'who has attained to the end of sciences.'

3, Sìladi settha patipatti paràmugena
Sisso-rasena saparattha ratena tena
Ananda nàma pathi tena tapo dhanena
Sankhepato nigadito Padasàdhanattho.

1. 'May the Supreme Lord named Sangharakkhita, by the acquirement of whose unparalleled patriotism* this great benevolent (deed) has been achieved by me, long exist like the sun!

2 and 3. 'The Padasàdana has been concisely commented upon by the ascetic known by the name of Ananda, (who is) bent upon doing good to himself and others; (who has) adhered to the principal (religious) usages of *Sìla* &c.; (and who is) a pupil† of the preeminent chief-priest named Medankara, that dwelt on the Mountain called Odumbara,—(was) rich in faith, (was) attached to (religious) duties, and (had) scratched off all sin by *Sallekhiya*.'‡

Payogasiddhi by Vanaratana, in the reign of one of the Buvanekabàhu's, is also a Pali Grammar upon the basis of Moggaláyana, from the Commentary to which Turnour has quoted in his introduction to the Mahavansa.

3. The next, and, by far the most numerous, class of Pali Grammars are founded on the principles enunciated in the *Sandhikappa*, usually called after the name of its author *Kachchàyana*. This, as I have already stated, is extant in Ceylon; and, from a list of Burman Pali works in my possession, I find that it is also found in that empire. The several other editions or revisions of Kachcháyana's Grammar, which, as remarked by Mr. Turnour, "profess, according as its date is more modern, to be more condensed, and methodized than the preceding one", are the Rúpasiddhi and Bàlavatára.

Buddhappiyo commences the Rùpasiddhi in these words: "Kachchàyananchàchariyan namitwà; nissàya Kachchàyanawannanàdin, bàlappabodhatthamujun karissan wyattan sukandan padarúpasiddhin."

* Lit. 'love for others.'
† Lit. 'Son-pupil.'
‡ 'Those religious observances which lead to the destruction of *keles*.'

"Reverentially bowing down to the Achárayo-Kachchàno, and guided by the rules laid down by the said Kachchàyano, I compose the Rùpasiddhi, in a perspicuous form; judiciously subdivided into sections, for the use of degenerated intellects (of the present age, which could not grasp the original.)"—*Mahàvansa*, p. xxvi.

The following is in the conclusion of the same work :—

"Wikkhyàtànandatherawhaya waragurùnan Tambapanniddhajánan sisso Dípankaràkkhyo Damilawasumatí dípaladdhappakàso Bàlàdichchàdi wásaddwitayamadhiwasan, sàsanan jotayí yo, soyam Buddhappi-yawho yatí; imamujukan Rùpasiddhin akàsi.

"A certain disciple of Anando, a preceptor who was (a rallying point) unto eminent preceptors like unto a standard, in Tambapanni, named Dípankaro, renowned in the Damila kingdom (of Chola) and the resident-superior of two frater nities, there, the Bàládichchá (and the Chudàmanikyo), caused the religon (of Buddho) to shine forth. He was the priest who obtained the appellation of Buddhappiyo (the delight o Buddho,) and compiled this perfect Rùpasiddhi."—*Mahàvansa*, p. xxvi.

Before I notice the principal and the oldest work with which we are concerned, viz., Kachchàyana's Grammar, I shall mention the names of some of the principal Comments thereon to which I shall have occasian to refer in the course of these notes; viz.

Nyàsa or Mukhamatta Dìpana
Kachchàyana bheda
Kachchàyana bhede *T*ìkà
Kachchàyana bhede Vannanà.
Kachchàyana Vannanà
Kachchàyana Sàra
Kachchàyana Sàra *T*ìkà
Sandhikappa Atuvà
Sandhikappa Viggahà.*

* For a list of Pali Grammars, see Appendix.

All these have been written expressly for the purpose of elucidating the text of Kachcháyana, which, I need scarcely say, is held in the same high estimation by Buddhists that Pánini is by the Brahmans.

Kachchàyana's Grammar is divided into eightbooks. The first treats on 'Combination', the second on 'Declension', the third on 'Syntax', the fourth on 'Compounds', the fifth on (Tadhita) 'nominal Derivatives,' the sixth on 'Verbs', the seventh on (Kitaka) 'verbal derivatives,' and the eighth on *Unnádi* Affix es.'

These are found subdivided into Chapters or Sections. But, all the aphorisms do not exceed six hundred and eighty seven.* The following extract embraces the writer's introductory remarks, together with the first Section of his Grammar :—

Se*tt*han tiloka m ahitan abhivandi yaggan
Buddhan cha dhamma' mamalan gana' mutta mancha
Satthussa tassa vachanattha varan subuddhun
Vakkhàmi sutta hita' mettha su Sandhikappan.
Seyyan Jinerita nayena buddhà labhanti
Tanchà'pi tassa vachanattha subhodhanena
Attan cha akkhara padesu amoha bhàvà
Seyyatthi ko pada'mato vividhan suneyya.

'Having reverentially bowed down to the supreme chief Buddha adored by the three worlds, and also to the pure *dhamma*, and the illustrious priesthood; I now celebrate† the (pure) Sandhikappa in accordance with the *Sutta*, to the end that the deep import of that teacher's words may be easily comprehended.

'The wise attain to supreme (bliss) by conforming (themselves) to the teachings of Buddha. That (is the re-

* *Satta situttana Sutta*
cha *sata* sun pam*a*n*ato*=687 Suttans.

† *Vakkhami* "I utter"—The true import of this word taken in connection with the allegation that 'Kachchayana published (pak*asesi*) his Grammar in the midst of the priesthood' may lead to the inference that it had at first only a memorial existence. But, since the same words are found used in works which were doubtless *written* from the beginning, the phraseology alone does not, I apprehend, warrant that inference.

sult) of a correct acquaintance with the import of his word. The sense, too, (is learnt) by a [non-ignorance] knowledge of characters and words. Wherefore, let him who aims at that highest felicity hear the various verbal forms.'

Lib. I. Section 1.

1. Attho akkhara saññàto.

The sense is known by letters.

2. Akkharà pàdayo eka chattàlisan.

The letters, *a* &c., are forty one *

3. Tattho dantà sarà *att*ha.

Of these the eight ending with *o* are vowels.

4. Lahumattà tayo rassà.

The three light-measured (are) short.

5. Aññe dìghà.

The others, (are) long.

6. Sesà byanjanà.

The rest are consonants.

7. Vaggà pancha panchàso mantà.

Each (set of) five to the end of *m* (constitutes) a class.

8. An iti niggahìtan.

The *An*† is a dependent.

9. Para samaññà payoge.‡

Other's names in composition.

10. Pubba' madho'-*t*hitam' assaran sarena viyojaye.

Let the first be separated from its (inherent) vowel, by (rendering) the *preceding*§ a consonant.

Such is the sententions brevity with which the Rules in Kachcháyana's Grammar are expressed. The author adopts three modes of explaining them. First, *Vuttiyá* or

* Moggallayana disputes the correctness of this *Suttan*, and says that the Pali, alphabet contains forty-*three* characters, including the short *e* (epsilon) and *o* (omicron.) The Sinhalese Alphabet, which is nearly as old as the Sinhalese nation also omits these. This is evidence of that language being derived from the Pali.

† The *anusvara*.

‡ Names or technical terms.

§ *Adho-thitam* "that which stands below [after such separation.]" The word *below* must however be understood to mean *preceding*; for in composition, which Eastern writers regard as a tree from *bottom to top*, the first-written character is considered as being at the *bottom or below* the rest.

Várttikas, comments to supply the deficiencies in the Suttas, and to render them clear; secondly examples; and thirdly explanatory notes on some of the principal grammatical terms in the shape of questions and answers. To these again are occasionally added a note to mark the exceptions to the Rule. In the examples mention is made of several of the places and towns which were rendered sacred by the abode of Gòtama, such as *Sàvatti, Patáli, Baranasí* &c.* There is also much correspondence between the Páninya Sutras and those given in Kacchàyana. E. G:—

1. Apàdàne panchamì *Panini* III. 4, 52.
Apadane panchami—Kachchayana.

So likewise:—

2. Bhùvàdayo dhàtavah. I. 3, 1.
Bhuvadayo dhatavo.
3. Kàlàdhvano ratyanta sanyoge. II. 3, 5.
Kaladdhana machchanta sanyoge.
4. Kartarì krit. III. 4, 6.
Kattari kit.
5. Asmadyuttamah. I. 4, 107.
Amhe uttamo.

Again, the text of Pánìnì is altered to meet the exigencies of the Pali Grammar, thus;

6. Tìnas trìni trìni pathama madhyamottamáh
Dve dve pathama majjhimuttama purisa. [I. 4, 101.

Tradition represents that, the whole work (including *Vutti*) as we now have it, was written by one and the same person. But this is contradicted by another Tradition. On this, I shall offer a few observations hereafter.

From its language, the Pali Grammar appears to be a very ancient work. It was probably written at a time when literature was usually carried on in the concise Algebraic form of

* These are doubtless, taken from "the contemporaneous History of Buddha,' which, as stated by Buddhagosa, "contains records such as these—' at such a period Bhagava dwells at Savatthi, or at the Jetavana vohara' . . . . . . 'he dwells at Rajagahan, or at the Veluvana Vohara'. . . . . 'he dwells at Vesali' &c.'

aphorisms. This is put down by Pr. Max Muller at 600—200 B. C., embracing the period at which the founder of Buddhism flourished, and which upon the best proof on which a date may be fixed in Asiatic History, was not only posterior to the *Mantas* (which are identified with the *Védas* * the *Vedangas* and *Veyyàkarana*, but subsequent to the *Mahà Bhàrata*,† *Rámàyana*; *Asvalàyana*‡ and *Paràsara*; and upon other data,—477 B. C.

To the indefatigable labours of the learned translator of the Maháyansa, whom I have so frequently mentioned in the course of these notes, were Europeans first indebted for the information as to the probable date of Kachchàyana's Grammar. In order to render my observations clear, Mr. Turnour's authorities on the subject are here extrated.

" In the commentary on the Rúphasiddhi we find the following distinct and important particulars regarding Kachchàyana, purporting to be conveyed in his own words :—

" Kachcháyano signifies the son of Kachcho. The said Kachcho was the first individual (who assumed that name as a patronymic) in that family. All who are descended from that stock are, by birth Kachchàyanà.

" (If I am asked) who is this Kachchàyano? Whence his name Kachcháyano? (I answer), It is he who was selected for the important office (of compiling the first Pali Grammar, by Buddho himself; who said on that occasion): ' Bhikkhus from amongst my sanctified disciples, who are capable of elucidating in detail, that which is expressed in the abstract, the most eminent is this Mahàkachchàyano.'

"Bhagawà (Buddho) seated in the midst of the four classes of devotees, of which his congregation was composed (viz.

* These are said, in the Buddhistical annals, to have been compiled by *Attaka*, Vessam itta, *Yamataggi*, *Angirasa*, *Bharadvaja*, *Vasettha*, *Kassapa*, and Bhagu.

† Mahabharata is frequently mentioned under the designati n of Itihasa. As valuyana is mentioned by Gotama. Vide extracts infra.

priests and priestesses, male and female ascetics:) – opening his sacred mouth, like unto a flower expanding under the genial influence of Surio's rays, and pouring forth a stream of eloquence like unto that of Brahmo—said: 'My disciples! the profoundly wise Sàriputto is competent to spread abroad the tidings of the wisdom (contained in my religion) by his having proclaimed of me that,—' To define the bounds of his omniscience by a standard of measure, let the grains of sand in the Ganges be counted; let the water in the great ocean be measured; let the particles of matter in the great earth be numbered'; as well as by his various other discourses.

" It has also been admitted that, excepting the saviour of the world, there are no others in existence whose wisdom is equal to one sixteenth part of the profundity of Sàriputto. By the Achàrayos also the wisdom of Sàriputto has been celebrated. Moreover, while the other great disciples also, who had overcome the dominion of sin and attained the four gifts of sanctification were yet living; he (Buddho) allotted, from amongst those who were capable of illustrating the word of Tathàgato, this important task to me,—in the same manner that a Chakkawatti ràja confers on an eldest son, who is capable of sustaining the weight of empire, the office of Parinàyako. I must therefore render unto Tathágato a service equivalent to the honor conferred. Bhagawà has assigned to me a most worthy commission. Let me place implicit faith in whatever Bhagawà has vouchsafed to propound.

" This being achieved, men of various nations and tongues, rejecting the dialets which had become confused by its disorderly mixture with the Sanscrit and other languages, will, with facility acquire, by conformity to the rules of grammar propounded by Tathàgato, the knowledge of the word of Buddho 'Thus the Thero Mahá Kachchàyano, who is here (in this work) called simply Kachchàyano, setting forth his qualification; pursuant to the declaration of Buddho, that " sense is represented by letters", composed the grammatical work called *Niruttipitako*.'* *Mahàvansa* p. xxvii.

Before I notice some of the objections urged against the above tradition, it may perhaps be convenient to refer to the various other Pali writers who have given it the sanction of their high authority.

Kachchàyana commences his work, as we have already seen, with *Atthó akkhara saññàto;* and it has already been shewn from the passage quoted by Turnour, that that Suttan was declared by Buddha himself. This is more clearly stated as follows in the

SUTTA NIDDESA.

Attho akkhara saññáto-ti ádi máha; idan suttan kena vuttan? Bhagavatà vuttan. Kadà vuttanti—Yama Uppala nàmakà dve Brahmaná *Khaya-vaya* kamma*tth*ánan gahetvà gachchhantà Nadì-tíre *Khaya-vayanti Kammatthá*ne karìyamàne eko udake machchan ganhitun charantan bakan disvà, udaka bakoti vicharati. Eko gha*t*e patan disvá gha*t*a pa*t*o ti vicharati, Tadá Bhagavà obhàsan munchitvà *attho akkhara saññàto*-ti vàkyan *th*apesi. Tesan cha Kamma*tth*á nan pati*tth*ahi. Tasmà Bhagavatá vuttanti vuchchati. Tan ñatvá mahà Kachcháno Bhagavantan yàchitvà Himavantan gantvá Mano-silà tale dakkhina disá bhàgan sísan katvá purátthima disàbhimukho hutvà *attho akkhara saññáto*-ti à dikan *Kachcháyana pakaranan* rachi.

'It is said that 'sense is represented by letters' &c. By whom was this suttan declared? It was laid down by Bhagavà. (To explain) when it was declared:—Two Brahman (Priests) Yama and Uppala, having learnt (from Gotama) the *khaya-vaya* branches of *Kammatthánan*† went away; and, whilst engaged in abstract meditation repeating 'Khaya-Vaya' on

* "Another name for the Rupasiddhi."—In the above note Turnour identifies Rupasiddhi with Niruttipitaka. But, it would seem that the latter is an original work of Maha Kachchayana, different from his Grammar, and different also from his theological work entitled the Nettipakarana. See *Kachchayana Vannana*.

† Studies such as abstract meditation &c., preparatory to the attainment of the paths leading to *Nibban*.

the banks of the *Nadí*, one of them saw a crane proceeding to catch a fish in the water, and began muttering* *Udako bako* 'water-crane.' The other, seeing a *ghate-patan* 'a cloth in a pot' began muttering *ghata-pato.* At this time Bhagavà by means of a light, which he issued, declared the sentence, *Attho akkhara saññàto*—'The sense is represented by letters.' Their Kammaṭṭhànan was also effectual. Wherefore it is said that this Suttan was declared by Bhagavà. When Mahá Kachchàna learnt this, he proceeded with Bhagavà's permission to *Himavanta.* Reclining in the *Mano-sila* region with his head towards the south, and facing the east he composed the *Kachchàyana-pakarana* consisting of (the Suttans) *attho akkhara saññàto* &c."

In the *atthakathá* to the *Anguttara Nikáya* Mahà Kachchàyana is spoken of;† and the Tika to the same work contains further particulars which are quoted in the following extract from

THE KACHCHAYANA VANNANA.

Achariyà pana lakkhana vutti Udáharana sankhátan iman Kachchàyana gandha pakaranan Kachchàyanattherena eva katanti vadanti. Tena áhá eka nipàta Anguttara tíkàyan 'Mahà Kachcháyanatthero pubba patthanà vasena Kachcháyna pakaranan, Mahà Nirutti pakaranan, Netti pakaranan, chàti pakaranattayan sangha majjhe pakàsesi.'

'Teachers say that this Kachchàyana *gandha pakarana* (Text or composition) which numbers *lakkhana* (Rules), *vutti* (supplementary notes), and *Udàharana* (Examples), was composed by Kachcháyana *thera* himself. Wherefore the Tika to the Anguttara of the *Ekanipáta* says; 'the thera Mahà Kachchàyana, according to his previous aspirations, published in the midst of the priesthood the three compositions, viz. *Kachcháyana Pakarana, Mahà Nirutti Pakarana,* and *Netti Pakarana.*'

* Or rather pondering on what he had observed.

† Vide extract therefrom infra.

Of the three books here mentioned the *Netti' Pakarana* is also extant in this Island; and it has been suggested by my Pandit that the style of this work, of which I give a specimen,* would seem to differ from that of the Grammar. There can be no question of this. The language of a work such as the Pali grammar, in which (to adopt the words of Professor Max Muller in respect of Pànini) the author "does not write and compose, but squeezes and distils his thoughts, and puts them before us in a form which hardly deserves the name of style,"† cannot bear any comparison to the style of a work on religion, where the object was to convince and fascinate the reader, and not to cramp the writer's ideas in small sentences with a view to render a facility to those who committed them to memory. Even in other languages works on science and religion written by the same person present the same diversity of style which the subject may demand. The one may be terse, sententious, and dry; and the other full, flowing, and elegant as is the case here. The difference of style, therefore, in these two works, does by no means furnish any ground for overthrowing the authorship ascribed to this *Páli Grammar*. And, I am again reminded by my learned Pandit that the metre of some of the gáthàs in Kacchàyana are different from those in the text-books of Buddhism such as Dhammapada; and that that difference would favor the belief that this grammar was written long after the Buddhist era.

I freely admit the force of the learned Pandit's observation, that the difference of metre (if, such were the fact) between confessedly Gotama's gáthàs, and all other Pàli writings (including Kachchàna's grammar) would establish a line of demarcation between two periods of literature. And I also confess that I have been disappointed in my search after a verse in the *Vasantatilaka* metre, such as *Setthan tiloka mahitan* &c.,‡ in any of the original writings in the Buddhist

* See Appendix.

† Sanskrit Literature p. 312.

‡ See the introductory Verses of Kachchayana quoted at p. xvi.

works. But, leaving this question for the determination of future researches, and of more competent scholars than myself, I may be permitted to remark that the absence of a particular metre in Buddha's lectures does not necessarily prove that it was unknown in his time. Different metres suit different compositions. There are some which are peculiarly adapted to the genius of the oldest form of the Pàli, before it received the elaborations of poets. Such are the Anus*t*ubh, the Tris*t*ubh, the Anus*t*ubh-tris*t*ubh, the Jagatì, the Tris*t*ubh-Jagatì, and the Vaitálíya metres which we frequently meet with in old writings. The Vasantatilaka is generally unsuited to the Pali, as it is to the Sinhalese, and other so-called Pràkrita dialects. Although compositions in that metre are occasionally found in works of both those languages; yet they have all the evidence of being forced, and abound with compounds, of which the really old Buddhist writings are comparatively free. This is doubtless the reason why this particular metre (Vasantatilaka) is not to be found in the lectures of Gotama, which were expressed, as occasions presented themselves, with a view to impart religious instruction, without study, and without any attempts at ornament. The case with the grammarian was, however, different. Except in the Suttans which were designed for instruction, he seems to have studied ornament. Perhaps too, he was fond of display. He, as we learn from himself, did not despise Sanskrit grammatical terms. He had no reason, therefore, to reject really Sanskrit metres in which he could with elegance depict the virtues of his Teacher. Hence the adoption in this grammar of metres which are not met with in original Buddhist writings.

There is not, therefore, I apprehend, sufficient evidence to set aside the popular tradition as to the author of this Grammar, which I perceive is supported by various considerations and inferences which may be drawn from several historical facts. That the *Màgadhí* which the Buddhists denominate the *Pàli*, was an actually existent form of speech in Behar at the time Buddhism arose, may be easily believed.* Yet, before this period when the Magadhas had but one common religion, and, perhaps, cultivated the language in which that religion was taught with greater zest, it is not improbable that the treatises to elucidate the vernacular *Mágadhà* were, as the Sinhalese Grammar are at the present day, limited. And this is obviously the reason why Kachcháyana, as he himself declares, had borrowed technical terms from *Sanskrit* authors.

PARA SAMANNA PAYOGE. (Vutti)—yá cha pana sakkata gandhésu samaññà ghosà' ti và aghosà' ti và tá payoge sati etthà' pi yujjante. 'In composition other's appelations. [Vutti.] Such (Grammatical) terms as are called *ghòsa*, (sonants) or *aghósa* (surds) in Sanskrit (gandhas†) compositions are here adopted as exigency may require.'

By 'Sanskrit' sources, perhaps, the writer meant the *Pràkrit* Grammars by Sanskrit writers, or such Rules of Pànini as are indicated in the following extract from the *Kavikanthapàsa* by Kedàra-bhatta:

> Pànini bhagavàn Pràkrita
> Lakshana mapi vakti Sanskrità danyat:
> Dìrghàksharancha kutrachi
> Dekàn màtrà mupaitìtì.

That is:—'Pànini, the Rishi, speaks also of the lakshana (or Grammatical Rules) of Pràkrita, besides the Sanskrit; and (says) that in some languages a long letter‡ becomes one syllabic instant.' But, whether this inference be well founded or not, it is quite clear that this was one of the earliest Pali Grammars, which borrowed its technical terms, not from *Pali* but, Sanskrit writers. Its object too, was to fix the Rules of

* See Sanyutta Nikaya—as to the Magadhi being the language of Magadha.

† This word is sometimes written *gantha*.

‡ The commentator explains that by a 'long letter' are meant the Sanskrit *e* and *o* which become short in some languages, or are each equal to one syllabic instant.

that language; since at the time Kachchàyana wrote his Grammar the Mágadhì, like other "dialects," had a tendency to become 'confused by its disorderly mixture with the Sanskrit and other languages.' This is a fact. As a vernacular dialect, the Màgadhì scarcely maintained its character in Asia till the age of Asòka. Two hundred years had hardly elapsed before its development was 'intermediate between the Pali and Sanskrit.' There must therefore, have been a gradual declension in Pali literature during those two centuries. Indeed this could not have been otherwise when we ascertain that the very pupils of Gotama had resorted to other languages for the elucidation of Buddhism. Hence the necessity for a compilation like Kachchàyana's—a work on Grammar 'for the easy comprehension of the word of Buddha'—*Sukhèna Buddha Vachanan ugganhissanti-ti;* and as *Kachchàyana* himself says in the opening of his work, written, not according to the vernacular dialect of the Magadhas, but 'in accordance with the (language) of the Suttans'—*vakkhàmi sutta hita' metta su Sandhikappan.*

These are not all the circumstances from which it may be inferred that Kachchàyana's Grammar was written at the first dawn of Buddhism. As was the case with all ancient nations, a sacred literature gave rise in Magadha to philological sciences. Religious doctrines when disseminated through a written medium, naturally led the Buddhists to Grammatical inquiries. The necessity for rescuing the *dhamma* from corruption, and for preserving their correct interpretations, as already seen, was a powerful inducement to Gotama's disciples to fix the rules of their Preceptors' words, the *Jina vachana*, as the Màgadhì is called in most ancient works.

It may, however, be asserted that neither was writing known six centuries before Christ, nor, consequently, were Buddhist doctrines recorded at that date. I have discussed this question elsewhere, and I may here state, as the result of those investigations, that at the time when Buddhism first started into existence, writing was known in Magadha as much as painting.* It was *practised* in the time of Gotama.† Buddhist doctrines were conveyed to different countries by its means.‡ Laws and usages were recorded.§ Little children were taught to write.¶ Even women were found able to read and write.|| The character used was the *Nágari.*** Vermilion was the 'ink', and metal plates, cloth, hydes, and leaves constituted the 'paper' of the time.†† That Buddhist annals therefore, were reduced to writing from the very commencement, is not only reasonable, but is indeed capable of easy and satisfactory proof.

To return to the subject. The literary qualifications of the théra Kachchàyana, seem to have been indeed such as to warrant the belief that he devoted his time to the elucidation of the *language* of Buddhism. He was, as is abundantly proved in the Pali works, a distinguished member of the Buddhist Church. He is also mentioned in the Tibetan Buddhistical Annals, as one of the disciples of Gotama; and it is expressly stated of him, that 'he recited the *Sútra* on emancipation in the *vulgar* dialect.' By 'the vulgar dialect' Mons. De Korési doubtless meant the language to which Colebrooke had previously given that appellation—*the Màgadhí.* Gotama himself states, that of all his pupils Mahà Kachchàyana was the most competent to elucidate his doctrines. In the very language of the sage, which is here quoted from the *Ekanipáta* of the *Angutta Nikáya:* Etanaggan Bhikkhavè mama sávakànan bhikkhúnan sankhittena bhàsitassa vitthàrena atthan vibhajantànan, yadidan Mahà

* Papanchasudaniya. lib. iii. in my possession.

† Id. also Maha *Vagga.* See *Chamakkhandaka* and a host of other authorities.

‡ Id. Sanyut Nikaya—&c. &c.

§ Sumangala Vilasini.

¶ Maha Vagga.

|| Sanyut Nikaya; Maha Vagga, and atthakatha to Dhammapada

** Papancha Sudaniya.

†† That such was the fact may be easily gathered from several authorities.

Kachchàno—' Priests, he who is Mahà Kachchàyana is the chief of all the *bhikkhus*, my pupils, who can minutely elucidate the *sense* of what is concisely expressed.' That this supremacy refers to the literary, and not the theological, attainments of Kachchàyana appears from the following comment which we extract from the atthakathà to the *Anguttara Nikàya.*

Aññe kira Tathàgatassa sankhepa vachanan Attha vasena và pùritun sakkonti vyañjana vasena và; ayan pana thero ubhayenàpi sakkoti: tasmà aggo-ti vutto.

' Some are able to amplify the concise words of Tathàgata *either* by means of letters, *or* by [shewing] their sense. But this thera can do so in *both* ways. He is therefore called *chief.*'

In the *Nyàsa* or the *Mukha matta-dìpanì*, which is supposed to be the earliest commentary on Kachchàyana's Pali Grammar, and, as may be proved, older than the *Rùpasiddhi*, the author of this Grammar is not only identified with the Kachchàyana thera, whose ' intellectual supremacy was extolled by Buddha'; but his memory is thus respected by an ' Obeisance.'

Kachchàyanan cha muni vannita buddhi-'massa
Kachchàyanassa mukha matta' mahan karrissan
Pàrampparà gata vinichchaya nichchhayan cha.

' Also (bowing down to) Kachchàyana, whose intellectual attainments had been complimented by Buddha, I shall comment upon the positive conclusions (Rules) which have been handed down by tradition as the very *oral* (teachings)* of this Kachchàyana.'

With reference to the name Kachchàyana in the above extract, the following passage occurs in the *Nirutti sàra Manjusa:* wherein also the writer acknowledges the consummate scholarship of the Grammarian.

* *Mukhamatta* ' the very (word of) mouth', a term which does not necessarily imply the absence of writing.

Kasi Kammàdinà vyàpàrena kachchati dippatíti Kachcho, thera pità tassa apachchan putto Kachchàyano Neruttukànan pabhava bhùto pabhinna pa*t*i sambhido etadagga *th*áne *th*apito khìnásavatthero, tan pana natvàna.

'By reason of the occupation of ploughing &c. [comes] *Kachchati* 'he shines.' Thence *Kachcho,* (the name of) the thera's father. His son is Kachchàyana—a thera, who was an *arahanta,* who was placed in the highest position, who had attained the *patisambhidà,** and who was the first cause (source) of all Neruttikà, [Grammarians or] philologers.'

Although it is stated† that Kachcháyana was residing at Avanti, the *pachchanta* or 'the foreign regions'‡, it is however expressly stated that this Grammar was written in the *Himavanta;* and from the mention of the principal towns celebrated by the presence and abode of Gotama, and especially that which had risen from a small village to the importance of a populous city in the time of the sage, I mean *Palàliputta,*§ it may be inferred that the writer took for his examples such of the names as were then of *recent* celebrity.

* See *Sivpilisimbia* in Clough's Dictionary. Turnour has defined this to be 'the attainment of the four gifts of sanctification.'

† In the *Chammakkhandaka* Section of the *Maha Vagga.*

‡ Dr. Muir in his *Sanskrit Texts,* says that 'the people whom Yaska designates *Prachyas,* or *men of the East,* must have been the Kikatas or the Magadhas, or the Angas, or the Vangas.'—p. 371. In the Buddhist annals however, the word *Pachchanta* is used to designate all the countries beyond the *Majjhima desa,* which is thus defined in the *Maha Vagga*: 'Here the *Pachchanta* are these Countries. On the East [of Majjhima] is the market town called Kajangala, and on the West Maha Sala. Beyond them is the great country of Pachchanta, and this side of it is the Majjha. On the South-east is the river called Salalavati. Beyond it is the Pachchanta country, and this side of it the Majjha. On the South is the town called Setakanni. Beyond it is the Pachchanta country, and this side of it the Majjha. On the West is the Brahman village called Thuna. Beyond it is the Pachchanta country, and this side of it the Majjha. And on the North is the mountain called Usuraddhaja. Beyond it is the Pachchanta country, and this side of it is the Majjha.'

§ It is stated in the Buddhist annals (see the first Banavara of the Parinibban Suttan) that this city, which in modern times has received the name of Patna, was built during the lifetime of Gotama, for the purpose of checking the Vajjians; and it is also stated that at the time it was built by Sunidha and Vassakara, two ministers of the reigning prince Ajatasatta, Gotama predicted its future opulence and grandeur as well as its partial destruction by fire and water.

As we have already seen, the Màgadhí scarcely maintained its original purity in the *Magadha desa* until the second ecumenial convocation; and the code of the Vajjian heretics, which was made at this time, and which may be clearly identified as the Nepal collection,* was in point of language "intermediate" between the Pali of Kachchàyana and the Dhammapada; and the Pràkrit of the Pillar-dialect.

These are important facts, which prove that the Grammar in question was composed in the golden age of the Pali literature—before it became interlarded with the Sanskrit, and before the language was so much neglected, (as at the time of the second convocation), that, except those who maintained the orthodox version of the Scriptures, literary men were unable to pay correct attention to 'the nature of nouns, their genders, and other accidents of Grammar, as well as the various requirements of style.'†

Nàma lingan parikkhàran àkappakaranàni cha
Pakatibhàvan vijahitvà, tañcha aññan akansute.

Thus, when the uniform and popular tradition stated in the above extracts, which there is no reasonable ground to set aside, is coupled with the many inferences to which I have directed attention; it is, I apprehend, very clear that Kachchàyana, the author of *Sandhi-kappa,* was one of the eighty eminent disciples of Gotama. As such, he must have flourished in the latter-half of the sixth century before Christ.

Against this popular belief I have been referred by several friends to another name of Kachchàyana, the author of the *Abhidharma Jnàna prasthàna,* mentioned in the following account of Hiouen-thsagn, the Chinese traveller of 629—645, A. D.

Après avoir fait environ cinq cent li, au sud-est de la capitale (de Chìnapati), il arriva au couvent appelé Ta-mo-sou-fa-na-seng-kia-lan (Tâmasvana-sanghâ râma), ou le convent

* See Appendix. † Dipavansa.

de la Forêt Sombre. On y comptait environ trois cent religieux qui suivaient les principes de l'école des Sarvàstivàdas. Ils avaient un extérieur grave et imposant, et se distinguaient par la pureté de leur vertu et l'élévation de leur caractère. Ils approfondissaient surtout l'étude du petit Véhicule. Les mille Buddhas du kalpa des sages (Bhadrakalpa) doivent, dans ce lieu, rassambler la multitude des Devas et leur expliquer la sublime loi. Dans la trois centième année après le Nirvàna de Sàkya Tathàgata, il y eut un maître des Sàstras, nommé Kâtyâyana, qui composa, dans ce couvent, le Fa-tchi-lun (Abhidharma-jnàna-prasthàna.)—*Mémoires sur les Contrées occidentales par Hiouen-thsang, liv. iv. p.* 200.

'Having travelled about five hundred *li* southwest of the capital (of Chínapati) he arrived at the monastery called Ta-mo-sou-fa-na-seng-kia-lan—(Tamasvana Sanghàràma) or the monastery of the dark-forest. About three hundred Religieux are reckoned in this place, who follow the principles of the *Sarvâstivàdas* school. They maintain a grave and imposing exterior, and are remarkable for purity of virtue, and elevation of character. They are engaged in the profound study of the little vehicle. The thousand Buddhas of the Kalpa of the wise men (Bhaddrakalpa) were bound to assemble, in this place, the whole multitude of the Devas, and expound to them the sublime law. In the three hundredth year after the nirvána of Sàkya Tathàgata, there was a master of the Sâstras, named *Kátyâyana*, who composed in this monastery, the *Fa-tchi-lun* (Abhi-dharma-jnâna-prasthâna.)'

Here there is nothing to establish the identity of persons. The age too, given by the Chinese pilgrim, does not throw any light on the subject. If Kàtyàyana, the author of *Abhidharma-jnâna Prasthâna* lived 300 A. B., he flourished after Asòka, and, according to the same authority quoted by Cowell, in a 'Monastère fondè par Asoka'; and at a time when he was sure to have figured very conspicuously in the Budhistical annals of Ceylon.

The absence, however, of any notice regarding him, proves, as I apprehend, what the Chinese traveller himself indicates, that Kàtyàyana of *Tamasvana Sanghàràma* was one who followed the principles of the *Sabbatti vàda**-school, and, therefore, one of the seventeen sects mentioned in the Dípávansa—'who distorted the sense and phraseology (of the scriptures); omitted a portion of the original (compilation) and of the *gàthás;* substituted others (in lieu of them); disregarded the nature of nouns, their genders, and other accidents, as well as the various requisites of style; and corrupted the same by different substitutions.'

Now, it is quite clear, from the evidence contained in the above passage, as well as from that furnished by the style of the Nepal scriptures, and also from the statements in the Chinese accounts, that the language used by these sectarians was, as stated by Professor Burnouf, 'one intermediate between the Pali and the Sanskrit'; that it was called the *Fan*, or the *Brahman* language, as that word is unmistakeably used in the following passage—Le dieu *Fan* (Brahman) et le roi du ciel (Indra) établirent des règles et se conformèrent au temps;' and that it was a language with the *dual* number, and therefore the *Sanskrit*, as moreover the name *Abhidharma jnàna prasthàna*, the work itself attributed to Kàtyayàna clearly indicates.

It is also stated that the Buddhists had an object in ascribing this Grammar to Kachchàyana. Professor Max Muller traces the *animus falcendi*, to a 'tendency of later Buddhist writers to refer the authorship of their works to names famous in ancient Brahmanic history.'—p. 303. There is, I believe, no foundation for this assertion. 'One swallow does not make summer.' Much less does a single instance prove a practice. One solitary exception is here made the rule, especially in regard to a question of *custom*—'the tendency of a people to do certain acts.' If, therefore, no other names but "*Kachchà-*

* See appendix.

yana" can be pointed out in support of this allegation, the allegation itself, I apprehend, is disproved.

But, to take a brief excursus into the subject, nothing can be clearer from the history of Buddhism, as we find it in the annals of Ceylon, than that the Buddhists, in imitation of their teacher, have always attempted to draw a distinction between themselves and other sects, especially the Brahmans. This will be found to be the case, even where there is no substantial difference between them. Although Buddhism, I am persuaded, arose out of Brahmanism, and although the very doctrines of the former are built upon those of the latter; yet there is scarcely a single subject upon which the doctrines of both are identical. Gotama, it would also seem, never lost an opportunity to draw some distinction between his own doctrines, and those of the Brahmans. Take, for instance, the doctrines of 'the Creation'; of [*átman* or *attha*] 'the soul'; of [*Nirvána* or *nibban*] 'eternal bliss' &c. &c.; and none can fail to perceive the attempt that is made by Buddhists to vary the Brahman doctrines. In this endeavour they have got into confusion, as in the case of *Nibban*, which even Nágasena pronounces to be 'a mystery.'

I may also allude to the institution of *Castes*. Gotama varied the Brahmanical doctrine on the subject. He differed from them as to its origin. He abolished that distinction among the priesthood. Although he never preached against it in a *social* point of view, and never affirmed it to be sinful, and pernicious to *society*; yet to set aside the pretensions of the 'twice born' he declared the *universal equality* of mankind in a *religious* point of view.

Khattiyo se*tt*ho jane tasmin ye-gotta pa*t*isàrino
Vijjà charana sampanno so se*tt*ho deva mànus.

'Amongst mankind, who are scrupulous in regard to their lineage, the *Khattiya* is supreme; but he who is endowed with *Vijjà* and *Charana* is supreme, both amongst devas and men.'

The *Vijjâ* and *Charana* are also thus defined by the Buddhists :—

Vipassanà-ñàna manomayiddhì
Iddhippabhedo picha dibha sotan
Parassa cheto pariyàya ñánan
Pubbènivà sànu gatancha ñànan.
Dibbancha chakkhà sava sankha yocha
Etàni ñànàn idhattha vijjà
Alankarun yà muni dhamma deham
Visesa sobhà guna majjhu peta.

'Here the eight *Vijjà* are the (following heads of) knowledge ;—abstract devout meditation ; power to assume any corporeal figure whatever at one's will ; the various other attributes of *iddhi ;** divine hearing ; knowledge of that which is produced in another's mind ; knowledge of the state of previous existences ; a divine perception ; and the extinction of (distressful) desire. These, which are peculiar attributes or qualities, embellish the [*dhamma*] religious-body of Buddha.'

Sìlan varan indriya san varocha
Mattà sità jà-gariyà'nu-yogo
Saddhà hirottappa bahussutat-tan
Parakkamo cheva satì matìcha.
Chattàri jhànànicha tàni' mànì
Tìpancha dhammà charanàni jaññà
Etehi vijjàhicha sampayogo
Sampanna vijjá charano munindo.

'Know that these fifteen constitute the *Charana ;* (viz.) observance of the supreme precepts, subjugation of the passions, eating ordinately,† wakefulness,‡ faith, shame (for sin), fear (of sin), much hearing (study), prowess, retentive memory (*sati*), understanding (*mati*), and the four jànas.§

* For an explanation of this, see Hardy on Buddhism, p. 500.

† Which is explained to be—' to eat only to live for religion—but not to live to eat only.'

‡ Refraining from much sleep—which the recluse is restricted to the middle watch of the night, or four English hours at midnight.

§ Abstract meditation which leads to the entire destruction of all cleaving to existence. See Gogerly's Essay C. B., A. S. J. ii. 15.

By the association of these with the foregoing *Vijjá* the supreme Buddhà was endowed with *Vijjá* and *Charana.*'—*Pradípikáva.*

The anxiety of Buddhists not to identify themselves with Brahmans appears also from the meanings which the former attach to the very words borrowed from the latter, *e. g.*

Brahmachariyà, 'the Brahman in his noviciate' is interpreted to mean 'the whole course of Buddhist religious duties.'* Take again the word *Valabá.* Between it and the Sanskrit word *badavà*, there is but the difference of the two dialects; for the interchange, occasionally, of *b* and *v*, and the change of the Sanskrit *d* into *l*, in the Pàli, is well known. Taking this, therefore, to be the Sanskrit word *badavà* we find that the Buddhists, whilst adopting the Brahman word for "*Aurva*, sub-marine fire, called *badava* or *bàdava*, and personified as the son of the Saint Urva", assign to it the like meaning of 'a sub-marine fire', but, with a view to differ from the Brahmans, explain it to be—not the *deva* of the Hindu Pantheon, 'who, consisting of flames but with a mare's head sprung from the thighs of Urva, and was received by the ocean', but—as Milton describes it,

————————'a fiery deluge, fed
With ever-burning sulphur unconsum'd.'

"The unquenchable fire of hell, so rigorous that its contact with water only inflames it the more."† And the *badavàmukha* 'the mare's mouth', wherein the Hindu Urva entered, is also known to the Buddhists as *valabámukha;* but they define it to be 'a pool or hollow in the trough of the Sea, occasioned in stormy weather by the waves rolling towards the Meru or the Sakvala-gala.'

To return to the alleged 'tendency of later *Buddhists* &c.' I have closely searched, but in vain, for a single instance (Kachchâyana excepted) in which the Buddhists of any period might be charged with such a weakness.

* See remarks of Mon. Burnouf in his *Histoire du Buddhisme*, 1. p. 141.

† Attanagaluvansa, Cap. ii. § 1.

Take, for instance, the *Rùpasiddhi* or *Bàlavatàra*, and other Pali Grammars which have already been noticed. There is no correspondence between the names of their reputed authors, and the "names famous in ancient Brahmanic history." Take also such names as Mihindu, Buddhagosa, Ananda, Buddhapiya, Vanaratana, Moggallàyana, and Anòmadassi, and we look in vain for their celebrated prototypes 'famous in Brahmanic history.' True, some of the Buddhist names are Brahmanical, and for the simplest of all reasons, that Buddhism arose out of Brahmanism, and on Brahmanical soil; and that some of 'the most famous in Brahmanic history', such as *Amara, Purushottama, Hemachandra*, &c., have embraced the new religion. Moreover, in the East, Brahman appellations were anciently, as they are at present, common names. Amongst the coolies in the Coffee and Cocoanut plantations of Ceylon do we meet with many a *Parasi Rámă, Chandra*, &c., &c.; yet, with the exception of the Patronymic *Kachcháyana*, it is difficult to find a single name of a Buddhist writer, which can be 'referred to similar names amongst the Brahmans famous in history.'

The reason too, for the anxiety evinced by Buddhists not to identify themselves with Brahmans, may be easily explained. It was to remove the reproaches of the Brahmans, such as the following, which *Kumârilá* casts upon the Sàkya fraternity.—"These Sákyas, Vaiseshikas, and other heretics, who have been frightened out of their wits by the faithful Mimansakas, prattle away *with our own words as if trying to lay* hold of a shadow.*

Having thus noticed the arguments for and against the alleged date and authorship of this Pali Grammar, it is indeed a matter of curious inquiry, especially in view of the similarity between it and Pànini;—'what relationship does the Pali Kachcháyana bear to its Sanskrit prototype? And here I shall first dwell upon the alleged identity between the author of the *Pràkrit Prakàsa*, and Kachcháyana. Professor Cowell,

* Max Muller's Sanskrit Literature p. 84.

the erudite translator of the Pràkrit Prakàsa, thus notices the subject :—

" Kàtyàyana has always been the reputed author of the Vàrtikàs, or supplemental remarks on the ancient Grammar of Pànini ; and both names are found in the accounts of the Chinese Buddhist Hiuan-thsang, who travelled in India in the first half of the seventh century of our era. Pànini is called Pho-ni-ni, and described as the founder of music, which appears to be the nearest Chinese expression for a Grammarian ; the passage relating to Kàtyàyana is as follows.* ' *Tchi na pou ti (erigé par les Chinois)*, limite de l'Inde du Nord. . . . . Au sud-est de la grande ville, à 500 *li*, monastère de *Tha mo sou fa na* (forêt obscure) ; lá a vécu le docteur *Kia to yan na*, 300 ans aprés le Nirvána† Monastère fondé par Asoka.' The Buddhist traditions in Ceylon all agree in calling the author of the earliest Pali Grammar Kachcháyano ;‡ and although this is said to have perished, yet when we remember how very closely allied Pàli is to Pràkrit, and that Kachchàyano is simply the Pràkrit form of Kátyáyana, there can be little doubt that the Prákrit grammar of the one and the Pali grammar of the other, are only the Brahmanical and Buddhist versions of the same tradition."—p. viii.

The learned Professor's argument amounts to the following :—' Kàtyáyana alias Vararuchi was the writer of the Páninya-*Várttikas.* Kachchàyana, between whose name and that of Kàtyàyana there is only the difference of dialects, was the author of a Pali (Pràkrit) Grammar. Vararuchi was, moreover, the writer of the *Pràkrit Prakàsa.* Things which are equal to the same thing, are equal to each

* Quoted in the Appendix (p. 382) to Remusat's translation of the " *Foe Koue Ki* ou Relation des royaumes Bouddhiques." See also M. Julien's Hist : de la vie de Hiouen Thsang, p.p. 102, 165.

† The common date of the *Nirvana* of Buddha is B. C. 543 ; but Hiuan Thsang (as quoted in a note to p. 237) gives several different dates as current in India in his time, the latest of which is about B. C. 360.

‡ See Turnour's "Mahawanśa", Introd : p.p. 25—27.

other. *Therefore*, Vararuchi was Kàtyàyana;—Kàtyàyana, Kachchàyana;—and Kachchàyana, Vararuchi. Therefore, the Pali Grammarian and the Pràkrit writer were identical!

This reasoning is certainly inadmissible. Identity of names does not prove identity of persons.* It is possible to point out from History several Kàtyàyanas, and as many Vararuchi's. They are, like *Kàlidàsa* and *Kàsyapa* in India, or, as *Smith* in England, common names. We have no better authority than the idle tale of a *Vrihat Kathà*, which abounds with the "marvellous,"† to prove that Kàtyáyana was called Vararuchi; and. even admitting for the sake of argument, and upon the authority of the *Kathà Sàrit Ságara*, and Hema-chandra, that such was the fact; it is remarkable that, when people speak of the author of the Vàrttikàs, they generally name him Kàtyáyana—*not* Vararuchi; and that when they allude to the writer of the Pràkrit *Prakàsa* they call him Vararuchi, *not* Katyàyana—shewing that they were two different men. There is indeed no tenable evidence of the identity between Panini's Commentator, and the author of the *Pràkrit Prakàsa;* none, indeed, to shew that the latter was the same individual that wrote the Pali Grammar.

The internal evidence, however, contained in the *Pali* and *Pràkrit* Grammars, satisfactorily proves that they were written by two different men, and at comparatively two remote times from each other.

Kachchàyana was a Buddhist, not only upon the authority of the Rúpasiddhi, but the testimony which confirms it, viz. the internal evidence of the fact in the Pali Grammar. Kachchàyana opens his work with a salutation to "Buddha of infinite knowledge," whereas Vararuchi, I believe it will be admitted, was of the Brahman faith. This is not all. There

* Professor Goldstucker says in his work on the Age of Panini: "In general sameness of names, like that of *Katyayana*, can never prove the identity of persons, [who bore them]; there is nothing proved by it, except that both belonged to the same family, or ('*resp.*') were followers of the same School, the *Katas*."—p.p. 187-8.

† Vide extract from Dandialankara, *infra*.

is no correspondence whatever in either arrangement, sentiments, or words, between the two works. According to Professor Lassen (Inst : § 6.) "Each (of the six dialects, of which the Pràkrit Grammarians treat) "descends by one degree of purity below the preceding one, so that the last is more remote than any of the former, from the common source." In this view of the case, the *Màgadhì* takes a third place in the list of "scenic dialects." Yet it is a well established fact, even in the opinion of M.M. Burnouf and Lassen, (Essai sur le Pali, p.p. 138 ff.) that "when the Pali (Màgadhì) as a derivative from the Sanskrit, is compared with other dialects, which have the same origin, it is found to approach far more closely than any of those others to that common source. It stands, so to speak, on the first step of the ladder of departure from Sanskrit, and is the first of the series of dialects which break up that rich and fertile language." This discrepancy, therefore fully proves that Vararuchi treats of *Pràkrit* dialects, especially the Mágadhí, of an age much later, as the language shews,* than the text-books of Buddhism. His grammatical rules of the principal Pràkrit, which Lassen denominates the Dialectus Præcipua', are designed for a modified form of the Pali—after it found a retreat in Ceylon, and degenerated from the form in which we find it in Kachchàyana, and Dhammapada, and before it assumed the shape of the present Mahàràshtrí. This I shall endeavour to shew hereafter. Suffice it however to state here that the Pràkrit-Màgadhì of Vararuchi is different from the Pali, and from every dialect which is supposed to have risen from it.

It would thus appear, that the author of the Pràkrit Prakàsa, and Kachchàyana, were different persons ; and, upon the evidence of religion it may be inferred, that the latter was also different from the Brahman sage of the Pàninya-*Varttikas*.

In view, however, of the correspondence between Pà-

* See comparative Tables, *infra*.

niní's Sanskrit Grammar, and Kachchàyana's Pali work—a correspondence which is not limited to one or two stray instances, but found in different chains of *Sútras*, and which may be detected not merely from the similarity of thoughts, but from the sameness of language—it may be inquired which of these works was prior in point of time?

This question may be considered in two different points of view; 1st, whether Kachchàyana availed himself of the same Grammarians to whom Pànini himself was indebted? or, 2ndly, whether the Sanskrit author, whose grammatical terminology the Pali writer chiefly adopted, was Panini?

So far as my researches have extended, and they are indeed very limited, the only circumstance which favors the first hypothesis is, that some of the technical terms in Kachchàyana, *e. g.*, *Panchamí* and *Sattamí*, for the 'Benedictive' and 'Potential' moods, which are not found as a *fifth* and a *seventh* division of the verb, are different from the names given to the same by Pànini. The *Balàvatàra* explains (panchamì sattamí tyayan pubb'àchariya saññà) that '*Panchamí* and *Sattamì* are the appellations of former teachers'; and the *Mahà Sadda Níti* states, that these appellations are in accordance with Sanskrit Grammars, such as the *Kàtantra*,* a comparatively modern Grammar, as stated by Colebrooke. These statements however are of no value. The expressions "former teachers" and "the Grammars *such as* the *Kàtantra*" are too vague and indefinite. Upon their basis no conclusions can be drawn. By "former teachers" we may fairly infer those who lived before Kachchàyana, or before Pànini; and who can say that they did not likewise adopt the same appellations which "such Grammars as the Kàtantra" use in regard to the *Benedictive* and *Potential* moods? It is indeed probable that Pànini, like Kachchàyana, adopted certain, and rejected certain other, technical terms, &c., of former Grammarians. My acquaintance with the Sanskrit literature is far

* I have not been able to procure a copy of this, for the purpose of comparison.

too limited to draw any further inferences. But all circumstances considered (to some of which I shall hereafter refer), I cannot refrain from the conviction that Kachchàyana had Pànini before him when he composed the Sandhikappa. If such were the fact, should not the Sanskrit Grammarian be placed before the Buddhist era?

This question, as indeed every matter relating to Asiatic History and Chronology, is one of considerable difficulty; and I must most distinctly disclaim the slightest pretention to give any definite proof on the particular question, especially when I find such eminent Sanskrit scholars, as Wilson, Bohthling, Weber, and Max Muller, have failed to do so. All I desire however, in view of the evidence which the Pali Grammar reveals, and the historical incidents which the Pali Buddhist annals disclose, is to attract public attention to a few inferences and deductions which may be drawn from them, and which do not precisely accord with the views expressed by the learned scholars abovenamed.

Experience has proved, that whatever weight might be attached to facts stated in Brahmanical works, no reliance could be placed upon their chronological calculations. All that may be depended upon to a certain extent are their popular traditions, when supported by the testimony of other, especially the *Buddhist*, nations. The popular tradition then, as to the age of *Pànini*, which is current not only among the Brahmans of India, but among the Buddhists of Ceylon, is exactly what is stated by Colebrooke in the following passage.

"Pànini, the Father of *Sanskrit* Grammar, lived in so remote an age, that he ranks amongst those *ancient* sages, whose fabulous history occupies a conspicuous place in the *Puràнas* or Indian Theogonies. The name is a patronymic indicating his descent from *Panin*, but according to the *Pauràнica* legends, he was grandson of Devala, an inspired legislator."*

* Colebrooke's Miscellaneous Essays. Vol. ii. p. 4.

Against this popular belief, several writers have quoted the passage wherein Pànini mentions *Yavanàni* as a name of a *lipi*, or writing, "the alphabet of the *Yavanas.*" The inference sought to be deduced, viz., that the Yavanas, who were a "head-shaving race"* were *Ionians*, or Bactrian *Greeks*, who could only have been known in Asia after the invasion of Alexander the Great,† is indeed unfounded.

Few subjects in the history of the East, are capable of more satisfactory proof than that the *Yavanas* or *Yonas* had been known before Gotama Buddha.

The identification of *Yavanas* with Mohammedans, is also open, in the opinion of Professor Wilson, to the objection that the former are mentioned in works prior to the Mohammedan era.‡

In one of Asoka's inscriptions, the Girnar, *Antiochus* is called the *Yòna ràja*, 'the king of the Yonas.' The Milindappanna speaks of *Milinda* as a *Yona* king. Whether he be identical with *Meneander*, and the Yonaka country with *Euthydemia*§ remains to be proved. From the following extracts, however, we glean the facts ; that Milinda was born at *Kalasi* in *Alasadda*, 200 Yojanas from Sàgal; and that Sàgal was only twelve *Yojanas* from Cashmir.

Ràjà àha bhante Nàgasena yo idha kàla kato Brahma loke uppajjeyya yocha idha kála kato Kasmìre uppajjeyya kochira taran ko sìga taran'-ti. Samakan Mahà ràjà'ti. Opamman karohì'ti—kuhinpana Mahá ràja tava jàta nagaranti—At thigàmo bhante *Kalasi* gàmo nàma yatthàhan jàto'ti—Kìva dùro Mahà rája ito Kalasi gàmo hotíti—Dumattàni bhante yojana satànìti—kíva dùran mahà ràjà ito Kasmíran hotíti-Dvedasa bhante yojanànìti—Ingha tvan mahà ràjà Kalasigàman chintehíti—Chintito bhanteti—Ingha tvan Mahà ràja

* "Sagara made the Yavanas *shave* their heads."—*Vishnu Purana*, iv., 3.

† See Pr. Benfey's Article on India.

‡ Wilson's Hindu Theatre, II, p. 179.

§ Vide Wilson's Ariana, p. 230.

Kasmíran chintehíti—Chintitan bhanteti—Kataman nukho mahà ràjà chirena chintitan kataman sígataranti—samakan bhanteti. Eva mevako mahà ràja yo idha kála kato Brah maloke uppajjeyya yocha idha kàla kato Kasmìre uppajjeyya samakan yeva uppajjantìti.

"The king said, Lord Nágasena (suppose) one who dies here (Sàgal) is born in the Brahma world; and another who dies here is born in Kashmir: which of them is born sooner, and which of them later? *Priest*—Monarch, at the same time? *King*—Give an illustration. *Priest*—Monarch, which is the City of thy birth? *King*—Lord, I was born in a place which is called *Kalasi gàma*. *Priest*—Monarch, how far is *Kalasi gáma* from hence? *King*—Lord, about 200 yojanas. *Priest*—Monarch, how far is Kasmir from hence? *King*—Lord, Twelve yojanas. *Priest*—Monarch, think quickly of *Kalasi gàma*. *King*—Lord, I have thought. *Priest*—Monarch, think quickly of *Kasmir*. *King*—Lord, I have. *Priest*—Which of them, Monarch, hast thou taken shorter time to think, and which of them longer? *King*—Lord, equal time. *Priest*—So likewise, Monarch, he who dies here, and is born in the *Brahma lòka*; and he who dies here, and is born in Kasmir, are both born at the same (period of) time."

Again:—Thero àhakuhin pana mahà ràja tava jàta bhúmìti'—'Atthi bhante *Alasando* nàma dípo tatthàhan jàtoti'—'kíva dúro mahà ràja ito Alasando hótìti'—'dumattàni bhantè yojana satà niti.'

"The Priest asked, Monarch, where is the land of thy birth? Oh! Lord, there is an island named *Alasanda*. I was born there. Monarch, how far is *Alasanda* from hence (Sàgala)?—Lord, about two hundred yojanas"

In the following passage Isiodorus mentions *Ságal* and Alexandria in the same sentence—*et Sigal urbs, ubi regia Sacarum, propeque Alexandria urbs et non procul Alexandriapolis urbs.* From the Mahawansa, moreover, we learn that *Alasadda* was the Capital of the Yona country. The mention of *dìpo* in reference to Alasanda, in one of the above extracts, presents no valid objection against its identification with Alexandria ; for Pali writers, and Buddhists in general, like the ancient Greeks, had a very vague notion of the Geographical position of countries.

Perhaps the *Milindappanna*, as well as the Inscriptions do, not furnish conclusive proofs on the subject ; since they were clearly *after* the date of *Asoka*, who is expressly mentioned therein. Nor indeed are the *Nàtakas* of much value, for the same reason. But the same objection does not apply to *Manu*, or the *Mahà Bhárata*, in both which ancient works the *Yavanas* are mentioned.

Manu states* that the following tribes were originally Kshatriyas, but have gradually sunk to the state of Vrishalas (*S*udras), from the extinction of sacred rites and from having no communication with Brahmans ; viz. Paun*d*rakas, Odras, Dravi*d*as, Kāmbojas, *Yavanas*, *S*akas Pāradas, Pahlavas, Chìnas, Kirātas, Daradas, and Khasas.

" These tribes of Kshatriyas, viz., *S*akas, *Yavanas*, Kāmbojas, Dravi*d*as, Kalindas, Pulindas, Usìnaras, Kolisarpas, and Mahìshakas, have become Sudras from seeing no Brahmans."†

The facts contained in the above extracts are supported in the Buddhistical annals ; and in quoting therefrom it becomes my privilege to adduce the authority to which Mr. Turnour referred, but which he failed to adduce, to prove that 'Yavana (yóna) is mentioned anterior to Alexander's invasions in the ancient Pali works'‡ Whether the Buddhist Pitakattáya was written after the death of the Sage, or before (and that it was at the period of the Buddhist era is also capable of satisfactory proof), Gotama, whose age is firmly established, has spoken of the Yavanas ; and in special reference to the distinction of *Aryas* and *dàsyas*, which was recognized in

* Chapter x. 43. 44.

† Anusasana Parva, verses 2103 et seq.

‡ See Turnour's Introd. to Mahavansa, xl., vi.

the pachchanta (foreign) countries such as Yona and Kamboja.

In the *Majjhima Nikàya*, from which I shall again quote, Gotama is said to have asked :

Tankin maññasi Assalàyana? suttante 'Yona Kambojesu aññesu cha pachchante mesu janapadesu vevannā ayyocheva dàso cha hòti—ayyo hutvà dàsohoti, dàsohutvà ayyohotì'ti.

'Assalàyana, what thinkest thou of *this*? Hast thou heard, that in *Yona* and *Kamboja*, and in other foreign countries, there are various ayyas* (superiors) and *dàsas* (inferiors); that superiors become inferiors, and inferiors superiors'?

It is said in the commentary that the above was said to illustrate (such a case as) this :

Bràhmano sabhariyo vanijjan payo jento Yonaka rattan và Kamboja rattan và gantvà kàlankaroti,—tassa gehe vayappatto dàso hoti; Bràhmanì dásenavà kammakàre navà saddhin vásankappeti; etasmin dàrake jàte so puriso dàsova hoti; tassa jàta dàrako para dàyajja sàmiko hotimatito suddho pitito asuddho—so vanijjan payojento majjhima padosan gantvà bráhmana dàrikan gahetvà; tassà puchchhismin puttan patilabhati, sopi màtitova suddho hoti pitito asuddho. Evan Bráhmana samayasmin yeva jàtisambhedo hoti—ti dassanattan etan vuttan.

'A Brahaman, provided with merchandize, having gone with his wife either to the country of Kamboja, or the country of Yona, dies. There is a grown up *dása* or laborer in his house. The Brahmanì lives either with the *dàsa* or the laborer, and begets a child for him;—that person is still a *dàsa*. The child that is born for him, who is pure as regards the mother, and impure as regards the father, becomes the lord of the inheritance. He (too), provided with merchandize, goes to the Majjhima region, and takes to him a Brahaman lass. She too gets a son, who is pure only on the mother's side, but impure on that of the

---

* For the Brahmanical definition of this word as well as *dasa*; See. Dr. Muir's Sanskrit Texts ii. pp. 379, 380.

father. Thus according to the very observances of the Brahamans there is a distinction of tribes.'

Whilst the authority above quoted satisfactorily explains the reason why, as in *the Hero and the Nymph*, Kàlidàsa has applied the term *Yavana* to *menial females*; it also establishes the fact that the *Yavanas* were ante Buddhistical.

It has also been stated by Professor Max Muller that since *Pànini* refers to the *Unnâdi-sûtras*, which mention *dinàrah* 'the Roman *denarius*', *Jinah* 'synonimous with Arhat a Buddhist saint', *tirîtam* 'a golden diadem', *stûpah* 'the Buddhist topes'; the Sanskrit Grammarian was *after* Buddha.* The learned Professor himself has rendered it very probable that all these words were introduced into the *Unnâdisûtras* 'after the general spreading of Buddhism, and the erection of Topes in India.' This was, however, upon the supposition that the *Unnâdi sûtras*, which are now extant, were identical with the Sûtras of the same name quoted by Pànini. But, the proof is indeed wanting to show that such was the fact; and the non-existence of the many Grammatical works to which *Pànini* refers, and the anxiety evinced by the Brahmans to place that sage as *Pàninyàdyah*, may fairly lead to the inference that all those works, including the particular *Unnàdi* sùtras referred to by Pànini, had been long ago lost.†

Since these sheets have gone to the press, and the two first sheets have been printed, I have received from England the invaluable work of Professor Goldstucker on the age of Pànini; and I here avail myself of that consummate scholar's remarks on the *Unnàdi* Sùtras, which directly bear upon the subject.

'It is true (says he) that this grammarian (Pànini) speaks twice of *Unnàdis*, but he *never* speaks of Unnàdi-*Sùtras*.

---

* Sankrit Literature p. 245.

† 'None of the more ancient works seem to be now extant'—Colebrooke's Essays ii. pp. 5, 6.

The former term merely implies a list of Unnàdi affixes, and may imply, according to analogous expressions in Pànini, a list of words formed with these affixes; but it can never imply a work which treats of these affixes and these formations, like the Unnàdi Sùtras which we are speaking of. Between a list of Unnàdis—affixes or words—and Unnàdi-Sùtras, there is all the difference which exists between a lexicographical and a grammatical work. All the conclusions, therefore, which are based on the identity of both, vanish at once —p. 159.

Again, says the same writer: 'Had Pànini not written the five Sutras (1, 2, 53-57) in which he explains the method of his grammar, or had he explained all the technical terms used by him, the absence of a definition of such terms in the Unnàdi-Sùtras would not justify us in arriving at any conclusion as regards the mutual relation of the two works. But since we know that Pànini does not define all his terms; and, on the other hand, that a treatise like the Unnàdi-Sutras uses those terms which are defi ned by him, and *exactly in the same sense in which they occur in his work*, the only possible conclusion is that this treatise was written later than the Grammar of Pànini.'—p. 170.

I have examined the Unnàdi-Stùras with the assistance of my Pandit; but have not been able to find any correspondence between them and the *Unnàdi* in Kachchàyana's grammar—a circumstance which favors my belief that the former work was also later than, the Pali grammar. This therefore accounts for the mention of 'the Roman *denarius*'* and 'the Buddhist *sthùpa*' and '*Jina*, the founder of a Buddha sect' &c.; although the two last, I may remark, had an origin before the age of Gòtama, as may be shewn from the sermons of that sage himself.

* Indeed this word like the others, has claims to a higher antiquity than the age of Gotama. See *Dena* in Pr. H. Wilson's Glossary of Judicial Terms.

M. Reinaud in his 'Mémoire Géographique, Historique et Scientifique Sur l' Inde &c. (Paris 1849) says.

'*Hiouen Thsang* attributes to Pànini, as he does to many other notable personages of Buddhism, two existences; the first he refers to an epoch in which the life of man was longer than at present, and the second about the year 500 after the death of Buddha; that is, in the time of Vickramaditya, a century after the reign of Kaniska. In his first existence, Pànini professed Brahmanism; but in in his second, he, together with his father, was converted to Buddhism.'—p. 88.

Founded upon this "Ghost-story", it has also been supposed by Professor Weber that Pànini should be placed six centuries after Gotama Buddha, or at 140 A.D.* But the legendary tale which *Hiouenthsang* relates, and which is quoted below, far from countenancing this conjecture, merely places him, "*at the epoch* when the life of man was reduced to a hundred years." This need not necessarily have been, as we again ascertain from the Buddhistical annals, *after* Gotama Buddha. It is stated in the *Buddhavansa* that.

'At the particular period (of the manifestation of the great elect) the term of human existence was one hundred years; and that it therefore appeared to be the proper age in which his advent should take place.'

This subject may therefore be dismissed by simply subjoining the following translation† of the passages referred to in *Hiouen thsang*:—

'Having travelled about twenty *li* north-east of the town, *Ou-to-kia han t'cha* (Udakhànda?) he arrived at the city *Po-lo-tou-lo* (Sâlâtura), the birth place of *Rishi Po-ni-ni* (*Páni-ni*) author of the treatise *Ching-ming lun* (Vyâkaranam.)

'During the times of a remote antiquity, the words of the language were extremely numerous; but after the world had

---

* See Professor Max Muller's remarks hereon in his Sanskrit Literature p. 304 et seq.

† For which as well as various other passages from French and German writers my acknowledgements are due to my Teacher J. B. Blake Esq,

been destroyed, the universe was found void and waste. Some Gods of an extraordinary longevity descended on the earth to serve as guides to the nations. Such was the origin of letters and books. At the conclusion of this epoch their source enlarged itself, and became boundless. The god Fan (Brahman), and the king of heaven (Indra) established rules and conformed to the times. Some heretic Rishis compos,-ed, each of them, some words. Men used them as models, carried on their work, and rivalled with each other in preserving tradition; but students made vain efforts, and it was difficult for them to comprehend their meaning.

'At the epoch when the life of man was reduced to a hundred years, the *Rishi Pánini* appeared, who received instruction from his birth, and possessed an immense understanding. Grieved at the ignorance of the age, he longed to abolish all vague and false conceptions, to extricate language from superfluous terms, and to establish its laws. As he was travelling for the purpose of research and instruction, he met the God *Tseu thsai* (Isvara Deva), and set before him the plan of the work he was meditating.

'Very well said the god *Tseu-thsai* (Isvara Deva) you may reckon on my assistance.

'Having received his instructions the Rishi departed He then gave himself up to profound researches, and employed all the energy of his intellect. He collected a multitude of expressions, and composed a vocabulary which contained a thousand slokas; each sloka consisted of thirty-two syllables. He sounded to their utmost limits, knowledge both ancient and modern; and having brought together, in this work, letters and terms, he enclosed it in a sealed envelope, and presented it to the king, who equally prized and admired it. He made a decree, which ordered all his subjects to study and teach it. He added that he, who should be able to recite it from one end to the other, would receive a reward of a thousand pieces of gold. Hence the reason, (thanks to the lessons of successive teachers) that this work is still held in great estimation. Hence it is that the Brahmans of this city possess substantial knowledge, and talents of a high order, and are always distinguished by the extent of their knowledge, and the rich stores of their memory.

'In the city of *Po-lo-tou-lo* (read *So-lo-tou-lo,* Sâlâtura) there is a *Stûpa*. It was in this place that a *Lo-han* (an *Arhat*) converted a disciple of *Ponini*. Five huudred years after is *Jou-lai* (the Tathàgata) had left the world, there was a great *'Olohan* (Arhat) who, coming from the kingdom of *Kia-chi-milo* (Cashmire) travelled for the purpose of converting people. When he had arrived in this country, he saw a *Fan-tchi* (a Brahmachârin) occupied in whipping a little boy, whom he was teaching. "Why do you ill-treat that child ?" said the *Arhat* to the *Fan-tchi.*

'I am making him study,' replied he, 'the treatise of the doctrine of sounds, (ching-ming Vyâkaranam) but he makes no progress.'

'The Arhat seemed amused, and suffered a smile to escape him. The old *Fan-tchi* said to him, "The *Cha-men* (sramanas) possess a tender and compassionate heart, and they pity the creatures that are enduring pain. A man full of humanity smiles upon occasion. I should wish to learn the cause.

'It is not difficult to make you acquainted with it, replied the Arhat, but I fear I shall produce in you a hesitancy of belief. You have, doubtless, heard of a certain Rish[1] named *Ponini*, who composed the treatise *ching-ming-lun,* and that he has left it behind for the instruction of the world. The *Po-lo-men* said to him—The children of this city who are all his disciples, revere his virtue, and the statue, erected to his memony, exists at this day.

'Well said the *Arhat*, this child, to whom you gave life, is actually that *Rishi*. In his former existence, he used his strong memory in studying profane writings: he did not speak, but of heretical treatises, and did not seek at all the truth. His genius and his science perished; and he coursed though, without stopping, the circle of life, and of death. Thanks to a remnant of virtue, he has been permitted to become your dear son. But profane writings, and the eloquence of the age only impose a useless labour. Can they be compared to the sacred instructions of *Jou -lai* which, by a mysterious influence, affords understanding and happiness. ?

'In former times, there was, on the shores of the Southern Ocean, a whithered tree whose hollow trunk afforded an asylum to five hundred bats. One day, some merchants halted at the foot of this tree. As there prevailed at the time an icy cold breeze, these men, who were tormented with cold and hunger, collected together sticks and thorns, and lighted a fire at the foot of the tree. The flame increased by degrees, and soon set the withered tree on fire.

'At this moment there was one of the merchants who began, at mid night, to read with a loud voice, the collection of the *O-pi-ta-mo* (Abhidharma.) The bats, tormented as they were by the heat of the fire, listened however, with desire to the accents of the law, endured the pain without quitting their retreat, and there terminated their existence. In consequence of this virtuous conduct, they obtained the honor of being born again in the class of human beings. They left their families, gave themselves up to study, and, thanks to the sounds of the law which they had formerly heard, they acquired a rare understanding, obtained altogether the dignity of Arhat, and cultivated from age to age, the field of happiness.

'During this latter period the king *Kia-ni-se-kia* (Kanish'ka) and the Honorable *Hie* (Arya-Parsvika) assembled five hundred sages in the kingdom of *Kia-chi-mi-lo* (Cashmire) and composed the *Pi-po-cha-lun* (the Vibhásha sástra). All these sages were the five hundred bats who had formerly inhabited the cavity of the withered tree. Although I possess a limited intelligence, yet I am one of them. But, men differ from one another, either by the superiority, or mediocrity of their genius. Those essay their flight, while these creep in obscurity. And now, O man full of humanity, you must allow your dear son to leave his friends. In performing this act, that is, embracing the life of a religieuse, one acquires in effable merit.

'Having finished his discourse, the Arhat gave proof of his divine power by his immediate disappearance.

'The Bráhman felt himself penetrated by faith and reverence; and, having loudly expressed his admiration, went and related the event in the neighbourhood. He also permitted his son to embrace the life of a Religieuse, and devote himself to study. As for himself, he was immediately converted; and showed the greatest esteem for the *Three Gems.* The men of his village followed his example, and, even at this day, the inhabitants are confirmed in their faith, day by day.'

Professor Bohtlingh, in his introduction to Pánini, advances the following arguments founded, as it would seem, on nearly the same authorities as those already quoted.

'As respects the age (he says) in which our Grammarian lived, I will produce some citations which will give some weight to the received opinion, that *Pánini* lived in the 4th Century, according to our chronology.

'*Amara-Sinha,* the most ancient lexicographer whose work is extant, lived, as universally received, in the middle of the first centry after Christ. In his work, we meet with a multitude of grammatical expressions and affixes, which occur also in *Pànini.* From this circumstance alone, one should not venture to decide absolutely on the high antiquity of *Pànini;* for, as we have early enough remarked, *Pánini's* grammatical terminology is easily discovered amongst his predecessors. By means of the following passages, however. I trust, I shall be authorized to draw a conclusion.

Amara Kosha (S 363, p I. and S. 378 12 and S 384 25 of Colebrook's edition.) It is said, that the word *Rātra* at the end of a compound, is masculine except when a numeral precedes; in this case it is a neuter.

According to Pànini (II 4. 29), *Ràtra* at the end of a compound is always masculine; *Kàtyàyana* also appears to maintain the rule unrestricted; compare with II. 4. 29— S. 363. Z. 4. (Colebrooke's) (S. 384. 26.) *Pathah Sankvyavyayat parah* ("*patha,* on a numerable or an undeclinable word following, is at the end of a compound neuter.)" *Pànini* (II, 4. 30.) allows only *Apatha* to be a neuter; *Kàtyàyana* enlarges the rule, in the same manner as *Amara Sinha*; compare with II. 4. 30.—S. 368. Z. 4. (Colebr. 385. 15.) *Punayasudinàmyò twahah parah,* "*Aha,* on *punaya* and *sudina* following, (is a neuter.)" With *Pànini, Aha,* at the end of every compound, is a neuter. Both opinions are given by Kātyāyana (compare with II. 4. 29.) The passage next following is most decidedly only half intelligible, without consulting our grammarian S. 374. Z. 3. (S. 393. 45. C.) *Anághantàstetarak tàgharthe.* The derivatives in *An* &c. in the signification of "coloured thereby" &c. (are all of three genders.) *An* is the first affix in that division of grammar in which the *taddhitas* and their significations are treated of; compare IV. 1. 83. The first signification of these affixes, in the formation of adjectives, is *Tenaraktan*; compare IV. 2. 1.

'It is indeed, by no means proved hereby that Pànini lived three centuries before *Amara Sinha.* But then this opinion will acquire probability, when it is stated that *Amara Sinha* is still more recent than Patangali. In this case we shall still have, between Pànini and Amara Sinha, four Grammarians; Kàtyàyana, the author of the *Paribáshā,* the author of the *Karika,* and *Patangali.*

'Tradition makes *Bhartrihari* the brother of *Vickramadit ya,* the author of the *Karika.* Were this point settled, *Patangali* would be at most a contemporary of *Amara Sinha's.* This tradition is contradicted by another; according to which *Patangali* is removed to a high antiquity, and constituted a mythological being in the shape of a Serpent. We shall not, however, take our refuge, by proving the worthlessness of one story by means of another, whilst we have at our command an historical testimony in the annals of *Kashmere.* The passage contains a grammatical difficulty, which may however, be removed by a small alteration. The verse is expressed in the Calcutta edition as follows (1. 176.)

Chandràcharyádibhirlabdhadesan tasmat tadàgaman.
Pravartitan sahabhashyan svan cha vyákaranan krit.

'Troyer (in his recent edition of this chronicle, *Ràjàtaringini*) reads *Chandra vyàkuranam* for *svan cha vyàkaranam,* and translates " Tchandràtcharya and others after receiving the commands, explained his (the king Abhimanyu's) *Sāstra,* and composed a large commentary and a grammar bearing the name of Chandra." Seeing, for ought that I know, that nothing is said any where about Abhimanyu's having composed a *Sāstra,* the word *pravartitan* can have no grammatical reference to *tadàgaman*; for this word is of necessity a masculine. To join *tadàgaman* as an adjective to *labdhàdesan,* and to render it " to come thither (to Abhimanyupura) or to him according to the command received by him" would be too forced. We read *labdhvàdesan;* then can *tadàgaman* be easily united with *Adesan.* Professor Herr Lassen, whom I consulted on this passage, proposed to me to read *tadàgame* by which the difficulty would be removed. "The causal from *pravart* has here, assuredly, no other signification than ' to set up a thing, to introduce a matter.'" The full sense of the verses will accordingly be the following: " when the teacher Kandra and others had received the command from him, (the king Abhimanyu) thither, (or to him) to repair, they produced the *Mahabàshya* and composed an accurate grammar." To corroborate this translation I put down here a quite similar passage from the same work (IV. 487.)

Desàntaràdāgamayya vyàchakshanàn kshamàpatih.
Pràvartayata vichchinnan mahabashyan svamandale.

" After the king (Gayàpida,) had brought in expositors from other lands, he introduced into his land the worn-out (no longer extant in a perfect condition ?) *Mahabàshya* again." M. Troyer renders vichchinnan *Mahabàshyan* by " the large well divided grammar," and remarks in a parenthesis, that this is *Pànini's* Grammar. In the first verse that learned man has translated *Mahabhàshya* quite commonly "a large commentary," as I conjecture, from this ground that it appeared to him improbable that the study of grammar was pursued already in the twelfth century according to our reckoning. (M. Troyer maintains strongly the chronology of the Cashmirian chronicle.) From this can we explain only his remarks on every passage: "The titles of the books *vyàkarana*, and *Upadêsa*, appear amongst the Buddhists, to be equivalent to those of the "*puràṇas*" and "tantras" (See the Memoir of Mr. Hodgson in the Transactions of the Rl. As. Soc. of Great Britain and Ireland, Vol II. parts I. and II.

'*Kandra* occurs in a memorial verse in union with the following ancient grammarians. *Indra, Kasakritsna, Apisali, Sâkatàyana, Pànini, Amara*, and *Ginendra*. *Bhattogi* mentions him and his followers, the *Kandras*, often.

'The age of the king *Abhimanyu*, in whose reign *Kandra* lived, may be fixed in several ways, all of which lead to the same result. Under *Abhimanyu*, there appeared in Cashmere, the *Bodhisatva Nagârjuna*, whose birth the Tibetans place 400 years after Buddha's death, therefore in the year 143 or 144 before Christ. His preaching as well as the reign of *Abhimanyu* may be accordingly fixed for the year 100. We maintain the same number, when we adhere to the chronicle of Cashmere. *Asoka*, the forty-eighth king of the second period is, without doubt, the grandson of *Kandragupta*. *Asoka* is removed from his grandfather forty-nine or sixty-two years; the beginning of his reign will fall in the year 250 before Christ. Five kings, according to the annals of Cashmere, divide *Asoka* from *Abhimanyu*. Let us allow each of them as well as *Asoka*, to reign on an average twenty-five years; we then have the wished for number of years for *Abhimanyu*. We arrive close to the same result when we follow the Chinese narrative. This narrative places *Kanishka* the last of the Turushka princes, and the direct predecessor of Abhimanyu 400 years after Buddha's death, that is, in the year 143—144 after Christ. Now, since we have discovered, that *Patangali's Mahabhashya* through *Kandra* in Cashmere, already in the year 100 before Christ, came into general use, we are fully authorized to put back the composition of the great commentary on *Pànini's* Sûtras to the year 150. Between *Patangali* and *Pànini*, there are, as we have remarked above, three Grammarians known to us who furnish us with contributions to *Pànini's* grammar. We need accordingly to place the interval between merely two or fifty years, to reach the year 350, in which, according to *Kathâ-saritsâgara*, our Grammarian is to be placed.'*

Professor Max Muller in reviewing the above arguments says Professor Bohtlingk "endeavored to shew that the great commentary of Patanjali, which embraces both the Varttikàs of Kàtyàyana, and the sûtras of Pànini, was known in the middle of the second century B. C. It is said in the history of Kashmir, that Abhimanyu, the king of Kashmir, sent for Brahmans to teach the Mahàbhàshya in his kingdom. Abhimanyu, it is true, did not reign, as Professor Bohtlingk supposed, in the second century B. C., but, as has been proved from coins, by Professor Lassen, in the first century A. D. But even thus this argument is important. In the history of Indian literature, dates are mostly so precarious, that a confirmation even within a century or two, is not to be despised. The fact that *Patanjali's* immense commentary on *Pànini* and Kàtyàyana had become so famous as to be imported by royal authority into Kashmir in the first half of the first century, A D, shews at least, that we cannot be very far wrong in placing the composition of the original grammar and of the supplementary rules of Kàtyàyana on the threshold of the third century B. C. At what time the Mahà-

* Introduction to Panini by Bohtlingk—See contra by Weber in his Introduction.

bhàshya was first composed it is impossible to say.* Patanjali, the author of the great commentary, is sometimes identified with Pingala; and on this view, as Pingala is called the younger brother, or at least the descendant of Pànini, it might be supposed that the original composition of the Mahàbhàshya belonged to the third century. But the identity of Pingala and Patanjali is far from probable, and it would be rash to use it as a foundation for other calculations.'†

All these arguments Professor Max Muller characterizes as "entirely hypothetical." Indeed they are; and the reader cannot fail to perceive that though it is quite correct to fix the date of Pànini at some time before *Amarasinha*, yet

---

* The following observations have an important bearing upon the question :—

' This is the only date, the fixing of which is called "*impossible*," in Muller's Ancient Sanskrit Literature; and as it has hitherto been my fate to differ from this work in all its chronological views, I seem merely to follow a predestined necessity in looking upon the date of Patanjali as the only one which I should venture to determine with anything like certainty.

' I do so, because Patanjali, as if foreseeing the conjectural date which some future Pandit would attach to his life, or the doubt that might lift him out of all historical reach, once took the opportunity of stating a period before which we must not imagine him to have lived, while on another occasion he mentions the time when he actually did live.

' "If a thing," says Panini, "serves for a livelihood, but is not for sale" (it has not the affix *ka*). This rule Patanjali illustrates with the words "Siva, Skanda, Visakha," meaning the idols that represent these divinities and at the same time give a living to the men who possess them,—while they are not for sale. And, "why?" he asks. "The *Mauryas* wanted gold, and therefore established religious festivities. Good; (Panini's rule) may apply to such (idols, as *they* sold); but as to idols which are hawked about (by common people) for the sake of such worship as brings an immediate profit, their names will have the affix *ka*."

' Whether or not this interesting bit of history was given by Patanjali ironically, to show that even affixes are the obedient servants of kings, and must vanish before the idols which *they* sell, because they do not take the money at the same time that the bargain is made—as poor people do,—I know not. But, at all events, he tells us distinctly by these words that he did not live before the first king of the Maurya dynasty who was Chandragupta, and who lived 315 B. C. And I believe, too, if we are to give a natural interpretation to his words, that he tells us, on the contrary, that he lived *after the last king* of this dynasty, or in other words later than 180 before Christ. But he has even been good enough to relieve us from a possibility of this doubt when commenting on another rule of Panini, or rather on a criticism attached to it by Katyayana.'—*Goldstucker's "Panini" p. p.* 228—9.

† Professor Max Muller's Sanskrit Literature p. 240.

no valid ground has been shewn to determine *that* as having been *after* the Buddhistical era.

A fact, however, may be here cited from the Buddhistical annals, which apparently countenances the conjecture of Professor Max Muller. It is this; that *Dévala* is mentioned as a contemporary of Gotama.

The *Atthokathà* to the Buddhavansa after alluding to the birth of *Siddhatta* before he became *Gotama-Buddha* says:— 'At that period a certain *tápaso*, named *Kàladewalo*, who was a confidant of the màharàja Suddhodano, and who had acquired the eight *samàpatti*, having taken his meal,—for the purpose of enjoying his noonday rest,—repaired to the *Tàwatinsá* realms. He there found the host of *dewatà*, in the *Tàwatinsa* realms, revelling in joy, and in the exuberance of their felicity, waving cloths over their heads, and asked, 'Why is it that ye thus rejoice, in the fulness of the heart's delight? Tell me the cause thereof?' The *dewatà* thus replied, 'Blessed! unto the ràja a son is born, who seated at the foot of the bo tree, having become Buddho, will establish the supremacy of *dhammo*: and we shall be blessed with the sight of the many attributes of his Buddhohood, and with the hearing of his *dhammo*. It is from this cause that we rejoice.'

'Thereupon the said Dewala the tápaso, on hearing this announcement of theirs, descending from the supreme Dewalòka enchanting with its golden glitter; and entering the palace of the monarch Suddhodana, seated himself on the pre-eminent throne erected therein. He then thus addressed the ràja who had accorded to him a gracious reception. 'Ràja to thee a son is born: him I will see.' The ràja caused the infant, richly clad, to be brought, in order that he (the infant) might do homage to the *tàpaso, Dévalo.* The feet of the great elect, at that instant performing an evolution, planted themselves on the ja*tà* (top-knot of *Devalo*) which glittered, from its hoariness, like unto the fleecy white cloud impregnated with rain. There being no one greater to whom reverence is due than to a Buddho elect, who had attained the last stage of existence,—instantly rising from the throne on which he was seated, (*Dewalo*) bowed down with his clasped hands raised over his head, to the Buddho elect; and the Ràja also, on witnessing this miraculous result, likewise bowed down to his own son.

'The *tàpaso* having perceived the perfection of the immortal attributes of the elect, was meditating whether he would or would not become the supreme Buddho; and while thus meditating, he ascertained by his power of perception into futurity, he would certainly become so; and smiling said, 'This is the wonderful mortal.' He again thus meditated: 'am, I or am I not destined to behold his achievement of Buddhohood?' and said, 'No, I am not destined: dying in the interval, though a thousand *Buddhà* be henceforth manifested, it will not be vouchsafed to me to participate in such a blessing: I shall be regenerated in realms inhabited by incorporeal spirits: never shall I behold the wonderful mortal: a mighty calamity is impending over me.' Having thus divined, he wept.

'The bystanders remarking, 'our *ayyo* (revered teacher) having this moment smiled, has now commenced to weep,' inquired, 'Is there any misfortune impending over the infant of our ruler?' The *tàpaso* replied, :unto him there is no impending calamity: beyond all doubt he is destined to become Buddho.' 'Why dost thou then weep?' 'I am not destined to see so wonderful a mortal as this, on his attaining Buddhohood: most assuredly unto me this is an awful calamity. I weep in the bitterness of my own disappointment.'

If the Kàladèvala ascetic here mentioned 'who had acquired the eight samàpatti,' and Dèvala 'the inspired legislator' of the Hindu Pauranic legends were identical, we might indeed be warranted in placing Pânini, as 'the grandson of Dèvala,' in the third century B. C., or in the third century A. D. But, this is by no means satisfactorily proved. There is the same difference between their names as between Sàkatâyana and Kàtyàyana. The *Pauranic* legend is also contradicted by *Bhottagi*. Professor Bothlingk says: "Pànini is, according to Bhottogi, a descendant of Pâninâ, who is either a *grandson.* or more remote descendant of Panin." Be this how ever, as it may. Without at all impugning the authenticity or genuineness of the Pali Atthakathà to the Buddhawansa, it may be stated that the identification of these two persons involves us in this difficulty, viz. that to other well-known Hindu works and writers, whom Gotama unmistakably mentions, we must in that case, assign a post-Buddhistic date.

At the time Gotama appeared, the *Vedangas* had been in existence. At the time the Vedàngas were composed, 'the period of inspiration,' according to Brahmans and even Buddhists, had long before ceased.* Their authors too, claimed no inspiration for themselves. They merely rendered the study of "the revealed literature," easier. Devala, as an "inspired legislator'" must therefore belong to a period before the *Vedànga* literature, and anterior to the appearance of Gotama Buddha. Hence the non-identity between *Devala* and *Kàla devala.*

If, again, Pànini lived two or three centuries after Buddha, we are sure to have in his sùtras, some allusion to the sage or his remarkable doctrines, which, as M. Burnouf says, 'found numerous recruits among those who were frightened by the difficulties of Brahmanical science.' There is however no such allusion; and the word 'Stûpah,' if it were not a later introduction, means, 'not a Buddhist tope,' but simply 'a heap of earth,' as it is said to have been used in the Vedas.

To place Pànini *after* the Buddhist era (supposing that I have correctly fixed the age of Kachchàyana) is indeed to affirm that the proud Brahamans were indebted for their Grammatical principles to those who had ceceded from their Church, and who were availing themselves of the Brahaman literature; and at a time too, when Buddhism with the language in which it was promulgated, was fast disappearing in Hindustan. This is indeed so very improbable, especially in view of the fact expressly stated by Kachchàyana, that he had adopted

* Gotama himself says that long before his advent the Brahamans had fallen off from their high sanctity.

terms given by *Sanskrit* Grammarians; that it may reasonably be concluded that Pànini was before Kachcháyana, and therefore before Gotama Buddha.

Professor Goldstucker says: 'Though Yáska be older than Pánini, and Pánini older than Kátyáyana, there still remains the mystery as to the era of Pánini. No work of the ancient literature, within my knowledge, gives us the means of penetrating it. But as the remotest date of Hindu antiquity which may be called a real date, is that of *Buddha's* death, it must be of interest to know whether Pánini is likely to have lived before or after this event.

'Not only is the name of *Sákyamuni*, or Sákya, never adverted to in the Sùtras of Pánini, but there is another fact connected with this name which is still more remarkable.

'The great schism which divided ancient India into two hostile creeds, centres in the notion which each entertained of the nature of eternal bliss. The Brahmanic Hindus hope that their souls will ultimately become united with the universal spirit; which, in the language of the Upanishads, is the neuter Brahman; and, in that of the sects, the supreme deity, who takes the place of this philosophical and impersonal god. And however indefinite this god Brahman may be, it is nevertheless, to the mind of the Brahmanic Hindu, an *entity*. The final salvation of a Buddhist is entire *non-entity*. This difference between the goal of both, created that deep and irreconcileable antagonism which allowed of none of the compromise which was possible between all the shades and degrees of the Brahmanic faith, from the most enlightened to the most degenerate. The various expressions for eternal bliss in the Brahmanic creed, like *apavarga, moksha, mukti, nihsreyasa*, all mean either "liberation from this earthly career" or the "absolute good;" they therefore imply a condition of hope. The absolute end of a Buddhist is without hope; it is *nirvána*, or extinction.

This word means literally "*blown out*;" but there is this difference, if I am not mistaken, between its use in the Brahmanic and in the Buddhistic literature,—that, in the former, it is employed, like other past participles, in any of the three genders, whereas in the latter it occurs only in the neuter gender, and there, too, only in the sense of an abstract noun, in that of *extinction*, *i. e.*, absolute annihilation of the soul. I have no instance at my command in which *nirvàna*, when used in the classical literature, implies any other sense than the sense "*blown out*," or a sense immediately connected with it. Thus Patanjali, when illustrating the use of this past participle, gives the instances: "the fire is *blown out* by the wind, the lamp is *blown out* by the wind;" and Kaiyyata who, on the same occasion, observes that a phrase, "the wind has ceased to blow," would not be expressed by "*nirvàno* vátah, but by *nirvàto* vátah," corroborates the instances of Patanjali with one of his own: "blowing out (has been effected) by the wind." But Pánini, who teaches the formation of this participle in rule VIII. 2, 50, which has indirectly called forth all these instances, says: "(the past participle of *và* with prefix *nir* is) *nirvàna* (if the word means) '*free from wind*,' (or, 'not blowing, as wind')."

'This is the natural interpretation of Pánini's rule. *Kàtyàyana*, it is true, gives a Várttika, which corrects the word *aváte* into *avàtàbhidhâne* "(if it have) not the sense of wind (or of blowing);" yet it is very remarkable that Patanjali, in commenting on this Várttika, does not interpret its words in his usual manner, but merely adds to them the instances I have just named; it is remarkable, too, that he introduces them with the observation: "(this Várttika is given in order to show) that (nirvána) is *also* or is emphatically used in the following instances." Still he has no instance whatever for the sense stated by *Pànini*, and his word "*also*" or "emphatically" does not appear to be justified by the criticism of Kátyáyana, which simply corrects the word *aváte* into *avàtábhidhàne* without any additional remark.

'In short, my opinion on this Vàrttika is analogous to that which I have expressed in previous instances. The sense of *nirvàna*, "free from wind (or not blowing)," had become obsolete in the time of Kàtyàyana, who merely knew that sense of it which found its ulterior and special application in the *nirvána* of the Buddhistic faith. But since there is no logical link between this latter word and the *nirvàna*, "wind-still," of Pànini; and since it is not probable that he would have passed over in silence that sense of the word which finally became its only sense, I hold that this sense did not yet exist in his time; in other words, that his silence affords a strong probability of his having preceded the origin of the Buddhistic creed.' *

Dr. Weber after reviewing the remarks of Professor Goldstucker,† concludes by exclaiming—"And this then is all wherewith Goldstucker is able to prop up his opinion of

---

* Goldstucker's Panini, p 225 et seq.

† As follows :—'As by the general reception of Goldstucker's results, a relatively chronological result only concerning Panini's connection with the work in question has after all been attained; let us now proceed to the crown with which he has adorned that work, if his which awaits this consummation, viz., the demonstration that Panini must have lived before the time of Buddha. This indeed, which, if true discloses an important discovery, is founded upon two points. First, upon this, that Panini does not mention the name of Sakyamimi. Now we learn from Goldstucker himself (p. 18. vide supra p. 48.) that nothing is to be inferred from that circumstance—"sometimes the words which belong to his (Panini's) province will be at the same time also of historical and antiquarian interest; but it does not follow at all, that, because a word of the latter category is omitted in his rules, it is absent from the language also." The second point is, that Panini mentions indeed the word *nirvana*, but in the sense of "free from wind, wind-still," and not in the sense in which the word is held by the Buddhists :—"and since it is not probable that he would have passed over in silence that sense of the word which finally became its only sense, I hold that this sense did not yet exist in his time: in other words that his silence offers a strong probability of his having preceded the origin of the Buddhistic creed," (p. 227.) It is quite evident from this passage that this exposition stands in direct opposition to the above-cited earlier expressions of Goldstucker's from p. 18. It is also again to be observed that the word avate in "nirvano 'vate" *Pan*. 8. 2. 50., in the sense of "free from wind," as a possessive adjective, is not the "natural interpretation," but a *perfectly arbitrary* one, blundering against Panini's usage of language, as well as against the sense in which the commentary understands it. The word avate rather stands in juxtaposition with the words asparce anapadane, avijigishayam in the sutra immediately preceding, and is to be understood, with them, as *Karmadharaya*. The sutra subsequently says, "Nirvana [it is

Pànini's priority to Buddha—a daring undertaking indeed ! and at the same time an ignominy of all that speaks to the contrary, which excites surprize" ! The learned Doctor then proceeds to adduce proofs in support of his own opinion—that Pànini was later than Buddha; and produces four items, such as the frequent mention of bhikshu, sramana, chìvara, munda, &c. &c.; 2. That the Buddhists themselves consider Pànini as having lived after Buddha's time. For (says he) Burnouf informs us from the Aryamanjusrí Mûlatantra, " It is thus that Sâkya predicts the future advent of Nagarjûna 400 years after him. He likewise announces that of Pànini, of Chandragupta, and of Aryasangha" ; 3. That Pànini's vocabulary is proof of the proposition; and 4. That no mention is made, among other names, of Pànini in the *Rik* or *Rik. Sanhita.*

Taking the last ground first, it appears to me that (without entering into other questions which arise upon this point), the inference here sought to be deduced is of no greater weight than the like inference drawn by Professor Goldstucker

---

the past perf. pass. of the root *va*] "out of the wind" or, "when there is no wind," that is to say, nirvana is not from the wind which blows out, it is blown out, it has ceased to blow, but from the regular part p. p. *nirvata*. From other things on the contrary, things that are blown out are blown away; for example, according to Patangali for the fire, a light, or as the Calc. Scholiast (how correctly ?) adds that *nirvana* is used for *bhikshu*. This last example is, from Panini's frequent mention of bhikshu, directly such a one as to lead one to suppose that by his rule he had it quite particularly in his eye. But I add that this is a mere conjecture, which may probably be so, but can be of no value anywhere as a proof. I have therefore also in these Studies, IV. 89., where I treat of intimations found in Panini's vocabulary concerning his time, only very briefly pointed them out in the note on the expression *nirvana* in VIII. 2. 50. If I had at all believed that that word must of necessity relate to *bhikshu*, or indeed that it could bear that signification which suits the '*nirvana* of the Buddhistic faith," I would throughout have laid quite another weight upon it. In truth, both words—and it is therefore that Goldstucker's reciprocal exposition of nirvana has failed—have nothing to do with each other. The nirvana of the Buddhistic faith is by no means a neuter of the part perf. passive, which may have acquired an abstract signification, but it is wholly a noun substantive, as niryana, nirmana in the sense of "the blowing out" "the extinction." It is so regularly formed that Panini had not the least occasion to make mention of it, while the irregularly formed past. perf. passive *nirvana* instead of *nirvata*, required altogether a special rule."—*Weber's Indische Studien*, p. 136 *et seq.*

from the fact, that no mention is made of Sàkya by Pànini. As to Pànini's vocabulary, I fail to perceive anything which leads to a conclusion one way or the other; and the words given by Dr. Weber as "actually Buddhistic terms" prove, in my humble opinion, nothing. For the Buddhists have scarcely any words which they have not taken from the Brahmans;* *e. g.* the titles *veyyàkarana* and *Upadesa,* to which reference is made in one of the above extracts, are for the *Abhidhamma-pitaka,* and "the hymns of joyous inspiration" of the Buddhists. It would also appear from the Buddhist works that the Lokàyata or the Jainas† had an existence before Gotama. The Jainas had doubtless their *bhikkhu* mendicants, their *Samana* or *Sàvaka* hearers. They wore *chivara* robes; and had, like the Yavanas, their heads bare. It would, therefore, to say the least, be rash to affirm that the other words given by Dr. Weber as "actually Buddhistic terms" had not been known to other pre-existing Sectarians; more especially as we find in the text books of Bhuddhism that Brahmans had frequently addressed Buddha with the epithets "S(r)amana bhavat Go(w)tama."

We are also told that the Buddhists themselves consider that Pànini is *after* Gotama Buddha. This is a mistake. There is no such belief entertained by the Buddhists in Ceylon. There is no mention of Pànini in any of the Ceylon Buddhist works. The authorities referred to are from the Nepaul works, and they are indeed no authorities at all. The prophecies which are related in them are the interpolations of seceders from the Buddhist Church. The predictions given in some of our own books regarding persons who lived after Gotama, such as Wijaya, Asôka, Nàgasena, &c., are the additions of zealous Buddhists, anxious to up-

---

* Vide Supra p. xxxiii. et seq. "The technology of the Buddhists" says Pandit Rajendralal Mittra, "is to a great extent borrowed from the literature of the Brahmans............... Their metaphysical terms are exclusively Hindu, and the names of most of their divinities are taken from the Hindu Pantheon"—*Lalita Vistara* p. 3.

† See extract in proof of this, *infra.*

hold the characters of whom they wrote, and to procure for their acts all the authority and weight with which such a prediction on the part of the sage was calculated to invest them. And, I may conclude by remarking, that the works themselves, in which these pretended prophecies* are recorded, are comparatively modern works; and therefore not the text-books of Buddhism.

To return to the subject. The proof adduced by Professor Goldstucker is not the only evidence on this matter. It is capable of more satisfactory proof. The best mode in which the dates of authors may be ascertained, in view of the scanty information which Asiatic biography affords us, is by the references which are made by writers whose dates have been ascertained. Now, few dates have been better ascertained than that of *Gotama Buddha.* If it be not 543; it is assuredly 477 B. C. If, therefore, the personages, who figure most conspicuously in Brahmanic history, are unmistakably mentioned by Gotama, there can be but little doubt of their existence having been anti-Buddhistic. By an investigation into the Buddhist Literature, we obtain a result which, to say the least, is satisfactory. According to Sha*d*gurusishya's Commentary on Kàtyàyana's, *Sarvànu krama*: (and here I am indebted to Pr. Max Muller for the extract, see his *Sanskrit Literature,* p. 230, et seq.) Saunahotra, a descendant of Bhàradvàja of the race of Angiras, who entered the family of Bhrigu, took the name of Saunaka;' the Reverend Asvalàyana was Saunaka's pupil;' and Kàtyàyana studied the works of both Saunaka and Asvalàyana.' The same authority places Vyàsa about the same date, if not a little anterior to Saunaka. And V*yàsa,* we learn from other Brahmanical sources, was the son of Parà-

* See Turnour's exposition of these frauds, in the Bengal Journal of the Royal Asiatic Society for September, 1837, with reference to the Nepaul "amplified [vaipulya] sutras," says the learned Rajendralal Mittra, "they allude to individuals who lived long after the days of their alleged author, and claim a degree of elaboration and finish, which leave no doubt as to their having been compiled at a much later period."—*Lalita Vistara,* p. 16.

sara. If therefore, we adjust these names according to their dates, we obtain, 1 Paràsara, 2 Vyàsa, 3 Saunaka, 4 Asvalàyana, and 5 Kàtyàyana. These facts may perhaps be relied upon : but I must object to their being applied to the "idle stories" of Kathà Sàrit Sàgara of Dr. Somadeva of Kashmir, or to any chronological calculations being built upon their basis.

I have already had occasion to refer to this, which is the same work in substance as the Vrihatkatha. It is confessedly not a book of any authority.—It is a compilation of fables, abounding with the "marvellous." It was composed without reference to History or Chronology. It has not even followed the chronological system of his contemporary *Kalhana Pandit*. The author has strung together various stories without order or date; and, I am persuaded, no one would be more amused than Somadeva himself, if now alive, at the historical importance attached by Europeans to his "ghost stories,' lost in the unfathomable depths of his "Ocean-of-Rivers-of-Stories." It may indeed be asserted, (says Professor Wilson) that the *Càthà Sàrit Sàgara*, or rather the *Vrihat Cathà*, is not a much better guide than the *Bhòjaprabanda*, and that a collection of idle tales is bad historical evidence : it must be remembered however, that those tales are not of *Sòmadeva's* invention : he has only the merit of telling them in his own way, and of having collected them together from various quarters. Thus we have most of the legends relating to Vikrama, which constitute the *Sinhàsana Dvdtrinsati* and *Vetala Pancha Vinsati*, and we have also a very considerable portion of the *Hitopadesa* or *Panchatantra* comprised in this selection.'*

Be the authenticity of the matters in Sòmadva's work, however, as it may. It cannot for one moment be maintained that it lends any authority to the identity (upon which several writers have based their inferences) between king Nanda in connection with whom Kàtyàyana is mentioned, and the

* Professor Wilson's Sanscrit Dictionary, pp. x: xi.

predecessor of Chandragupta :* My pandit has shrewdly intimated to me the probability, in view of the age of Asvalàyana, as it appears from Buddha's discourses, and the shifts to which Somadeva resorts to connect Kàtyàyana's story with other fables, that the mention of Channakka and Nanda, had led the writer to identify some previous Nanda with the predecessor of the Sudra king. This is not unlikely in the same manner that the Nepaul Buddhistical writings, to which M. Burnouf assigns a Cashmirian origin, had mistaken Dharmàsoka for Kàlàsoka : and I need hardly add that no inference can be drawn from the mention of *Channakka*. No arguments are indeed necessary to prove that the scheming, and treacherous Purōhita Brahman Channakka, who figures so conspicuously in the Hindu Nàtakas and in our own Buddhistical annals, was different from the venerable sage Saunaka, the preceptor of Asvalàyana " celebrated among the rishis as the glorious, having seen the second Mandala, and who heard the collection of the Maha Bharata."

Nor has this, I believe, been attempted. But the authority upon which the identity between the writer of the Varttikas and the minister of King Nanda of Pàtaliputta is attempted to be established, would have us believe that the former was also the contemporary of *Pànini* 'and actually defeated Pànini in a grammatical controversy.' ! !

To return from this digression : the dates of *Paràsara* and *Asvalàyana*, however, may be ascertained from the Buddhistical annals. True it is that we cannot fix them exactly; but if it can be shewn that they had an existence before Gòtama Buddha, it is sufficient for our purpose. Now, any one who has the slightest acquaintance with the history of Buddhism, and the disputes which the principal fraternities of Brahmans are said to have had with Gotama, cannot fail to identify the youth mentioned in the following extract, (the

---

* Professor Max Muller himself has fairly stated the weight due to this authority. See pp. 242.

first) with one of the descendants of Paràsara, the Hindu sage ;—and likewise the *mànavo* in the second extract, with a descendant of the notable *Asvalàyana* of Hindu legends.

In the *Majjhima Nikàya*, from which I have already quoted, at p. xlv., the following passage occurs :—

1. Evan me sutan : ekan samayan Bhagavà Kajangalàyan vihariti Mukheluvane. Athakho Uttaro mànavo Pàràsariyante vàsi yena bhagavà tenupasankami...... .... Deseti no Uttara Pàràsariyo brahmano Sàvakànan indriyànan bhàvananti ? Deseti bho Gotama Pàràsariyo brahmano sàvakànan indriyànan bhávananti.

'Thus have I heard. When, at a time, Bhagavà dwelt at Mukheluvana in Kajangala, a youth (named) Uttara, a pupil of the *Pàràsariya* fraternity, went to the place where Bhagavà was................. ...... (Gotama inquired) Uttara, does the Brahman (your teacher) of the Pàràsariya fraternity teach *Indriya bhàvanà* to pupils ? Sir, Gotama (replied Uttara) the Brahman of the Pàràsariya fraternity does teach Indriya bhàvanà to pupils.'

In the Assaláyana Suttan, where a dialogue is given between Gotama and one of the *Assalàyana* family, a distinguished member of the Brahman fraternity, as to their alone being 'the highest' race, 'the purest,' 'the projenitors of Mahà Brahmà,' and who had 'sprung from his mouth ;' the following passage occurs :—

2. Evan me sutan : ekan samayan bhagavà Sàvattiyan viharati Jetavane .... Tena khopana samayena nànà verajjakànan brahmanànan panchamattàni Brahmana satáni Sàvattiyan pativasanti kenachadevakaraniyena. Atha kho tesan Brahmanànan etadahosi : 'Ayan kho samano Gotamo chatuvannin suddhin paññàpeti ; konukho pahoti samanena Gotamena saddhin asmin vachane patimantetun'ti. Tena kho pana samayena Assalàyano nàma mànavo Sàvattiyan pativasati ;—dhàro vuttasiro sàlasavassuddesiko jàtiyà ; tinnan vedànan pàragú sanighandu ketubhànan sakkharappabhedà-

nan itihàsa panchamànan; pàdako veyyakarano lokàyata mahà purisa lakkhanesu anavayò.

'Thus have I heard: At a time Bhagavà dwelt at Jetavana in Sàvatti; and at that time about five hundred Brahmans of different countries,* also resided there for some purpose. They thus thought: 'this Samana Gotama proclaims the purity of (all) the four classes: who is able to dispute with Samana Gotama on this matter?' At this time there lived at Sàvatti a youth named Assalàyana. He was young, head-shaven,† and about sixteen years of age (from his birth.) He had mastered the three Vedas, which, with (the supplements) *Nighandu, Ketubhà,* and the distinction of *Akkhara* (letters) &c., have *Itihàsa* for a fifth.‡ He was a Pàdaka,§

---

* By 'different countries' says the Commentator, 'are meant Anga and Magadha.

† Assalayana was of the Bhagu (Bhrigu) family, and this, therefore, agrees with the Brahmanical account—that 'the Bhrigus have their heads quite shaved.'—*Grihya-Sangrah parisishta.*

‡ The above enumeration of Brahmanic sciences may not be unimportant in the identification of the person, who is said to have been accomplished in them. The three *Vedas* are here unmistakably mentioned. They are, as we learn from the *Ambatta Suttan, Irubbeda* (Rig. Veda) *Yajubbeda* (Yajur), and *Samaveda,* made by Attaka and other religious Sages. The fourth Veda, which is here omitted, is elsewhere stated to be the *Attabbana* (Atharvana) Veda, 'made in subsequent times by impious (wicked) Brahmans, introducing life-slaughter, and other irreligious ceremonies, such as sacrificial torments &c.' The fifth veda is called *Itihasa* [puravutta pabandho Bharatadhiko] 'compositions of ancient times such as Bharata &c.' It is also here stated that the three Vedas included '*Nighandu, Ketubha,* and the distinctions of *Akkhara* &c' These are doubtless the supplements to the Vedas, viz. the *Vedangas,* which are also expressly mentioned in the Buddhist annals. By Nighandu is meant, as Professor Roth says, 'a collection of difficult and obsolete words, which formed a basis for instruction in the mode of expounding the Veda." *Ketubha* is explained in the Glossary to be [ketubhanti kiriya-kappa vikappo kavinan upakaraya Sattan] 'a science which is an auxiliary to poetry.' As a supplement, however, to the Veda, Ketubha can only be identified with the Sanskrit *Nirukta,* a science serviceable for the understanding of the Vedic hymns;

Tasmad Vedarthava'-bodhaya upayuktan Niruktam.

'Hence the *Nirukta* is serviceable for the understanding of the meaning of the 'Vedas.' '*The distinction of Akkhara* &c., may also be identified with the Brahmanical *Siksha,* which Sayana defines to be "the science of the pronunciation of letters, accents, &c.'

§ Padaka.—This word is not explained in the glossary. From its being however mentioned immediately before Veyyakarana, I am inclined to believe that it is a

and a Veyyàkarano (grammarian). He was accomplished in Lokàyata,* and in the science of *Purisa-lakkhanà.*†

More direct evidence than the above, can scarcely be adduced of the identity of persons in Asiatic History: and, if, as I apprehend, Assalàyana here named, was a descendant of Asvalàyana, 'celebrated amongst the Rishis', the claims of Pànini to an antiquity remoter than Gotama, are undoubted. It may thence be concluded, that the Buddhist Grammarian availed himself of the Pàninya Vyàkarana, between which and the Pàli aphorisms there is so much correspondence.

But, there is the same correspondence between the Sanskrit *Varttikas,* and the Pali *Vutti.* Was, therefore, Kàtyàyana anterior to the Buddhist Pali Grammarian?

I believe it is not stated that Kàtyàyana was a pupil of Asvalàyana. All that is alleged in respect of the former, is, that 'he, having mastered the thirteen books of Saunaka and of his pupil, composed several books himself.' What time, therefore, elapsed between them does not appear; nor is there any valid reason to admit between them 'only an interval as large as that between teacher and pupil, or between father and son.'‡ If, however, such was the fact, Kàtyàyana may, for the reasons already adduced, be placed before Gotama; for, all the testimony adduced in favor of Pànini's antiquity applies equally to Kàtyàyana.

But, supposing for the sake of argument, that Katyàyana's

Pali expression for the Sanskrit *Nairuktas*, or 'Etymologists,' a large class 'who made the verbal origin of all words the leading principle of all their researches,' as opposed to another school also mentioned in the text viz. the *Vaiyakaranas* or 'Analysers,' who, according to Professor Max Muller, p. 164., 'following the lead of Gargyo the etymologist, admitted the verbal origin of those words only for which an adequate grammatical analysis could be given.'

* The system of Atheistical philosophy taught by *Charvaka.*

† A science which teaches of the temper or fortune of a person, and of the lineaments of his body. The Commentator on the text, says that there was a work on the subject, consisting of 16,000 heads of instruction.

‡ Muller, p. 239.

Varttikà were post-Buddhistical, and after the age of Kachchàyana; and that it is very improbable that the former availed himself of the language of a *Buddhistic* Pali writer: I beg to submit that this hypothesis does not shake the testimony in regard to Mahà Kachchàyana's identity with the author of Sandhikappa; for all that may be fairly inferred in that case, is, that the *Vutti* in the Pali work, like the *Varttikà* to the Sanskrit Grammar, were written at a subsequent period and by a different person.

In noticing this question, it must be borne in mind, that although tradition in one voice ascribes the authorship of the Pàli Suttans in the Sandhikappa to Mahà Kachchàyana, yet that writers are divided in their belief as to the *Vutti* having been written by that distinguished hierarch of the Buddhist Church.* This very difference of opinion disproves the alleged "tendency of later Buddhist writers to refer the authorship of their works to names famous in ancient Brahminic history."—(Max Muller, p. 303.)

Such are the facts and circumstances connected with the age and authorship of this Grammar, to which I desire to attract public attention. It is indeed possible that future researches may enable me to adduce more satisfactory proofs upon those points, or materially to qualify the inferences and conclusions here drawn. But, so far as my humble researches have hitherto extended, I incline to the opinion that this Pali Grammar was written by *Mahà Kachchàyana* in the latter-half of the sixth century before Christ.

As already stated this work is intended to illustrate the grammar of the language of Gotama Buddha's discourses. This may lead to the inference that it was, in some degree, different from another dialect which had also received the appellation of Màgadhí. Be this however, as it might. The Páli is essentially the language of Buddhism. Nothing is known definitely of the state of its cultivation previous to the establishment of Buddhism by Gotama.

---

* See Appendix.

All that may be confidently advanced of times previous to the Buddhist era, is that in remote antiquity a tribe of people settled themselves under Bhàrat in the *Aryadesha* or *Aryàvarta*, the region commonly known as Central India, between two lines of mountains the *Himalayà* on the North-East and the *Vindhya* on the West.* According to the traditions current in India there were numerous kings from the war of the Mahà Bharat to a comparatively very late period; but all the dynasties, though existing in different parts of the *Aryadèsha*, were founded by one and the same race of people, whom we may designate the *Arians*, consisting of four classes, the *Kshestriyas*, or the royal (military) tribe—the *Brahmans*, or the sacerdotal class—*Vaisya*, or the commercial—and the *Sudra*, or the servile.† Of the several dynasties, one was that of *Magadhas*. It numbers a connected chain of thirty-five kings from *Sahadeva*, who reigned at the termination of the war of Mahà Bharat, to the Buddhistical era in the reign of *Ajàtasatta*.

The religion of the Magadha people was doubtless Brahmanism from a very early period, though at the Buddhistical era, it branched off into different sects.‡ Yet the undoubted existence at this time of a cultivated dialect, peculiar to the Magadhas, called the *Màgadhí*, proves that, whilst sharing with the Brahmans their religion, the Magadhas had a language of their own, fundamentally the same as the Sanskrit, and exhibiting the nearest relation to the earliest form of the language of the Brahmans.

Although there are now several dialects, including the Pali, which receive the name of *Pràkrita*, it may nevertheless be gathered from a variety of circumstances to which I shall hereafter refer, when I come to speak more particularly of the relation which the Màgadhi bears to the Sanskrit,—that

* British Asiatic Society's Journal, vol. xvi, p. 190.

† See Colebrook's Miscellaneous Essays ii. p. 178. Also American Oriental Journal iii. p. 314.; and Gotama Buddha's account of them in Bengal Asiatic Society's Journal, Vol. vii., p. 698.

‡ See my Lecture on Buddhism, p. 5, et seq.

the language which had at first received the name of *Pràkrita* is either now entirely lost, or has been absorbed into other forms of speech, leaving behind but few, if any, traces of the parent stem.

It is also very probable from historical and philological considerations, that the *Màgadhi* and the *Sanskrit* are two of those forms. Against this view of the question may be urged the absence of a *Màgadhí* literature before the Buddhistical period, and the undoubted existence of the Sanskrît.

The existence of a Sanskrit literature, before the Buddhistical era, was owing to the pre-existence of Brahmanism ; and if Buddhism had existed in Magadha before 628 B. C., we should doubtless have some evidence of the existence of the *Màgadhi*. But, such was not the fact. Till Gotama proclaimed his religion, and sought to disseminate it, far and wide, throughout Asia, the kings of Magadha had no necessity for a display of their language. Till then they had no religious feuds; no sectarian animosities. Till then there had been no contentions with any who held an antagonistic faith. Both the Magadhas and their Arian brethren were the adorers of the same gods. Their sacred books, through which alone the existence of a literature may be ascertained of nations of antiquity, were identical with those of the Brahmans. Although they had a language of their own, the *Màgadhi* ; yet they had little to record in it apart from religon, to the exposition of which the Brahmans had laid exclusive claims ; and if they had a literature of their own, which doubtless they had, its destruction through the agency of Brahmans, is sufficiently proved from the political changes which Magadha underwent in the fifth century, and, above all, from the fact that not many centuries after their promulgation, the sacred scriptures of Buddha were re-transferred from Ceylon to India.

When, however, the Magadha kings had embraced a new faith, a necessity arose which had not existed before ; and that was the recording of the doctrines of Buddhism in books

And, although they shared the fate of their scientific works, yet by the early transfer of the former into different countries at a time when the Buddhists had not been subjected to the oppressions of the Brahmans, we have some means of knowing the existence of the *Màgadhi*, and that it had already attained the refinement it now possesses, at the time of Gotama Buddha's advent.*

The absence, again, of a literature is not proof positive of the non-existence of the language itself, just as the absence of Sanskrit Inscriptions of a data anterior to the Buddhist era, is no evidence of the previous absence of the Sanskrit language. The non-existence moreover, of historical or literary records, testifies nothing further than the imbecility, or the apathy of a people, who had no taste for literary pursuits, or a regard for history, or historical proceedings. This, indeed, was the case with the early Brahmans, as well as the early Magadha princes. At first both had a common interest, and possessed in common a literature which was inseparably connected with their religion also common to both; and, therefore there was no inducement to raise monumental erections, which in comparatively later times were the result of a rupture of those ties which had formerly bound them together—the consequence of a new faith —the work of vain kings, wishing to proclaim th supremacy of a particular princedom, and to disseminate the tenets of a newly embraced creed.

The most important fact, however which demonstrates the existence of a *Màgadhì* literature before the Buddhist era is that furnished by the language itself, viz.—*its high state of cultivation at the period above mentioned.* This proves that it had been in existence for a long time previously. For it could not have attained its perfection in a day. It must have been the work of time, the result of ages, the slow progress of innumerable changes. A considerable period too,

* Turnour's Mahavansa—Int. p. xxvii.

must have intervened between the time when it first started into existence, and the period at which it was so much celebrated as to induce Pali scholars to designate it the *Múla bhàsà*, 'the original language'

There are two theories current with regard to the comparative antiquity of the Sanskrit and Pali. Some regard the former as the original, and the latter as a *derivative* from it; whilst others affirm the superiority of the Pali over the Sanskrit, and assign to it an origin before the language of the Vedas. But, nearly all Brahman and European writers on the subject, are agreed in considering the several Indian dialects, which are generally designated the *Pràkrita*, as inferior in structure to the Sanskrit, and, therefore, as being deduced from it.

These are questions which are involved in doubt and obscurity; and upon which there is still great misapprehension. The uncertainty which prevails on the subject, appears to me to originate in the minds of men, who, without paying sufficient attention to a most important consideration—the history of Buddhism and of its language, the Pali, suffer their judgment to be swayed by two circumstances, viz., the superior structure of the Sanskrit, and the comparative antiquity of its records.

Those who assign to the Sanskrit a superiority over the Páli do so upon the grounds that the former is more "finished" and "elaborate" than the latter; and that the Pali cannot be traced, through its literature or religion, to a period before Gotama—whereas the Vedas and the Mahà Bhàrata* are confessedly of a much anterior date.

I readily accord to the Sanskrit, as to its "wonderful structure" and "refinement," the superiority, which one of its most accomplished and able students, Mr. Colebrooke, assigns, when he declares it to be—'a most polished tongue, which was gradually refined, until it became fixed in the classic

* Prof. Lassen's Ind. Ant. 1, 489-491.

writings of many elegant poets, most of whom are supposed to have flourished in the century preceding the Christian era.' I also admit the existence of positive evidence to prove that the Vedas, and therefore the faith it proclaims, had been known before Gotama established his religion by means of the Màgadhì.

But these admissions, I presume, do not affect the theory of some of our ablest pandits, viz., that at a very remote period, some *one Prákrita* [' mother'] dialect, which can no longer be identified, or may not now be in existence in its original development, was the principal tongue of the Arians; and that the *Páli* (not the dialect spoken at present in Magadh or Behar, nor the Mágadhì of the Indian Grammarians), and the Sanskrit, are both branches of the same unknown original stock.

In the investigation of this subject, it may not be unprofitable to notice, to the extent of our limited information and means, (1) the subdivisions of the principal Indian languages; (2) the number of dialects comprehended in the term *Pràkrita*; (3) the acceptation of that term by nations and literary men; (4) its correct signification; (5) the conjectures as to its identification; (6) its relationship to the Sanskrit; and (7) its high state of cultivation and decline in Asia.

I. As to the classification of Indian languages, we have the following interesting passage in the *Dandialankàra*, or as it is otherwise called, *Kàvyadarsha.*

Tade tadvànmayan bhúyas *
Sanskritan Pràkritan tathà;
Apabhransascha misranche
Tyàhuràptàschatur vidham.
Sanskritan nàma daivivà
Ganvàkhyàtà mahàrshibih;

* Tadeva vaumayan vidyat—Lassen p. 33. I am indebted for the text to a Sinhalese copy.

Tadbhavan Tatsaman Desì
Tyanèkah Pràkritakramah.
Mahàràshtràsrayàm bhàshàm
Prakrishtam Pràkritam viduh ;
Sàgarah sùkti ratnànàm
Setubandhàdi yanmayam.
Saurasenìcha Làtìcha
Gowdìchà'nyàpi tádrisì ;
Yànti Pràkrita mityèva
Vyavahàreshu sannidhim.
'Abhiràdi girah kàvye
Shv'apabhransa itismritah ;
Sastreshu Sanskrità danya
D'apabhransa tayoditam—
Sanskritam sarga bandhàdi
Pràkritam skhanda' kàdiyat ;
Oushàradì-ny'apabhranso
Nàtakà ditu misrakam.
Kathàdi sarvabhàshàbih
Sanskritenacha baddhyate ;
Bhútà bhàshà mayim pràhur
Atbhùtàrtham Vrihatkathàm.

That is to say—' Preceptors declare that the (above) compositions consist of four kinds (of language); Sanskrit, Pràkrit, Apabhransa,* and Misra. The speech of the gods, which is defined by great sages, is named Sanskrit. The Pràkrit is of various orders; viz. *Tadbhava* (born of the Sanskrit,) *Tatsama* (which is equal or similar to the Sanskrit), and *Desi* (provincial or local). The language current in Maharàshtra is known as the principal Pràkrita—that which is an ocean to gems of beautiful language, and that in which Sètubandha,† &c., are composed. The

* The Commentator says—' pure Sanskrit, pure Prakrit, pure Apabhransa, and a mixture of these with the Paisachi &c.'—

† Professor Cowell states in the introduction to his Prakrit Prakasa, that this a 'rare and ancient Prakrit poem' the knowledge of which he derives 'from Dr. Hofer's interesting article in his *Zeitschrift*'—p. x.

languages of Saurasena, Làta, Gowda, and such like,* are usually† treated under the very name of Pràkrita. Dialects like the Abhirà‡ &c., are (alone) reckoned as Apabhransa in poetry; but in the *Shàstras*§ all languages besides the Sanskrit receive that name. Compositions which are divided into chapters, are in the Sanskrit language; those which are (skandaka) composed in one entire body, are in the Pràkrita; those like the *Aushra* are in the Apabhransa; and the *Dràmas* are (misra) in a mixed dialect. Historical writings &c. are composed in the Sanskrit, as well as in (other) dialects; but the *Vrihatkathà* of marvellous import, is said to be only in the speech of the demons.'

Obs.—(*a*) The division of languages here spoken of, is founded upon the authority of Brahman writers, and their usages. That division is into four; viz., Sanskrit, Pràkrit, Apabhransa, and Misra—epithets which have certain meanings, and which are descriptive of the different languages for which they are names. The *Sanskrit* is 'the language of the gods'—that is, the sacred language of the Brahmans, in which historical writings, and the Shástras are composed, having subdivisions.

The Prakrit is various, or, in other words, has 'several orders' or 'dialects'; and is divided into three classes, viz., *tadbhava*, *tatsama*, and *desi*. The first comprehends "derivatives," those which have sprung from the Sanskrit which have undergone various mutations in course of time and which may yet be traced to the parent stem. The second includes 'sister-dialects,' those which are *tatsama* 'co,-equal' or, 'similar,' or 'bear a resemblance to the Sanskrit; and which stand in fraternal connection with the Sanskrit—*not* in the relation of descent from it—*not* be-

* The Commentator understands by 'such like,' the languages of Magadhi (Pali). and *Panchala* (Zend.)

† 'Usually'—that is 'in practice,' 'by custom' or 'usage.'

‡ *Abhirà*—a dialect of herdsmen, of people of the lowest tribe.

§ By the *Shastras* are meant the works of the Brahmans—their scientific books.

gotten by it ;—but sprung from the same shoot with it. The third is a name for *provincial dialects,* or *non-Sanskrit* languages,—those which cannot be traced to a Sanskrit origin, or do not exhibit any evidence of fraternity to it. They are *dèsi,* peculiar to a country, or, as the Sinhalese call them, *nipan* 'born in a country,' and therefore *local.*

Of these various Pràkrit dialects, the Mahàràstri is in the estimation of my authority, the best cultivated dialect. Perhaps, it was, at the time *Dandi* wrote, which is supposed to have been in the twelfth century of the christian era—* '*an ocean to gems of beautiful language*'—a dialect, which, like the 'vast profound' abounded in gems of lofty expressions—(that is ; rich in expression, and copious as a language), as evidenced by works like the *Sétubandha* &c. Prákrit compositions, unlike the Sanskrit works, which are subdivided into chapters, are only in entire books.

Although by *Pràkrita* such languages as the above are alone indicated ; yet (says Dandi) 'the dialects of Saurasena ; Láta, Gowda, and such like (by which the commentator says the *Màgadhí* and *Panchàli* were meant) are usually treated under the very name of *Pràkrita.*'

The name of the third division of languages is *Alpabhransa* or 'the ungrammatical'—'a jargon ;' such as the *Abhiri* and *Chandàli*—dialects used by herdsmen, and by persons of the lower orders ;†—for compositions in which, Dandi refers the reader to *Oushra.*

Misra is the name of the last division of languages,—that dialect which contains a *Mixture* of all the other classes of language—not a mixture of merely words, but entire passages of different languages interlarded with the Sanskrit as in the dramas.

Another division of languages, as stated by Dandi, and according to the *Shástras* of the Brahmans, is into *Sanskrit*

---

* See Professor H. H. Wilson's Preface to the Dasakumara Charita p. 4.

† Colebrook's Essays ii. p. 61.

and *Apabhransa,* the latter including all dialects besides the Sanskrit. Historical compositions are written in all the languages comprised under these two heads; but *Vrihatkatha* alone (which abound with the 'marvellous') are to be found in the speech of the *demons,* by whom I understand the barbarians, or the aboriginal inhabitants of those provinces which were afterwards peopled by the Arian race.

Obs.—(*b.*) The above inferences which are forced upon us by the phraseology adopted by *Dandi* and by the explanations of his Commentator, authorize five important conclusions, 1st, That although the *Prakrita* has become manifold, or has assumed diverse forms; yet it may be regarded as *tatsama,* or, as having a fraternal relation to the Sanskrit. 2 That the principal Prakrit dialect, which (whether rightly or wrongly we shall not here pause to consider) is generally regarded as the *Maharastri*—is rich in expression, and copious as a language; 3. That although originally there was but one *Prakrita* dialect, many tongues have nevertheless been by the *usage* of Brahmans improperly comprehended under the appellation of *Prakrit;* 4 That all dialects except the Sanskrit are by them designated *Apabhransa* 'the ungrammatical;'* 5. That the Pali (Mágadhi) and the language of Punjab (Panchàla) may be regarded as two dialects bearing some particular relation to each other.†

II. The dialects which receive the designation of the *Pràkrita* are many; and they are to be generally found in the dramatic writers. The Commentators, Grammarians, and

* This last fact accounts for the common acceptation of the term Prakrita, to which I shall hereafter refer.

† Professor Wilson, speaking of the Pali, says "It is, as Messrs. Burnouf and Lassen remark, still nearer to Sanskrit, and may have prevailed more to the North than Behar, or in the upper part of the Doab, *and in the Punjab,* being more analogous to the Sauraseni dialect, the dialect of Mathura and Delhi, although not differing from the dialect of Behar to such an extent as not to be intelligible to those to whom Sakya and his successors addressed themselves."—*Journal of the Royal Asiatic Society xii. p.* 237.

Rhetoricians, who have written on the language s contained in the Hindu plays variously define them, with reference to the patois of the drama; and there seems to be much misapprehension, and much more confusion in their classification.

1. Monsieur Adolphus Fredricus Stenzler in his preface to the Play entitled the *Mritcha Katika*, after quoting from a Commentator states:

Dialecti non Sanskritœ, quœ in dramates adhibentur, sunt aut *Prakritœ* aut *apabhransicœ*. Pràkritœ dialecti sunt Sauraseni, Avanti, Prachyà, Màgadhì. Apabhransicœ dialecti sunt Sakàrà, Candàlì, Sabarì, Dhakki.'*

2. The same Commentator, to whom Monsieur Stenzlir was indebted for the above, also states:—

'Màgadhyavantijà Pràchyà Saurasenyardha Màgadhi
Bàlìkà Dàkshinàtyàcha sapta bhàshàh prakìrtitàh.'

That is: 'It is declared that there are seven dialects (in Dramatic works) Màgadhì, Avanti, Prachyà, Saurasenì, Ardha-Màgadhì, Bahlìkà, and Dakshinàtyà.†

3. There was a tradition current, in the thirteenth century, that there were only six Indian dialects which received the name of *bhàsha*; and hence the appellation of *Shad-bhàsha parameshvara*, to one who is a proficient in six languagesl These are enumerated in the *Ratna-kosha*; and they are—

---

* Mr. Colebrooke on the authority of *Kullaka Bhatta* on Menu ii. 19, identifiee Sauraseni as the language of Saurasena, another name for the country of *Mathura*. Avanti is *Oujin*, or as the Singalese call, *Udeni*; and the language of which is supposed to be the *Malava*. *Prachya* is the language on the East of India. It is identified with the *Gowdi* or *Bengali* by the Commentator on the Sahityadarpana. *Magadh.* is the language of Magadh or Behar. It is at present a corruption of the ancient lani guage of tha t country. The original is alone preserved in Ceylon and Burmah. *Sakari*, and *Sabari* have not been identified; Candali is supposed to be the dialect of herds men of the lowest tribes; and Dhakki is probably *Dhakshinatya*; see next note.

† *Ardha-Magadhi* is a corrupt dialect of the Pali. It may be identified with the Magadhi of the Prakrit Grammarians. Bhalika is supposed by Mr. Colebrooke to b. the language of *Balkh*, in the *Transoxana*, a country famous for its horses and situated on the North of India—*Dakshinatya* is identified by the Commentator of the *Sahitya darpana* as the country of *Vidarbha*, which is said to be the modern *Berar*.

'The Sanskrit, Pràkrita, Màgadhì, Sauraseni, Paisàchì, and Apabransa.'

4. In the *Selalihini-Sandesa* the philological acquirements of Totagamuva, a Ceylonese, who lived about 1415 A.D.*, are said to have been so vast that Brahmans visited him from India to pay the homage due to a *Shadbhàshà-parameshvara.*† The six bàsas with which he was acquainted are enumerated thus—'The Sanskrit, Pàli (Màgadhì), Pràkrit, Sauraseni, Paisàchi, and Apabhransa.'

5. Hemachandra, a Grammarian of the Jaina sect, who flourished in the thirteenth century, and wrote a *Pràkrit* Grammar as an eighth *adhyàya* after the seven *adhyàyas* of his Sanskrit Grammar‡ enumerates also six *bashàs;* and they are Pràkrit *bhàsha* (which Mr. Cowell calls 'principal pràkrit') the Sauraseni, Magadhì, Paisachì, Chulika Paisachì, and the *Apabransa bhasha.*

6. Mr. Colebrooke gives the following translation of a passage§ in a work on Rhetoric compiled for the use of *Mànïkya Chandra* a king of Tirhat, but the name of the work is not given:—'*Sanscrita, Pracrita, Paisachi* and *Màgadhì* are in short the four paths of poetry. The gods, &c., speak *Sanscrita;* benevolent genii, *Pràcrita;* wicked demons *Paisachi;* and men of low tribes and the rest, *Màgadhì.* But sages deem Sanscrit the chief of these four languages. It is used three ways; in prose, verse, and in a mixture of both.'

'Language again, the virtuous have declared to be four fold, Sanscrita (or the polished dialect) *Pràcrita,* (or the vulgar dialect) *Apabhransa* (or jargon), and *Misra* (or mixed). *Sanscrita* is the speech of the celestials, framed in grammatical institutes; *Pràcrita* is similar to it, but manifold as a provincial dialect and otherwise, and those languages which are ungrammatical are spoken in their respective districts.'

* See my Sidath Sangara Intr. p. clxxxviii.

† See Introduction to Tudave's Selalihini Sandsa.

‡ See Prakrit Prakasa by Cowell; Introduction p. xi.

§ Miscellaneous Essays, ii, p., 1.

7. Vararuchi in his *Prákrit Prakasa* gives a principal Pràkrita, supposed to have been the Maharastri, and enumerates three others, the *Sauraseni*, *Magadhi* and *Paisachi*, for the elucidation of which he assigns but a very small portion of his work.

Obs.—From the above authorities, taken in connection with the foregoing historical notices on the Pàli language, several important facts may be deduced. First, that there was originally but *one* language which received the name of *Prakrit*, and that since it became 'manifold as a provincial dialect,' its name has been applied to other tongues: and this is attested by another fact, that the farther back we go in point of time in search of the *Prakrit*, the fewer are the dialects treated of by authors under that name; and that Vararuchi, the Pràkrit Grammarian of the times of Vikramàditya, treats chiefly of one *Pràkrit* dialect, the 'dialectus principua" of Professor Lassen. From the names, too, given to the *Shad-bhasha* of comparatively an ancient date, it may be inferred that the many varieties given in modern works under the name of *Pràkrit* are merely "the subtle refinements of a later age," in order to distinguish the fifty-six* different languages "spoken in their respective districts," some of them being *Misra* or mixed; and that philologically speaking languages were originally three-fold, viz., those which have been designated by the epithets *Sanskrita*, *Pràkrita*, and *Apabhransa*. These in the language of the Brahman Rhetorician above quoted upon Mr. Colebrooke's authority, were 1st, "the speech of the celestials framed in Grammatical Institutes;" 2nd, a "dialect *similar* to the last;" and 3rd, a "language ungammatical."

* From the Sanskrit are usually enumerated fifty-six dialects as known in India the principal of which are the Pali, long since the dead and sacred tongue of the Buddhists; the Magadhi, a more recent form of Pali, and an ancient dialect of a great part of Behar, also a dead language; various forms of Prakrit; besides nine-tenths of Hindi. Bengali, Maharatti, Gujarati, and the rest of the fifty-six dialects" —*Journal of Royal Asiatic Society*, xvi p. 174.

The first, it would seem, became early fixed, as the dialect of the Vedas—the last was the spoken language of the rude aborigines of the Dekhan—and the second, the speech of different Arian nations, which underwent different modifications; such as the Pali of the Sinhalese; the Bactrian-Pali* of the bilingual coins of the Greek kings; the idiom of the *Zendavastâ*; † the dialect of the Nepal Buddhists, and the Jains; the speech of the mass of the people with whom the Greeks came in contact after Alexander's invasions; the language of Asoka's Inscriptions; and the Prâkrita of the plays.

Although the original Pràkrit has thus undergone different changes in different countries; yet it is clear that the differences which at first distinguished several Pràkrit dialects from each other, were not such as to render any one of them altogether unintelligible to the great mass of the people. This was, obviously, the reason why the Màgadhì, "the speech of the Brahmans and the Aryas" ‡ is represented as having been generally intelligible to Gotama's varied congre-

* Several inscriptions, as obtained from the Topes excavated, or as forwarded by travellers from within the ancient limits of Bactria, were nearly deciphered, so that very little remained to perfect this discovery also, and to establish that the *ancient Pali language*, or something very closely resembling it, prevailed over all those countries"—Bengal Asiatic Society's Journal vii. p. ix.

† It is a question well worthy the attention of the learned, whether or not every fact stated in respect of the Zend in the following extract is not equally applicable to the Pali? Professor Max Muller says: "It is clear from his (Burnouf's) works, and from Bopp's valuable remarks in his comparative grammar, that Zend in its grammar and dictionary, is nearer to Sanskrit than any other Indo-European language. Many Zend words can be re-translated into Sanskrit simply by changing the Zend into their corresponding forms in Sanskrit........ Where Sanskrit differs in words or grammatical peculiarities from the Northern members of the Arian family, it frequently coincides with Zend. The numerals are the same in all these languages up to 100. The name for thousand, however, (*sahasra*) is peculiar to Sanskrit, and does not occur in any of the Indo-European dialects except in Zend, where it becomes *hazanra*........ These facts are full of historical meaning; and with regard to Zend and Sanskrit, they prove that these two languages continued together long after they were separated from the common Indo-Eupean stock"—*Professor Muller's Last Results* &c. pp. 112.

‡ See extract from *Vibhanga Atuwa*, post.

grations; why the ancient Translators of several Sinhalese books* into the Pali say, that by such transposition they "would render a facility to both the inhabitants of this island, and *of other lands*;" and why Buddhaghosa, a consummate Sanskrit scholar of the 5th century, preferred the *Pàli* to the Sanskrit in translating the Sinhalese Atthakathà.

III. As to the acceptation of the term *Pràkrita* amongst nations and literary men;—

1. Mr. Colebrooke, according to a forced etymology, says 'the most *common* acceptation of this word is *outcast*, or men of the lowest class; as applied to a language it signifies *vulgar*.' †

2. Cowell, the translator of the *Pràkrita Prakàsa*, says "Pràkrit is the common name given to the various dialects which sprang up in early times in India from the corruption of the Sanskrit, and as the word is used by grammarians, it signifies, '*derived*, thereby to denote its connection with the original Sanskrit." ‡

3. The authority upon which the above opinions are founded, is taken from *Hemachandra*, who defines—*Prakritih Sanskritam tatra-bhavam tata àgatam và pràkritam*—'Pràkrit has its source in Sanskrit, and is that which springs or comes from it.'

Obs.—Though willing to admit the above to be the acceptation of this word *amongst the Brahmans* generally, to distinguish their so-called heaven-derived religion from other dialects; we cannot, however, receive such opinions without caution, and even distrust; for we perceive from the writings of the Brahmans themselves, both unwilling and prejudiced witnesses in this respect,—that the so-called "common acceptation" of the term, does not accord with facts, and the particular opinions expressed by the learned. For, if the Pràkrit is "equal" (or similar) to the Sanskrit; and, if moreover the

* Introduction to the Pali version of the Daladavanṣa.

† See his Miscellaneous Essays, ii. p. 2.

‡ See his Prakrit Prakasa xvii.

former is "an ocean to gems of lofty expressions;" with what justice or propriety can it be said that the Pràkrit is an "out-cast"—that it is "a vulgar dialect"—or that it is (apabhransa), a "jargon" destitute of grammar? A comparison of the Sanskrit with the Pali, clearly disproves the assertion of the *Shàstras*; and the result is not different when even the Pràkrit passages in the dramas are compared with the "speech of the gods."

4. Sir William Jones describes the Pràkrit in the plays to be little more than the language of the Brahmans, melted down by a distinct articulation, to the softness of the Italian.*

5. Professor H. H. Wilson from the testimony contained in the Dramas, written by Kàlidàsa, and in several 'finished modern imitations', treats the *Pali* under the designation of Pràkrit (under which appellation he includes 'three varieties more or less refined',) and adds: "the words are essentially the same in all, and all are essentially the same with Sanskrit, the difference affecting the pronunciation and spelling, rather than the radical structure, and tending generally to shorten the words, and subtitute a soft for a hard, and a slurred for an emphatic articulation."†

6. The *Kàvya darsha* defines the Sanskrit to be 'the speech of the devas,' and the *Pràkrita* to cousist of several dialects, of which some are born of the *Sanskrit*; and some which stand in equal relationship with it; and others which are native or vernacular—peculiar to certain countries.

Obs.—I am aware that some writers‡ have put a different construction upon this authority: and have interpreted it to mean that the Prakrits 'are composed of a three-fold element.' It is however submitted with much deference, that the differences noticed by Dandi are differences of entire *dialects*, or, as the commentator says, entirely '*pure* dialects

* Preface to the Sakuntala. † Hindu Theatre 1. p. lxiv.

‡ Dr. Muir's *Sanskrit Texts* ii p. 60.

and not differences of words in the same dialect. The context sets this at rest; for the writer enumerates 'several orders', or the '*various*' dialects of the Pràkrit, and not the words of which they are composed.

But to return from this digression:

7. "In reference to the meaning of the word Pràkrit," says Dr. Stevenson, "it may be observed that, among the Maràthi Brahmans, the term is often taken in its widest sense to signify the *natural* or vernacular language of any province in India. In a more restricted sense, it means any of the *ancient* dialects of the different provinces, and which as most of their books used till lately to be written in it, obtains, in the South of India, the appellation *Grontha*.*

8. The Sinhalese also give the name of *Grantha* to ancicent languages, and doubtless it is identical with the Indian ***Prakrita*** as may be seen from the enumeration of the qualifications of King Parakkramabahu III., 1267, A.D., in an extract from History given in my *Sidath Sangara* p. clxix.

9. "There are" says the Rig Veda, "four measured grades of language: with these intelligent Brahmans are acquainted. Three hidden in secret make no sign. The fourth grade of speech is *uttered by men*." Dr. Muir in his Sanskrit Texts p. 163, et seq., after quoting the above, and its comment, which concludes thus: —"the Brahmans speak two sorts of language; both that of gods and that of men—" says, "three of the ancient schools which are quoted, assert the current language (vyavaharika vak) to be the fourth kind of speech alluded to in the Vedic text, as being spoken by men;" and, after expressing a conjecture, that this was the Sanskrit (?) he adds:—"It is true that in the Brahmana which the author of the Parisishta cites, a remark is made (connected with what precedes) that the Brahmans *speak two languages, that of the gods, and that of men*; and this might seem to prove that, as in later times, a distinction was drawn at

* Kalpa Sutra, p. 132.

the time when the Brahmana was composed, between *Sanskrit*, the language of the gods, and the *Prakrit* the language of men."—p. 165.

Obs.—From the foregoing facts, deductions, and inferences it may be concluded that *an* "ancient," "cultivated," "natural or vernacular dialect," "similar to the Sanskrit" has continued to retain the name of Pràkrit, along with several provincial dialects, which are usually treated under the same name.

IV Like all the above grounds of evidence, the testimony derivable from the primary signification of the word *pràkrita* is against the so-called "common acceptation" of that word; and invests the language, to which it was originally given as a name, with a character for originality and independence equal to, if not higher than, the Sanskrit.

I am glad to find that Professor Lassen agrees with me in believing that *prakriti* is the "source" from whence *Pràkrita* is derived; but I am equally sorry that I am constrained to differ from him as to the meaning which he assigns to that word. In his *Institutiones Linguæ Prakriticæ* pp. 25, 26, the learned Professor says:—"Notatio vocabuli est a *Prakriti*, i. e. procreatrix, genetrix natura, unde *Pràkrita*, generatus, derivatus; derivatur enim hae linguae a Sanskritica aut directo aut una per aliam, quo sensu dicitur prakriti cujusvis linguae esse ea, a qua deducitur: *Prakritih Sanskritam, tatra-bhavam tata àgatam và Pràkritam.* Hemach: Cap. viii. § 1. 'Prakriti sive origo in Sanskrita est; in ea lingua ortum vel ex ea profectum quod est, id *pràkrita* s. derivatum est.' Opponuntur praeterea in aliis juncturis sibi *Sanskrita* et *Pràkrita*, ut de hominibus, qui quum justa cultioris vitae institutione imbuti sint, Sanskritici, sin minus, Pràkritici dicuntur, unde fit, ut pràkrita etiam notet hominem vulgarem. Pràkriticæ igitur linguæ etiam sunt vulgares, rusticae, provinciales."

Now, it is clear that if *Pràkrit* comes from *prakriti* (procreatrix, genetrix natura) 'nature', the former cannot mean, as stated by the learned Professor, "derived," but its very opposite —"the radical, or the root," and, when applied to a language, "the orignal lan guage from which another springs." That "the several Pràkrit dialects are *regarded*" [by modern Brahmans*] "as derivatives of the Sanskrit either directly or mediately" signifies nothing ; and cannot, I apprehend, affect the question any more than the dictum of the Buddhists, 'that the Pali is the [*mûla bàsà*] radical language' The only mode by which we may a scertain the correct meaning of *Pràkrita* is, I submit, as Professor Lassen himself has done, by tracing the word to its radical, primary, signification, in which sense, we may, considering the usages of the East, reasonably believe it was originally used.

By any other mode of determining the sense of this word we shall fail to obtain any information beyond the secondary sense, which, in the arbitrary usage of the *modern* Brahmans of the dramatic age, is assigned to this word —viz., that it is a name for "vulgar, rustic, and provincial forms of speech." The modern acce ptation of this word, is indeed inadmissible in an inquiry as to what language it was *ab initios* a name ? Words are like men. They grow into various shapes. They gradually lose their original forms. They undergo in process of time, so many changes both in body and sense, that we cannot often determine their original meaning by their "common acceptation" at the present day. If, for instance, desirous of ascertaining how the old Romans preserved their writings, we referred to the modern acceptation of the term *volumen*, it would give us an idea merely 'of writing preserved on paper folded, or bound like our books (volume) with a number of distinct leaves above one another. But, if we

* "It is in the period with which we are now concerned (says the same writer) viz., that between Vikramaditya and the later Gupta Kings, that the names Sanskrit for the classical language, and Prakrit for the forms of speech springing from it, must have arisen."—*Lassen's Ind. Ant.* ii. p. 1151.

traced the word to its original (prakriti) source, we should find that it meant 'a folding,' 'a roll'—and, therefore, that the Romans 'rolled up their writings' as a 'scroll,' or like 'the folds of a snake.' Suppose again, for instance, we were engaged in an inquiry as to whether the Kandians and the maritime Sinhalese were originally of the same stock; and we were in the course of our investigations furnished with two epithets, 'opposed to each other,' and by which the maritime natives were distinguished from the Kandians; viz 'the *high* Sinhalese' and 'the *low* Sinhalese.' By the adoption of the meanings which either ignorance or prejudice has assigned to them among some people, we must conclude that the first meant 'the Sinhalese strictly so called* and the second, 'the low' 'the inferior,' or (as the Brahmans designate the Prakrita) 'the vulgar.' But nothing could be more distant from the original signification of these terms as applied to the Sinhalese. The first meant 'those who occupied the *high*-lands of the Kandian country,' and the second 'those who inhabited the flat *levels* of the maritime provinces.'

In considering, therefore, the question as to the comparative claims of the *Pràkrita* and the *Sanskrita*, we should take their *primary*, not their secondary, sense—that which they radically import, not that which has been assigned by usage. In a primary sense also, be it remarked, those words are "opposed to each other"; *Sanskrita* conveying 'adornment' and *Pràkrita* 'the natural': and this it would seem is also proof of the *Pràkrita* being the 'original' form of language, and therefore, in a secondary sense, (to adopt the contemptuous expressions of the Hindus) 'the uncultivated savage,' 'the rustic,' or 'the vulgar' idiom from which the language of the Brahmans has arisen to the development of

* See Ceylon Branch Royal Asiatic Society's Journal, vii. p. 240.

the *Sanskrit,* 'the highly polished', or 'the civilized.'*

I have already shown that the word from whence *Pràkrita* is derived, was *prakriti.* It is thus defined by several writers :—

1. According to the Amarakosha (see pp. 32. 55) *prakriti* means in the Sanskrit 'nature' 'the natural state.'

2. Bopp defines it also to be '*natura r. kri facere præf pra s. ti*'—*Glossarium Sanscritum* p. 225.

3. Professor H. H. Wilson gives to it among other significations, the following ; 'Nature, in philosophy, the passive or material cause of the world, as opposed to the active or spiritual ;—the natural state, or condition of any thing ; a radical form or predicament of being ; cause, origin, a mother, the radical form of a word before the affixes forming cases, &c. are subjoined. E. *pra* implying 'priority' or 'precedence,' *kri* 'to make' aff : *ti.*'

4. The same meanings are assigned to its kindred expressions (*pakati*) in the Pali, (see *Abhidanapadìpika* p. 11.) and in the Sinhalese (see Clough and the *Sidath Sangara*).

Obs.—*Prakriti* is therefore, that which is natural, or the nature itself of a thing—that which is pre-eminent—that which is the natural and quiescent state of any thing—'not made.' Hence it is clear that the correct and primary sense of the word *Pràkrita,*—indeed that which was originally assigned to it, despite the so-called 'common acceptation,'—was 'original,' 'root,' 'natural.' By the Pràkrit was therefore, at first meant the original Indian language, as distinguish-

---

* Colonel Sykes, after alluding to certain doubts expressed by Professor Wilson as to how the descendants (the Prakrits) could have been so exquisitely refined as he found them in the Plays, if the parent (the Sanskrit) was comparatively rude, which he believes was the fact before the age of the classical language of the Hindu literature, says ; "A simple solution of Professor Wilson's doubts would be to consider the Sanskrit emanating from the Pali, [? I shall rather say—the one original Prakrit language which has assumed the form of Pali]—the perfect from the imperfect, the polished from the rude, and the expressive from the simple ; at least such is the natural progress of languages with growing civilization."—*Journal Royal Asiatic Society, vi. p.* 422.

able from the Apabransa 'the ungrammatical,' and the Sanskrit, signifying [from *sam* 'altogether' or 'together,' and *krita* 'done'= 'altogether' or' completely made, done, or formed'] that 'which has been composed or formed by art adorned, embellished, purified, highly cultivated or polished, and regularly inflected as a language.'

V. What then was this *original Pràkrit* language which was "similar to the Sanskrit ?" It would be in vain to look for it in any of the living languages of the world ; for it is an established fact in philology that all languages change * in course of time, even without the introduction of foreign elements. It can only be discovered, I presume, by the examination of the earliest writings of those languages which have ceased to be spoken.

Let us first examine the dramatic dialects with reference to the precepts of the Grammarians and Commentators.

1. It has been found by Professor Lassen and others who have examined these writings, (says Mr. Stenzler) † that, making great allowances for the errors of ignorant copyists, and the unauthorized alterations of learned transcribers, there is still a difficulty in reconciling the doctrines of the grammarians with the language of the dramas.

2. 'Much discrepancy' says Mr. Cowell ‡ exists between the Pràkrit of the grammarians, and that which we find in the plays.'

3. Professor Wilson, who was intimately acquainted with the language of the dramas, from his having translated them, says that the term Pràkrit, applied by grammarians 'to a variety of forms, agrees only in name with the spoken dialects.' 'The *Màgadhi by which name may be considered that dialect which is more ordinarily understood by Pràkrit,* is very different from the vernacular language of Magadh or

---

* Subodhalankara on Rhetoric.

† See his preface to the Mritchakatika.

‡ Prakrit Prakasa p vii.

Behàr. The *Sauraseni* is by no means the same with the dialect of Mathura, and Vrindavan, and the *Maharashtri* would be of little avail in communicating with the Mahárattas, or people of Maharastra. The other species enumerated, are equally inapplicable for identification with the dialects to which they might be supposed to refer.' *

4. 'Highly finished specimens are to be found in plays which are modern productions. The *Vedagdha Madhura*, for instance, consists more than half of high Pràkrit, and it was written less than three centuries ago.'—ib.

Obs.—This discrepancy may be accounted for by the following conjecture. The dramatic writers, whose age is fixed by Professor Lassen at 400–100 B. C, and, who wrote the great bulk of their plays in Sanskrit, were eminent *Sanskrit* Scholars. They indeed studied the Pràkrit languages; and, even if they did not, from the affinity of the Pràkrits to the Sanskrit, they found no difficulty for a display of their learning by improving upon several then existing Indian dialects. In doing so, according to the original aphorism of Bhárata, it was necessary "to employ choice and harmonious terms, and an elevated and polished style, embellished with the ornaments of Rhetoric and rythm." It may be then believed that they imitated the best writers with whom they were acquainted; that some authors gave preference to some writers as models for imitation, and others to others; and that some selected old, and others modern authors for their guide;—whilst, perhaps, the same writer in different plays adopted the language of both ancient and modern books. Hence 'the exceeding richness' of the Pràkrita in some of the plays, and its comparative inferiority in others,—and, perhaps, the same differences exhibited in the works of one and the same person. The Grammarians, on the other hand, especially Vararuchi, whom we regard,

* Wilson's Hindu Dramas, 1 pp. lxiii, iv.

according to Hindu traditions, as one of the 'nine gems' of Vikramaditya's Court, and therefore a writer of comparatively after times;* were led by different lights. The Pràkrita passages scattered throughout the Hindu dramas, did not afford them sufficient means to obtain an acquaintance with the whole extent of those languages. They found, probably, that one dramatic writer made one class of persons speak a particular dialect, when another put that into the mouth of other classes—thus rendering it difficult even to assign a name to the dialects used. It is also probable that the Grammarians sought in India for, and having found but few traces of, the principal Pràkrit, which tradition represented as a language which "abounded in gems of lofty expressions," and which, as stated in the Pràkìritadìpikà, "is the most excellent form of speech" took for their guide a then existing dialect of Maharastra.

This was probably a *modification* of the Pali. For, from the account of Fa Hiam, it would seem that Buddhism had flourished in *Mutra* from a very early period; and, consequently, its language, the Pali had been early introduced into that country. Yet, from its having been amalgamated with other Pràkrit dialects, and not become fixed as a dead language, as was the case with Pali in Ceylon, the Maharashtrì presents a great many corruptions, of which the Pàli is comparatively free.

The following comparative Table of the first thirty words in Vararuchi's Pràkrit Prakàsa, will render this manifiest.

samriddhi	samiddhi	samiddhì	'prosperity'
prakata	pàkata	paadam	'manifest'
abhijàti	abhijàti	ahijài	'family'
manasvinì	manassinì	manansinì	'wise woman'
pratipad	pàtipada	pàdivaà	'1stday l ½ mon
sadrikksha	sarikkha	sarichchham	'like'

* See Indische Altathumskunde ii., p. 1160.

prasupta	pasutta	pasuttam	'asleep'
prasiddhi	pasiddhi	pàsiddhi	'fame'
asva	assa	asso-àso	'horse'
ì-hat	ìsan	isi	'little'
pakva	pakka	pikkam	'cooked'
svapna	soppa supina	sivina	'sleep' 'dream'
vetasa	vètasa	vediso	'ratan'
vyajana	vìjanì	viano	'fan'
mridanga	mutinga	muingo	'drum'
angàra	angàra	ingàlo	'charcoal'
aranya	arañña	raññam	'forest'
sayyà	seyyà	sejjà	'bed'
saundarya	sundara	sunderam	'beauty'
trayodasa	telasa	teraho	'thirteenth'
âscharya	achchhariya achchhera	achchheram	'wonderful'
paryanta	pariyanta	perantam	'limit'
valli	valli	vellì	'creeper'
badara	badara	voram	'jujube'
lavana	lona	lonam	'salt'
navamallikà	navamallikà	nò mallià	'jasmine'
mayùra	mayùra mora	mora mauro	'peacock'
mayúkha	mayùkha	moho maùho	'ray'
chaturthì	chatutthì	chotthì	'fourth'
chaturdasì	chatuddasì chuddasi choddasì	chuddahì chaddahì	'fourteenth'

Having once identified the principal Pràkrit, with that which approached nearest to it, viz. a dialect of the Maharattas, different from the language which, like the Pali, was once greatly admired, and different also from the language now prevailing in that country, the Grammarians had no alternative but to seek for the Màgadhì in the speech of men living in Magadha. This too, was different from that which is in use there, and also greatly at variance with the original Màgadhì (the Pali) which was only preserved in Ceylon. Hence the discrepancy between the Grammarians and the dramatists—and hence also the difference between the Ceylon and Indian writers in respect of Màgadhì—the Sinhalese treating it as the *Pàli* (or the language of the text books of Buddhism) which found an early retreat in Ceylon, and the Brahmans identifying it with a modification of the same dialect greatly deflected from its original construction.

It would also seem from the foregoing observations that the dialect, which originally received the name of *the Pràkrit*, has in course of time, undergone a vast change in India, and that the patois of the dramas, does not furnish us with sufficient materials for its identification with any known dialect. Probably the Pràkrit of the Plays is a modification of the *Pàli;* and it is very probable that the principal *Pràkrit* of Vararuchi is a still greater modification of the *Pràkrit* of the plays. But of this we may be sure—that both have many traces of corruption, and that both have less claims for originality than the Pali. [See my comparative Tables *infra.*]

Another language which may demand attention here, is the so-called *Gàthà dialect* of the Nepal Buddhists. A solution of the difficulty as to its origin, will be given hereafter. In the meantime it is sufficient to notice what we gather as to its style, from the writings of a learned Hindu gentleman* and of M. Burnouf, viz. 'that the Buddhist literature of Nepal, from which the Sacred Scriptures of Tibet, Tartary, and China have been compiled, is in

* Article by Babu Rajendralal Mittra Esq., in the Bengal R. A. S. Journal for 1854, p. 604.

an ugly Sanskrit dialect, destitute of the niceties of the Sanskrit grammatical forms of declension and conjugation, &c.; that the authors have sacrificed grammar to the exigencies of metre; that it is in a mixed style of prose and *Gàthàs;* that it bears a strong resemblance to the Tantras of the 4th to the 7th Century of the Christian era—and that it appears to be the production of men to whom the task of compilation was assigned without sufficient materials at their disposal. In view of these peculiarities, Mons. Burnouf has pronounced the Nepal sacred scriptures to be a 'barbarous Sanskrit, in which the forms of all ages, Sanskrita, Pali, and Pràkrita appear to be confounded.'*

These peculiarities establish its inferiority to the Pali; and the dialect of the Pillar Inscriptions (which were recorded in the third century of the christian era,) being decidedly posterior to the language of Gotama, I shall, in search of this original *Pràkrit,* next betake myself to the Ceylon Pali, a dead language of antiquity, which came from Magadha, and has been preserved in Ceylon from the time almost of the Buddhistical era. Its identity with the *Màgadhà* of remote antiquity, is not only established by the history of Buddhism, and by the promiscuous use of the terms Pali and Magadh in Ceylon; but also from the extract above given, of the enumeration of the *shud bhàshà,* ante p. lxxxiii. Its great antiquity, and high state of cultivation in Ceylon, are made to appear from a variety of circumstances.

It is indeed a remarkable fact that all oriental scholars, who have made Pali the subject of study according to the different, though imperfect, opportunities they have had out of this island, have not failed to perceive something peculiar in the Pali, which distinguishes it from every variety of Sanskrit-idioms.

1. Professor Benfey in his *Ersch and Gruber's German Encyclopædia* p 194, characterises the Pali as 'the sacred lan-

* l'Histoire du Buddhisme Indien, p. 105.

guage of the Buddhist writings found in Ceylon and Trans-gangetic India, ... which is shown both by internal and external indications, to have been the vernacular dialect of central India, and which was diffused *along with the Buddhist religion in the countries above-named*, where it soon acquired the same *sacredness in the eyes of the Buddhists* which Sanskrit possessed, and still possesses, for the Brahmans. This language,' he continues (' though distinct proof cannot yet be adduced of the assertion,) is one of the very oldest of the Indian vernaculars, and was already in popular use at the period of the rise of Buddhism.'

2. Dr. Muir after citing the last authority, states. " But it matters little in what particular province we suppose the Pali to have originated, whether in Magadha, or in some country further to the westward: as the fact remains in any case indubitable, that it represents one of the oldest Prakatic dialects of northern India."—Sanskrit Texts p. 79.

Obs.—I may here remark in passing, that if the Pali represents, as it undoubtedly does, the oldest Pràkrit; and, moreover, if the Maharashtrì dialect is, as stated by the writer of Prâkrita-kalpataru, " the root of the other [Pràkrits];" i. e. those of which the Indians had any knowledge, or which have not been lost in India;—the inference is inevitable that the Pali, which had found an early retreat in Ceylon, is the parent of *all* Pràkrits, including the Maharashtrì. But to proceed: M. M. Burnouf and Lassen, who had but few Pali works within their reach, have not however, failed to perceive the nearest relationship of the Pali to the Sanskrit. Though I reluctantly, but respectfully, differ from them in the belief that the former is immediately derived from the latter; yet the facts which those learned writers record, are not without importance or value.

3. ' When the Pali, [say those learned writers in their Essai sur le Pali, p. 138] as a derivative from Sanskrit, is compared with other dialects having the same origin, it

is found to approach far more closely than any of those others to that common source. It stands, so to speak, *on the first step of the ladder of departure from Sanskrit,* and is the first of the series of dialects which break up that rich and fertile language.'

4. Dr. Muir, after subjecting the Pali to a comparison with the Sanskrit and Prakrit, concludes by saying, 'from this comparison it will result that the Pali stands nearer to the Sanskrit, and represents a more ancient phase of the vernacular speech of Northern India than is exhibited in the Pràkrit'

And he adds 'It has been demonstrated at length that it (the Pàli), in its turn, is more ancient in its grammatical forms than the Pràkrits are, and departs less widely than they do from the Sanskrit.'—p. 137.

I may also remark that entire sentences may be given of, and that whole passages may be composed in, the Pali wherein every word, every grammatical form, and every philological development most closely accords with even the *Sanskritized* idiom of the Brahmans. The following extracts, for example, from the Bhatti Kàvya, which abounds with specimens of the kind, authorize the above statement.

Chàru samìrana ramane
Harina-kalanka kiranàvalì savilàsá
Abaddha Ràma mohà
Velà mùle vibhàvarì parihìnà—p. 77.

'The evening, radiant with masses of moon-beams, and which filled (bound) Ràmà with affliction, was spent on the confines of the shore which was rendered delightful by reason of the (sweet) gentle breeze.'

Gantum Lankà tìran
Baddha mahà salila sancharena sahelan
Taruharinà giri jàlan
Vahantu giri bhàra sansahà gurudehan—p. 88.

'Let the monkeys, able to sustain the weight of mountains, convey the heavy-bodied rocky chain, so that we may in one line, get to the shores of Lankà, on a bridge constructed on the vast profound.'

To the above facts, all which are important in the consideration of the general question, as to the relationship of the Pali to Sanskrit, I shall add the testimony of eminent Oriental scholars, who notice the difference of the Pali from every dialect which is supposed to have arisen from the ancient Magadhì ;—its difference

1. From the dialect of the rock inscriptions ;*

" Now it is curious enough that some of the distinguishing traits of the pillar dialect are just such as are pointed out by the Grammarians of a later day as constituting the differences between Màgadhì and Pali." "The [same] language," Mr. Prinsep adds in another paper† " differs essentially from every written idiom : it is as it were intermediate between the Sanskrit and Pali."

2. From the Buddhist writings of Nipal ;

'They are' says M. Burnouf, " intermediate between the regular Sanskrit, and Pali—a dialect entirely derived, and manifestly posterior to the Sanskrit. ‡

3. From the Pràkrit dialects ;

'The Pràkrits do not represent the derivative form of speech which stands nearest to the Sanskrit ; and we are in a position to point out a dialect which approaches yet more closely to the latter than the Pràkrits do. I mean the Pali, or sacred language of the Buddhists ; a language which is extinct in India, but in which numerous canonical books of the Buddha religion, still extant in Burmah and Ceylon are written.' §

---

* 'We have seen (p. 72) that the Pali has some grammatical forms which are older than those of the inscriptions ; and *vice versa*.'—Dr. Muir, p. 137,

† Bengal Asiatic Society's Journal, vol. vi, p. 567,

‡ L' Histoire du Buddhisme Indien p. 105,

§ Dr. Muir's Sanskrit Texts, p. 65.

4. From the Màgadhì dialect in which the works of the Jains are written;

'On comparing the Mahawanso (says Dr. Stevenson) one of the sacred books of the Ceylonese with the Jain writings, I find considerable dissimilarity between the two dialects; the Pali approaching much nearer to the standard of the general Pràkrit, and having few, if any, of the peculiarities of the Màgadhì dialect, while the Jain works exhibit them by no means in a slight degree.' *

5. From the present language of Magadha or Behar;

'The Pali' says a writer in the Asiatic Journal, xviii. p. 764, 'being generally known by the name Màgadhì, was compared with the modern dialect of Magadh or Behar, and the comparison shews that they essentially differ. In those respects in which it differs from the Pali, it approaches the Prakrit or the sacred language of the Jains.'

6. And from the Màgadhì of the Indian grammarians :—

The following comparative view of the Pali, with the rules given by Vararuchi under the head of Màgadhì, will render their difference evident.

(i.) The first rule of Vararuchi is SHA SOH SAH. In the Pali there is no *S*. It has only the dental sibilant S. The inapplicability of the rule which states that in the peculiar dialect of Pràkrit termed Màgadhì, '*S* is substituted for *sh* or S,' is therefore, self-evident.

(ii.) JO VAH. The occasional substitution of *y* for *j* is no more a peculiarity of the Pali than of the Sanskrit or Sinhalese; e. g. *yàminì* or *jàminì* in Sanskrit, *yama* or *jáma* Sinhalese 'night.' The usual Pali *nija* is written in the Suttans with a *y*, as *niyan puttan* 'own son.' Instances like these are exceptions, not the rule, in those two languages. But neither in the instance given by Vararuchi, nor in the great majority of Sanskrit words with a j, is it changed into a *y* in the Pali. The reverse of what is given by

* Kalpa Suttra, p. 132.

Vararuchi may be regarded as the rule. Thus, *jàyate* 'he is born,' is the same in the Pali, and is not changed into *yàyade.* So likewise, *raja* is *rája,* and not *ràya* 'king'; *gaja* is *gaja* but not *gaya* 'elephant;' *vajra* is *vajira,* but not *vayara* 'diamond.' It is true that in words like *paryùshana,* the Pàli form is *payyùsana,* and not *pajjau-sana,* as in the common Prakrit. This peculiarity in the Pàli, however, does not indicate a change from j to y. It is simply the reduplication of y.

(iii.) The next rule, CHVARGASYASPRISHTATA TATHOCH-CHARANAH : seems to refer to a nicety in the pronunciation of the palatal letters, which we do not perceive in the Pali; and therefore proceed to the next;

(iv.) HRIDAYASYA HADAKKAH. This is equally inapplicable to the Pali. *Hridaya* 'heart' never becomes *hadakka,* but *hadaya,* in Pali. So likewise *hrisva* 'short' is not *hadasva,* but *rassa*; and *hri* 'shame' is not *hida* but *hiri.*

(v.) RYARJAYOR YYAH. The substitution here spoken, of *yy* for *ry* and *rj* may be regarded as the exception (and that of very rare occurrence) rather than the rule in the Pali. Thus *kàryan* 'to be done,' is not *kayye* but *kàriyan*; and *durjana* 'wicked' is not *duyyana,* but *dujjana,* in the Pali. So likewise *vìrya* 'exertion' becomes *viriya*; *bhàrya, bhariya* 'wife'; *aisvarya, issariya* 'prosperity'; and also *garjana* becomes *gajjana* 'noise'.

(vi.) KSHASYA SKAH. This is again different in the Pali. Thus *ràkshasah* 'demon' does not become *laskase* but *rak-khaso*; nor *dakshah* 'clever' *daske,* but *dakkho.* So like-wise, *vriksha* 'tree' becomes *rukkha* in the Pali; *kshamà kamà* 'forgiveness'; *dakshina, dakkhina* 'south'; *kshùra khùra* 'razor'; *kshetra, khetta* 'field'. This peculiarity will be found explained in another part of our observations, *vide infra,* § x.

(vii.) ASMADAS SAU HAKE HAGE AHAKE. The Sanskrit *ahan bhanàmi* 'I speak', is the same in the Pali; and does not become as stated here *hake, hage, or ahake banami.*

(viii.) Ata idetau lukcha. The Sanskrit *etad* (root) *eshah* (nom :) is said to be changed in the Màgadhì into *esa*, and *su* being added to it=*esà-su ;* and the latter affix being elided, the *a* in *esà* is changed into *i*, or *e*. This is not a peculiarity of the *Pali*, in which *eta* (root *eso*—nom :) becomes *esa ràja* (which is *esha ràjà* in *Sans :*) 'this king', and not as in the so-called Màgadhì *Esi laa ;* (! !) and similarly *esha purushah,* Sanskrit, becomes *eso puriso* in the Pali, but not, as in the Pràkrit Màgadhì, *esà pulise* 'this man.'

(ix.) Ktantad uscha : which is rendered by Dr. Cowell into English as follows : *U* is substituted when the affix *su* follows a word ending with the affix *kta ;* and also (as we infer from the *cha* of the *Sút :*) we may optionally use the *i* or *e* of the preceding Sút, or even elide the affix ; as hasidu or hasidi, haside, hasida, for hasitah 'smiling.' It is only sufficient to state here that the Pali knows no such thing, and that the Sanskrit *hasitah* is in the former simply *hasito*.

(x.) Naso ho va dirghatwamcha : That is to say '*ha* is optionally substituted for *nas*, the affix of the genitive singular, and at the same time the preceding vowel is lengthened, as *pulisàha* or *pulisassa dhane* for *purushasya dhanam* 'the man's-wealth.' The Pali form of this is *purisassa dhanam* wherein the Sanskrit inflexion *sya* assumes *ssa*, for the simple reason that the Pali dislikes the union of two consonants of different classes. It is further remarkable here that *dhane* of the Pràkrit-Màgadhì becomes *dhanam* (neuter) both in the Sanskrit and Pali, in which moreover the cerebral *n* is not used.

(xi.) Adirghas Sambuddhau. It is to be inferred from the examples given under this rule that in the Prakrit Màgadhì dialect the vocative inflexion *a* both in the singular and plural number is long. In the Pali, however, the termination of the vocative *singular* may be either long or short. (See *Clough's Bàlàvatàra* p. 19,) ; as *purisa àgachchha* or *purisà àgachchha*—'O ! man come.'

(xii.) CHITTHASYA CHISHTHAH. In shewing the difference of the Pali from the Pràkrit-Màgadhì, it is here sufficient simply to exhibit the Pali forms of the given examples.

Purushah tishthati *—*Sanskrit.*
Puriso titthati—Pali.
Pulise chishthadi—Mag : Prakrit.

(xiii.) KRINMRINGAMAM KTASYA DAH. Here again we cannot exhibit the difference of the Pàli from the Màgadhì Pràkrit better, than by placing the given examples in juxtaposition with their Pali forms.

Kritah 'done'		*mritah* 'dead'		*gatah* 'gone.'		*Sans.*
Kato	—	*mato*	—	*gato.*		*Pali*
Kade	—	*made*	—	*gade.*		*Mag-Pràk.*

(xiv.) KTVODANIH. The following comparative view of the examples given under this rule, shews the relationship of the Pali to the Sanskrit to be far nearer than that of the Prakrit-Màgadhì.

Sodvàgatah†	—*kritvàgatah*‡	*San.*
Sahitvá gato	—*katvágato*	*Pali*
Sahidani gade	—*karidani aade.*	*Prak M.*

(xv.) SRIGALASYA SIALASIALESIALAKAH. The difference between the Sanskrit *Srigàla* and the Pali *sigala* is, simply that occasioned by the absence of the Sanskrit *r* in the latter language. But Vararuchi gives the three following forms into which that word is changed in Màgadhì-Pràkrit; viz. *siálá, siale, siàlake.*

Obs.—From the above, and many a fact in the history of Buddhism, it may be inferred that there are few traces of the genuine Pràkrit in the existing Indian dialects; that the principal Prakrit, which distantly approaches to the Pali, is a corruption of the latter; that the patois of the dramas is an exhibition of it; and that the Grammarians, who subse-

* 'The man stands.' † 'Having borne went.' ‡ 'Having done went.'

quently framed rules for the formation of this corrupt idiom, had not the Pali, which had been banished the Magadha country along with the Buddhist religion. It may also be thence inferred that in very early times the Pali became mixed up with pure Sanskrit, as in the Nepal version; that it next assumed the form of the pillar dialect, and that at last it was reduced to the Màgadhì of the Jains, which distantly resembles the dialect of the grammarians. Buddhism, in a very early period of its history, doubtless, brought the Pali language to Ceylon; where, having soon become a dead language, its use was confined to the priesthood; and from the homage the Ceylonese paid to it as the language of the founder of their religion, it remained in the Island unaffected by those changes to which, as a spoken language, it was subjected in its migrations in India. Thus, its philological peculiarities, which will be noticed hereafter—its great age in this Island—its still higher antiquity in Asia—and the absence of any other Indian dialect which bears traces of so close an affinity to the Sanskrit as the Pali, when taken into consideration with the facts, that 'the Brahmans and Aryas' had for their *vyavahàrika vàk*, a dialect similar to the Sanskrit; and that that dialect is declared by Buddhagosa, himself a Brahman, to be the Pàli [Pràkrit]; we may indeed discover a few at least of the grounds upon which the tradition of the Buddhists is based, viz., that 'the Pàli was the *mûla bàsà*.'

VI. This leads us then to the consideration of the theory with which we have set out—that the Pali is "a sister-dialect of the Sanskrit, being probably derived from one and the same source."

In considering this subject we notice that the *Brahmans* regard the *Sanskrit* to be of divine origin, and as a direct revelation from their Creator; and that the *Buddhists* claim for the *Pali* an antiquity so remote that they affirm it to be a language 'the root of all dialects, which was spoken by Brahmàs, by men before the present *kappa*, by those who had neither heard nor uttered human accent, and also by supreme Buddhas'—

Sà Màgadhì mùla bhàsà
Nàrà yà yàdi kappikà;
Brahmànochassutàlàpà
Sambuddhà chàpi bàsare.

The above is found quoted by Mr. Turnour from the Payogasiddhi; and the following, to the same effect,* occurs in the

VIBHANGA ATTHAKATHA.

Tissadatta thero kira Bodhi mande suvanna salàkan gahetvà 'a*tt*hàrasasu bhàsàsu katara bhàsàya katemi—iti' pavàresi. Tan pana tena atthato uggahetvà pavàritan; napatisambhidàya *t*hitena; sohi mahàpaññatàya tan tan bhàsan kathàpetvà ugganhi: Tato uggahe*t*hatvà evan pavàresi. Bhàsan nàma sattà ugganhantìti vatvàcha panettha idan kathitan. Màtàpitarohi dahara kàle kumàrake manchevà pì*t*hevà nipajàjpetva tan tan kathaya mànà tàni tàni kichchàni karonti; dàrakà tesan tan tan bhàsan vavatthàpentu 'iminà idan vuttan iminà idan vuttan'ti gachchante kàle sabbampi bhàsan jànanti. Màtà Damilì pità Andhako tesan jàto dàrako sache màtu-kathan pa*t*haman sunàti, Dami*l*a bhàsan bhàsissati, sache pitu kathan pa*t*haman sunàti Andhaka bhàsan bhàsissati. Ubhinnampi pana kathan asunanto Màgadhikan bhàsissati. Yopi agàmake mahà raññe kathento nàma natthi sopi attano dhammatàya vachanan samu*tt*ha pento Màgadha bhàsa meva bhàsissati. Niraye tirachchhàna Yonian pettivisaye manussa loke deva loke-tisabbattha Màgadhika bhàsà eva ussannà; tattha sesa O*tt*à Kiràthà Andhaka Yonaka Dami*l*a bhàsàdikà a*tt*harasa bhàsà parivattanti. Aya'meva ekà yathàbhuchcha-Brahmavohàra-Ariya-vohàra-sankhàtà Màgadhika bhàsà eva na-pa-

---

* Parivattesi sabbapi Sihala*tt*hakatha tada,
Sabbesan mulabasaya Magadhayaniruttiya.—*Maharansa, p.* 253.

rivattati. Sammà Sambuddhopi tepitakan buddha vachanan tantin aropento Màgadha bhàsàya eva àropesi ; Kasmà evañhi atthan àharitun sukhan hoti. Màgadha bhàsàyahi tanti arû*l*hassa buddha vachanassa pa*t*isambhidappattànan sotapatha gamane-neva yanche sotena sangha*tt*ita matte yeva naya satena naya sahassena attho upa*tt*hàti ; aññàya pana bhàsàya tanti àru*l*hakan pothetvà uggahetabban hoti.

'Tissadatta thèra took up the gold broomstick in the Bô compound, and requested to know in which of the eighteen *bhdsas* he should speak ? He so (spake) from (a knowledge of those languages) acquired not through inspiration,* but, by actual study ; for being a very wise personage he knew those several dialects by learning : wherefore, being one of (such) acquirements he so inquired. This is said here (to illustrate) that men acquire a bhàsà (by study.)

'Parents place their children, when young, either on a cot or a chair, and speak different things and perfom different actions. Their words are thus distinctly fixed by the children (on their minds, thinking) 'that such was said by him and such by the other' ; and in process of time they learn the entire language. If a child, born of a *Damila*† mother, and an *Andhaka*‡ father, should first hear his mother speak, he would speak the *Damila* language ; but if he should first hear his father speak, he would speak the *Andhaka* language. If however he should not hear them both, he would speak the Màgadhi. If, again, a person in an uninhabited forest, in which no speech (is heard), should intuitively attempt to articulate words, he would speak the very *Màgadhì*. It predominates in all regions (such as) Hell ; the animal kingdom ; the *Petta* sphere ; the human world ; and the world of the *devas*. The rest of the eighteen languages—*Ottà, Kiràthà, Andhaka, Yonaka, Damila*, &c., undergo changes ;—but the

* Pa*t*isambhidaya—the four supernatural attainments peculiar to the highest order of Arahanta, including *inspired* knowledge.

† Damila (or Tamil) is the Pali form of *Dramida*, or *Dravida*.

‡ *Andhaka* is the Pali form of Andhra, the Sanskrit name for the Talugu—see *Caldwell's Dravidian Comp. Gram.* p. 5.

Màgadhì does not, which alone is unchangeable, and is said to be the speech of Brahmans and Ariyas. Even Buddha, who rendered his *tepitaka* words into texts, did so by means of the very *Màgadhì;* and why? Because by doing so it (was) easy to acquire their (true) significations. Moreover, the se nse of the words of Buddha which are rendered into doctrines by means of the Màgadhì language, is conceived in hundreds and thousands of ways by those who have attained the *pati-sambhidà* so soon as they reach the ear, or the instant the ear comes in contact with them; but discourses rendered into other languages are acquired with much difficulty.'

Now it is a fact that 'all rude nations are distinguished by a boastful and turgid vanity.' They invent fables to exalt their nationality, and leave records behind them to abuse the credulity of after ages.' They cannot speak of their race, or of their sacred languages without assigning to them an origin the remotest in the world. In 'a spirit of adulation and hyperbole' they exalt them as high as the object of their adoration and worship. This is peculiarly the case with Eastern nations.

Although such extravagantly high pretensions, are by themselves of no value; yet when some of these traditions are partially supported by the concurrence of other testimony, we may by a judicious exercise of our judgments in separating fact from fable, and reality from fiction, receive them, I apprehend, to the extent to which they are confirmed. Let us examine this confirmatory proof.

The term Pràkrita, as we have already seen, means 'root' or 'original;' and the Pali is the earliest exhibition of the Pràkrit. In this point of view, therefore, the Pali may claim greater originality, if not antiquity, than the Sanskrit, which is confessedly a dialect 'made' or 'done.' In other words, if the Pali, may be regarded as the prakriti, or an exhibition of the aboriginal tongue, there is nothing in the signification of the term *Sanskrita* to entitle the language for which it is a name, to be considered the source from whence the former is *derived*.

The facts, too, which we glean from history or find from natural causes, accord wonderfully with the import of the terms which we have above given, and with the belief that Pali is a Vyavahàrika idiom of the Sanskrit. For, whilst both the languages are fundamentally the same, the Pàli is simpler in its formation, and is more adapted to the vocal organs of men in a rude state of society, who, like children, avoid the sharpness of a union of heterogeneous consonants by the elision of the first, and the reduplication of the second.

These can scarcely be pronounced to be peculiar characteristics of a derivative tongue. For, we know that many nations both of the North and South-Indian class, in their attempts to beautify language, draw largely from the Sanskrit. The Tamils and the Hindus use a dialect full of Sanskrit words; and the modern Sinhalese with a view to beautify language, do not assimilate sounds, and shorten expressions, but *Sanskritize* our ancient simple language.* This was probably the case with the Sanskrit itself, which has no claims to originality.

The simplicity of the grammatical system in the Pali, as is indicated by the non-use of the dual number, the absence of certain elaborations of simple tenses,† the small number of verbal classes,‡ &c. 'look like the spontaneous substitution of practical to theoretic perfection in actual speech'.§ For, it is a fact consistent with natural events, that the less finished and elaborate system is usually ante-

* See specimen in my Sidat Sangara, p. xxxvi.

† See my Notes at the end of the First Chap. on Verbs.

‡ Also my notes at the end of the Chap. ii.

§ Professor Wilson's Hindu Plays, 1. p. lxv.

rior to that which is more so.* The presumption therefore is—not that the Sanskrit had an origin anterior to the Pràkrita, by which I here mean the Pali—not that it received the name of Sanskrit when in a rude state—not that the Pali-Pràkrit is a derivative of the Sanskrit;—but that the latter is only a more finished exhibition of the Pali, or of some unknown idiom from whence both have sprung. I may, in justice to the theory of the Buddhists, add, that many of the laws by which certain derived languages may be distinguished, do not govern the Pàli, *e. g.* The Pali has not rejected case-terminations for particles; and has not adopted auxiliary verbs in conjugation. It is indeed the Sanskrit which may be charged with using auxiliary forms altogether unknown to the Pali.† For, "the Sankrit verbs of the tenth class, and all derivative verbs, periphrastically express the reduplicated præterite by one of the auxiliary verbs,—*kri* 'to make', *as* and *bhû* 'to be.'‡"

The fact, as remarked by M.M. Burnouf and Lassen, that 'no grammatical form is to be found in the Pali, of which *the origin* [why not say, some *traces*] may not be discovered in the Sanskrit,"§ far from proving the Pali to be a *daughter*, establishes to my mind that she is, like the Zend, a *sister* of the Sanskrit. It would also seem that no inferences can be drawn by comparisons between the Pali and the Sanskrit‖ on the one hand, and, for instance, the Italian and the Latin

* 'I feel bound to concede that, by its greater simplicity of construction and superior facility of enunciation, the Prakrit may easily bear away the palm from its rival as a simple, yet polished and harmonious vehicle of human thought, admirably fitted to be the spoken tongue of a great and refined nation.'—Dr. Stevenson's Kalpa Suttra, p. 137.

† Panini iii., 1. 35. ff.

‡ Bopp's Comp. Grammar, ii., p. 841.

§ Essai Sur le Pali, p. 138.

‖ "From tho facts detailed in the preceding paragraphs (says Dr. Muir in his Sanskrit Texts ii. p. 274.) which prove that compound roots have been taken by the Indian grammarians for simple ones, and that old forms have been modified or lost in the modern, or even in the Vedic-Sanskrit, it is clear that that language (especially in its modern form) cannot always be regarded as a fixed standard, according to which the originality of the Latin and Greek [I would also add *the Pali*] forms could be estimated."

on the other; because the Sanskrit itself has undergone a great change, and the various influences which contribute to the corruption of languages are not the same both in Europe and Asia. And the differences must be great indeed between the languages (*e. g.* Sanskrit and Pali) of tribes who had continued together for several thousand years in the same country, subject to the same influences of literature, religion, and clime,* and who upon separation have changed their religious faith, and have ceased to speak their respective lauguages; and of those (*e. g.* Latin and Italian) of other tribes who have been 'separated for as many thousands of years, living in regions far apart from each other, under different physical conditions, and whose vernacular dialects are subject to the modifying action of different social, political, and religious institutions.'†

Yet it is a singular fact that, in some particulars in which the grammatical forms of the Pali differ from the Sanskrit, they agree with the structure of the Indo-European languages, and of the Pràkrit dialects. *e. g.* There is 'a concurrence of the Pràkrit with the old High German and the Latin of the 2d conj. in this point—that it in like manner has contracted the affix *aya* to *ê*.'‡ Compare Sanskrit *mànayâmi* 'I honor', Pali *mànêmi* Pràkrit *mànèmi*, Old-High German *var-manêm* 'I despise', Latin *moneo*:"§

Sanskrit.	*Pali.*	*Prakrit.*	*Old High Ger.*	*Latin.*
mànayàmi	mànemi	mànemi	var-manêm	moneo
mànayasi	mànesi	mànesi	manês	monês
mànayati	màneti	mànedi	manêt	monet
mànayàmas	mànema	mànemha	manêmes	monêmus
mànayatha	mànetha	mànedha	manêt	monêtis
manayanti	mànenti	mànenti	manênt	monent

* "In general it appears that in warm regions languages, when they have once burst the old grammatical chain, hasten to their downfall with a far more rapid step than under our milder European Sun."—Bopp's Comp. Gram. p. 711.

† "Closely related dialects are known to develope and change at very different rates of progress."—*Pr. Whitney, Am. Oriental Journal Vol. v. p.* 352.

‡ Also see Bopp's Comp. Grammar, p. 701.

§ Bopp's Comp. Grammar, pp. 109, 10. The examples of the Pali in the above table, have been introduced by me.

In regard to these weak verbs, (adds Professor Bopp) which have suppressed the first vowel of the Sanskrit *aya*, and give therefore *ya* as affix, we will here further recall attention to the forms *iga* (*ige*), which occasionally occur in Old High German and Anglo Saxon, whose connection with *aya* is to be traced thus, that the semi-vowel *y* has become hardened to *g* (comp. § 19.) and the preceding *a* weakened to *i*.' Hence the Pràkrit *padhijjai* 'is read', *gamijjai* 'is gone.'

If the Pali was immediately derived from the Sanskrit, it is sure to have those forms only which the Sanskrit adopts; and cannot possibly know any other forms which her Sisters had taken away, at their separation from the Indo-Ariyan speech. The existence however in the Pali of both forms known to the Sanskrit, and forms which her European-Sisters adopt, as in the instances cited under the causal form of the verb,*—establishes the belief of Dr. Weber, to which I shall hereafter call attention;—'the contemporaneous development of both the Sanskrit and the Pràkrit dialects from one common source, viz., the Indo-Arian speech.'

I may also here observe that among the more ancient Brahmans, none, notwithstanding their partiality to the Sanskrit, have expressly stated the locality† or the source of the dialect called by way of eminence, the Pràkrit. Comparatively later writers do indeed point at Mahàrashtrì as that principal Pràkrit;‡ but neither Vararuchi nor Bahàmaha has so stated it. The former who treats of four dialects, says that Paisàchi and Màgadhì are derived from the Saurasenì; and the Saurasenì had its source in Sanskrit; but he is silent as to the origin of *the Pràkrit*, to the elucidation of which he devotes the largest portion of his work.

* See my notes at the end of the Cap. iii. *infra*.

† 'No province is assigned however to the principal Prakrit dialect'—Lassen's Inst. Prak. § 3.

‡ Shadbhasha Chandrika.

It is however stated by those who maintain that the Pali, or the principal Pràkrit is a derivative, that the Sûtra (18) at the end of Cap. ix, in which Vararuchi refers the student to "the Sanskrit" for "the rest" or the remaining grammatical forms,* implies that the principal Pràkrit had its origin in the Sanskrit. This, however, is not the only inference. The fact from which that inference is drawn, is also consistent with the belief of the Buddhists—that the Pàli or the principal Pràkrit is a sister of the Sanskrit. For, if they were, like the Sanskrit and the *vyava-hârika vàk* of the Brahmans, two dialects which had a simultaneous origin, and merely differ from each other in some respects like the Attic and the Ionic; there was no necessity whatever to treat of, twice, the grammatical forms which were identical in both. Having a full and complete grammar of one (the Sanskrit), it was surely sufficient to shew the differences only by which the Pràkrit grammatical forms were distinguishable from those of the Sanskrit. Hence the simple reference—*Seshah Sanskritàt*—to 'the Sanskrit for the rest.'

I have already alluded to the fact that the Sanskrit had been in a state of transition until it became fixed as the classical language of the Brahmans. 'It shews clearly to be' says a late writer, 'the adaptation of some vernacular dialect to the state in which we find it, in order to form a characteristic language.' 'Its style exhibits all the traces of transition from the first efforts of expression to the highest refinements of grace and inflection, and its literature all the gradations from barbarism to sublimity, and from sublimity to refinement.' Some of the older compositions, such as a portion of the Vedas, prove this; for thier style, unlike the poetry of Kàlidàsa is rustic and irregular, and 'they are written in an ancient form of the Sanskrit, so different from that now in

* It is indeed remarkable that the Pali Grammarian, who has even borrowed technical terms from the Sanskrit, does not refer the Student for 'the remainder' to the Sanskrit, but to the Pali language, as the same is developed in the discourses of Gotama. See Cap. iv. § 36 *a*.

use, that none but the more learned of the Brahmins themselves can understand them.*

That the Pali, if it were not the *vyavahàrika vàk* of the Brahmans, had a contemporaneous existence with an old form of language, which has been cultivated to the development of the Sanskrit, appears not only from a comparison of the Pali with the oldest available Sanskrit, viz., the Vedas, but also from a careful examination of the oldest Pali alphabet.

To treat of the latter first: The earliest *records* are by Pali-speaking† Buddhists in an old type of the Nàgarì alphabet; and, judging by its internal evidence, 'it bears every impress of indigenous organization and local maturation.'‡ Although the age of this character is identical with that of Asoka (235 B. C.); yet that the same character had been in use for a considerable time before that date, may be easily believed. Indeed the following description given by King Pukkusàti of the characters in which the letter of his royal friend Bimbisàra was written, clearly shews that the same was the Màgadhì alphabet used in the time of Gotama Buddha.§ So tan pasàritvà 'manàpàni vata akkharàni samasìsàni samapantìni chaturassànì'ti àdito patthàya vàchetun àrabhi. That is, 'when he had unfolded [the gold plate 6 feet × ½, on which the epistle was written] he (observed) that the letters|| were indeed pretty—exact in (the forma-

* Elphinstone's India, vol. i., p. 72.

† Or, "*Magadhi*, by which name may be considered that dialect which is more ordinarily understood by *Prakrit*"—Wilson's Hindu Plays, i., p. lxxii.

‡ Prinsep's Indian Antiquities, ii. p. 43.

§ 'The alphabet which we possess, as used by the Buddhists of a couple of centuries later, was that in which their sacred works had been written by the contemporaries of Buddha himself, who died in 543. B. C.—*Prinsep's Indian Antiquities*, ii. p. 39.

|| This proves that the *cursive* departure from the *square* form should be dated *after* the Buddhist era; and that the latter was not, as supposed by some, confined to Inscriptions, from its being better suited for lapidary purposes. For, the Epistle of Brimbisara was written with "pure vermilion", a material, which, if 'the rounding of angularities' was known in his time, 'presented no difficulties to any series of curves or complicated lines.'

tion of) their heads—and quadrangular (in shape),—and that the lines were of even tenor; and he commenced to read it from the beginning.'—*Papanchasûdanîya.*

In alluding to the specimens from the Buddhist caves of western India, Mr. Prinsep remarks, "The old alphabet* appears to be *the very prototype* of all the Deva Nagari and Dakshini alphabets; and nothing in the pure Sanskrit tongue has yet been discovered, preserved in this character; indeed it would be impossible that it should, because, still more than the Pali, the alphabet is deficient in many letters absolutely necessary to Sanskrit Syntax."†

Col. Sykes, that enthusiastic advocate for the superior claims of the Pàli, has drawn all the inferences which may be drawn from the above facts; and I prefer to set them before the reader in his own expressive language: 'It is incredible,' he states, 'to suppose that the modern Sanskrit could have existed without symbols or a character to express its present richness, force, and beauty. How, then, are we to account for the fact of the modern Deva Nagari resolving itself into the ancient Pali letters, and those letters expressing *only*, not the Sanskrit language, but, the ancient Pali? I cannot see any other way of solving the question, than in the supposition, that at the period the primitive Deva Nagari was expressing the old Pali language * * * * the Sanskrit itself, if it existed independently from the old Pali, was in the same rude state with the Pali.'‡

---

* 'This primitive character may well have proved sufficient for all purposes of record, so long as the language it was called upon to embody remained as simple as that for expression of which we may suppose it to have been originally designed and adapted. On the introduction of the Sanskrit element, it was necessarily subjected to previously-needless combinations, and under this and other process, perhaps, lost some of the stiffness of outline, which it may, nevertheless, have retained together with its original literal simplicity among the vulgar, even in the presence of an improved style of writing, suited for more polished literature; as in the existing Orthography of Hindi, contrasted with the elaboration of Sanskrit alphabetial definitions.' *Prinsep's Indian Antiquities by Edward Thomas*, vol. ii. pp. 43, 4.

† Beng. Asiatic Society's Journal, vi. p.1043.

‡ See Journal of the Royal Asiatic Society, vi. p. 414.

I return to the language: It is indeed a very significant fact that many grammatical forms of the Pali, which may be distinguished from those of the modern Sanskrit, are identical with some of the *Vedic* peculiarities. This may be rendered evident by a few examples contained in the following notes, taken by me in the course of my studies: and I have no doubt that, with a more intimate acquaintance with these two languages than I possess, the list may be greatly enlarged.

(i.) The Vedas—and I shall here take an example from a portion which is not in metre—contain exceptions to the general rule in Sanskrit, by which a word ending in *e* or *o* when not combining with a following *a*, should cause its elision; as *Vasishteadhi* 'over Vasishtha.' This is frequently the case in the Pali. Thus, in the *Dhamma-Pada, dussìlo-asamàhito* 'a reprobate free from meditation.' It is remarkable that owing to this peculiarity Pali Grammarians do not make elision imperative in this case.

(ii.) I believe short vowels are rendered long in the Vedas. See Wilson's Sanskrit Grammar, p. 453. This is also the case in the Pali. Thus, *san rajjati* becomes *sà rajjati* 'greatly attached.' See *Bàlavatàra*, p. 14; *khantì paraman tapo* (instead of khantī short) 'Forbearance is the highest religious austerity'—*Kachchàyana. Evan game munì chare.* 'Thus, may the muni dwell in the village'—*Kachchàyana.* A long *i* is frequently rendered short in the Pali. Thus in the *Attanagaluvansa*, Chap. i. § 2.

'Yo bodhisatta gunavà sirī Sanghabodhi.' Again in the well known 'Ye dhammà hetuppabhavà' stanza of the Buddhists, *vàdì* is written *vàdī*; thus,

'Evan vàdi mahà Samano'

Thus also in *Kachchàyana's* Pali Grammar Bhó* vàdi nàma so hoti 'He is named Bho vàdī.'†

---

* 'Sir'—a term in the vocative, used amongst the Brahmans; and *Vadi*—'speaker'; thence a name for the Brahman—'venerable speaker.'

† These examples are taken from *Kachchayana*, lib i. Section 3.

(iii.) In the Pali as in the Vedas the cerebral *d* is very frequently changed into the Vedic *l* which is also found in the Pàli. Thus gûlha 'concealed'; da*l*ha 'hard'; and the common Sanskrit àru*d*ha becomes àrù*l*ha —See Bàlavatàra, p. 110.

(iv.) *Adukshat*, the Vedic form of *adhukshat* is in consonance with the Pali, wherein the aspirate dental is changed into the unaspirate; as *idha bhikkhave* or *ida bhikkhave* 'here, O priests'—See Bàlavatàra, § 24.

(v.) *Ange ange*, would be quite correct in the Pali, and so it is in the Vedic; although in modern Sanskrit the following short vowel should be elided, as angenge 'member, member.*

(vi.) The Pali *ayan so aggi*, which in modern Sanskrit should be written *ayansognih*, is found to agree with the Vedic *ayan so agnih*.

(vii.) Even the phrase *Hari Hari yàhi* in the Gìtagovinda, is more in accordance with the Pali than the modern Sanskrit.

(viii.) As in the Vedic Sanskrit, wherein the person plural *bhis* is not unfrequently retained instead of the substitute *ais* (*aih*) which is enjoined after nouns in *a*, the Pali invariably takes the former; as *devebhi* 'with god' *Buddhebi* 'by Buddha'; *rukkhebhi* 'with tree.'†

(ix.) 'The Pràkrit (says Bopp) has fully followed out the path commenced by the Veda dialect, and changed into *e* the *â* of *asmâ-bhis*, *yushmâ-bhis*, as also, in the locative plural, that of *asmâ-su*, *yushmâsu*; hence *amhe-hi*(*n*), *tumhe-hi* (*n*)‡ *amhesu*, *tumhesu*. Moreover, in Pràkrit, all other *a* bases, as well pronouns as substantives and adjectives, terminate the instrumental plural with *ehi* (*n*); and thus *kusmehi* (*n*) 'floribus', (from *kusma*,) answers to the Veda *kusumebhis*.' Comp. Gram. § 220.

---

* The same form of *sandhi* frequently occurs in the Rig Veda; e. g. *deva so apturah*, p. 72.

† The *bh* is sometimes changed into *h* in Pali; as *devebhi* or *devehi*.

‡ The *n* is lost in the Pali.

(x) The substitution of *ya* for *n* before (*u*) the sign of the instrumental case singular, is to be found in the Pali as in the Vedas, but with this difference—that the substitution is confined in the Pali to feminine nouns; as *dhànuyà* 'by a cow'; *yàguyà* 'with gruel.'

(xi.) In the Rig Veda, p. 60, *narà* is given for the dual vocative. The Pali, which does not recognize the dual, adopts this in the plural.

(xii.) Again *mitra varunà* (see Rig Veda, p. 63) which in the modern Sanskrit is changed into *mitra varunau*, is in accordance with the Pali.

(xiii.) The gender is found changed in the Vedas, as *madhos triptdh* 'satisfied with nectar.' Here *madhu* is masculine; and similarly it may be either masculine or neuter in the Pali.—See Bàlavatàra, p. 51.

(xiv.) The curtailment of the neuter plural of nouns in *a*, by the omission of *ni*, is as frequent in the Pali as in the Vedas. Thus *khettà* for *khettàni* 'fields'; *chittà* for *chittàni* 'minds.'—See Bàlavatàra, p. 44.

(xv.) In the Vedas *mri* 'to die', of the sixth conjugation is inflected as if belonging to the same class, (the first) to which it belongs in the Pàli.

(xvi.) One voice is used for another in the Vedas; as *brahmachàrina michchate* (for *ti*) 'he wishes for the religious student.' As the distinction of *àtmane pada* and *parasmai pada* is not strictly observed in the Pali, the above is equally admissible in that language, and the same sentence will serve as an example.

(xvii.) In the *àtmane pada*, the initial *ta* of a termination is rejected in the Vedas, as *dakshina tah saye* (*sete*) 'he sleeps on his right side.' So likewise in the Pali the above sentence may be correctly rendered thus; *dakkhina to saye* (*sayeyya* or *sayetha.*)—See Bàlavatàra, p. 104.

(xviii.) In the modern Sanskrit the infinitive is *tum;* but the Vedic shows different forms, amongst which we have *tave*, which, as well as *tum*, is found in the Pali. Thus the

Vedic *kàrtave* 'to do' becomes *kàtave* in the Pali.—See Bàlavatàra, p. 121.

(xix.) The Pali past participle pìtvàna 'having drunk' is nearer the Vedic *pìtvànan.*—See Wilson's Sanskrit Grammar, p. 477.

(xx.) "From the researches of M.M. Kuhn* and Benfey,"† observes Dr. Muir in his *Sanskrit Texts*, p. 168,, 'it appears that many words, which in modern Sanskrit are only of one, two, or three, &c., syllables, have in the Veda to be read as of two, three, or four, &c. syllables, i. e. as of one syllable longer, in order to make up the full length of the lines required by the metre employed by the Vedic poets. Thus tvam has to be read tuam; vyushtan as *viushtan*; *turyam* as *turiyam*; *martyàya* as *martiàya*; *varenyam* as *vareniam*; *amàtyam* as *amàtiam*; *svadhvaram* as *suadvaram*; and *svastibhih* as *suastibhih*. Now as this mode of lengthening words is common in Pràkrit, it would appear that the Prakrit pronunciation agrees in this respect with that of the *old* Sanskrit, in contradistinction to the more recent.'

Such are the relations which the oldest Sanskrit now accessible to us, bears to the Pali; and it must be borne in mind that the former is (1) a modification of two sorts of language, the *Vedic* or the sacred Sanskrit, and the vyavahàrika or the *Vernacular*;—that (2) the vernacular, or the 'current' language of the Brahmans was in course of time assimilated to their *Vedic* Sanskrit;—and (3) that the Vedas themselves have been tampered with, so that whilst they received additions and mutations in point of substance, the language itself has indeed undergone a considerable change in point of form. We have thus no truthful evidence of the normal development of the Vedic Sanskrit, and which, if we had, might, perhaps, exhibit that many other forms of

* Zeitschrift fur die Kunde des Morgenlandes, iii., 80.

† Sama Veda, Introduction, p. liii., ff.

the Pali, which are distinguishable from their corresponding forms in the Sanskrit, were at one time as much identical with the Anti-Vedic, as several remnants of the Vedic forms are decidedly the same in the Pàli. A few words may however be deemed necessary in support of the above propositions ; and

1. *That the Brahmans had two kinds of language.* It is a well known fact in the East generally, that nearly every nation has a book-dialect and a vernacular speech. Take, for instance, the Sinhalese. Our vernacular language is generally without the contrivance of *Sandhi* and *compounds ;* whereas the dialect in which our books are written cannot be understood without much reflection, and, in some cases, without a Commentary. The case was doubtless the same with the Sanskrit. Its refinement and development are such that no one can reasonably conclude that it was ever the *spoken* language (vyavahàrikavàk) of the Brahmans ; yet from several passages in the Sanskrit literature, the colloquial use of a modified form of the Sanskrit may be concluded. It would thence seem that their language was two-fold. A passage that we have already quoted (ante p. lxxxviii.) from the earliest Veda, sets this beyond doubt.

2. The development of the existing Sanskrit, other than the *Vedic,* indeed proves, that the *Vyavahàrika vàk* has been so assimilated to their sacred language, that—*vires acquirit eundo*—it has received additional refinement in its progress.

"The language of the Vedas (says Pr. Whitney) is an older dialect, varying very considerably, both in its grammatical and lexical character from the classical Sanskrit. Its grammatical peculiarities run through all departments : euphonic rules, word-formation and composition, declension, conjugation, syntax. Without entering into any specification of them, which would extend this paper beyond its proper limits, it will be enough to say here that they are partly such as characterize an older language, consisting in a greater originality of forms and the like, and partly such as characterize a language which is still in the bloom and vigor of life, its freedom untrammelled by other rules than those of common usage, and which has not, like the Sanskrit, passed into oblivion as a native spoken dialect, become merely a conventional medium of communication among the learned, been forced, as it were, into a mould of regularity by long and exhausting grammatical treatment, and received a development which is in some respects foreign and unnatural."* If it may be established that the Vedas were altered, it may indeed be concluded that the *anti Vedic* forms had been greatly different from the Vedic. This leads to the consideration,

8. *Were the Vedas altered by Brahmans?* Professor Wilson, in his Review of Professor Max Muller's valuable work on *Sanskrit Literature*, thus notices the subject.

"The first and most obvious conclusion to be drawn from the hymns of the Vedas, whatever may be their relative antiquity, whether twenty or twelve Centuries B. C., is that the religion which they inculcate is not that of the Hindus of the present day. The Brahman, who from the time of the code of Munu as we have it, had arrogated to himself the attributes of a god upon earth, is in the Veda only among seven, or even of sixteen priests, acting as a sort of master of the ceremonies, but not invested with any superior rank or authority. Of the distinction of caste, all the indications are faint and uncertain, with one exception—that of a remarkable hymn in the 10th Mandala, the tenor and style of which place it indisputably in a comparatively recent stage, and bring it at least to the Brahmanic period, by which time we know that the Brahmanical system had been organized. There is no mention of temples nor of public worship; the ceremonial is entirely domestic, and so far the formulæ, the language of the Suktas, still constitute the liturgy of the domestic rites of the Hindus.' It is very doubtful if images

* American Oriental Journal, iii., pp. 296-7.

were known, although mention of personal peculiarities, as of the handsome jaws of Indra, might be suggested by a sculptured representation of him. Something else may, however, be meant; but the great feature of difference is the total absence of the divinities, both nomina and numina, who have for ages engaged, and, to a great degree engrossed the adoration of the Hindus. We have no indications of a Triad, the creative, preserving, and destroying power; Brahma does not appear as a deity, and Vishnu, although named, has nothing in common with the Vishnu of the Puràṇas; no allusion occurs to his Avataras. His manifestation as Krishna, the favorite divinity of the lower classes, for some centuries at least, does not appear. As a divinity Siva is not named, nor is his type the Linga ever adverted to. Durgà and her triumphs, and *Kali* whom the 'blood of man delights a thousand years,' have no place whatever in the hymns of the Vedas. These differences are palpable, and so far from the Vedas being the basis of the existing system, they completely overturn it. It would be an interesting subject of inquiry to discover when and by what means the vast mass of the modern mythology of the Hindus sprang into existence and attained a circulation throughout India."*

The Buddhists enlighten us on this subject: and the following extracts show that not only were additions made to the Vedas, but that the Vedas themselves which are said to have been originally composed in accordance with the Buddhist doctrines of Kassapa, a so-called predecessor of Gotama, were in after times altered by the Brahmans.

In the *Ambatta Suttan*, Gotama declares that the *mantas* of the Brahmans (which are identified with the Vedas by the Commentators) were compiled by Attaka (a) Vàmaka, Vàmadèva, (a) Vessàmitta, (a) Yamataggi, Angìrasa, (b) Bhàra dvàja, (a) Vàsettha, (a) Kassapa (b) and Bhagu. (b) †

* Edinburgh Review No. 228, pp. 381-2.

† All these names are also given in the Abhidanapadipika. Some of them are the Rishis of the Rig-Veda.—See Max Muller p. 44 note. Names marked with an (a) may be identified with those given in Muller's Sanskrit Literature, p. 42; and for those marked with (b) See Max Muller, p. 378.

Te kira dibbena chakkhunà oloketwà parùpaghàtan akatvà Kassapa sammà sambuddhassa pàvachanèna salià sansandhetvà mante ganthesun. Aparà' paran pana Brahmanà panàti pàtàdìni pakkhi pitvà tayo vede bhinditvà Buddha vachane saddhin viruddhe akansu.—*Sumangala Vilàsinì.*

'Those sages after obtaining* the supreme discourses of Kassapa Buddha, through the medium of their divine eyes, compiled the Manta conformably to those discourses, without the mention of tormenting (sacrifices.) The Brahmans in course of subsequent times, however, set aside the three Vedas, and made (a different compilation) by departing from the words of Buddhism, and introducing (an authority for) life-slaughter &c.'

Tìsu vedesù'-ti àdisu Irubbeda Yajubbeda Sàma-veda sankhàtesu tesu vedesu: tayo eva kira vedà Attakàdìhi dhammikehi isìhi lòkassa sagga magga bhàvan' atthàya kathà; tenevahi tayotì vuchchanti. Athabbana vedo pana pachchhà adhammikehi Bràhmanehi pàna vàdhàdi atthàya kato, purimesucha tìsu vedesu teheva dhammika yàjayo apanetvà yàga vadàdi dìpikà adhammika sàkhà pakkhittà-ti veditabbà.

'*Tìsu Vedesu* i. e. the three Vedas called Irubbedda (Rig. Veda.)' Yajubbèda (Yajur), and Sàma Veda. These three Vedas were made by Attaka, and other religious sages for the attainment of the path of heaven by mankind: they are therefore called 'three.' The Athabbana (Atharvan) Veda, however, was since made† by irreligious (wicked) Brahmans with a view to introduce life-slaughter (animal sacrifices). Moreover, be it known, that they themselves introduced into the first mentioned Vedas, irreligious branches which proclaim sacrificial torments &c., after expelling virtuous promoters of sacrifices.—*Vimata Vinodana Tìkà.*

I have thus glanced over the peculiarities which distinguish the oldest from the modern Sanskrit—the structure of

---

* Lit. 'beholding.'

† See also Edinburgh Review, No. 288 p. 376.

the latter being that which may be regarded as the most expressive and harmonious that has ever been attuned to human utterance."

An examination of Pali Grammars establishes beyond all doubt the affinity which it bears to the Sanskrit (i.) "from which it differs only in such modifications as are exhibited by those European dialects which are most immediately derived from the unknown idioms of antiquity."*

(ii.) In a review of the Revd. B. Clough's Pali Grammar (see Asiatic Journal for 1827, p. 663) the writer bears similar testimony to the identity of Sanskrit with the Pali. He says, "every essential part of it (the Pali) is found in the Sanskrit. The vocabularies of its nouns and of its verbal roots are nearly the same. The Grammar is also formed on the same model, but is much more simple."

(iii.) Professor Bopp also thinks that "the relation between these two idioms (the Sanskrit and Pali) is nearer than that which subsists between most of the distinct branches of the Indo-European system, and that it may be compared to the degree of affinity which the Latin bears to the Greek."†

(iv.) Fausboll in his Introduction to the *Dhammapada* (p 6.) states the relationship of the Pali or Màgadhì to the Sanskrit, thus: "Inter literas buddhisticas sacras hunc librum antiquiorum in numero habendum esse *ex sermone*, quo utitur, elucere videtur, qui multis in rebus a sanscritico et quidem antiquissimo prope abest, et multum ab eo dicendi genere differt, quo utuntur Sutta prosaica et scholia Buddhaghosæ. Huc pertinent: nom. præs. participii in—*am*, ut *ganayam*, *rodam*; a. pers. plur. præs. medii in—*are*, ut *socare*, *upapajjare*; dat. gerund., ut *netave pahàtave*; præterea formæ, quales sunt: *karoto* et *kubbato* (karontassa) *káhiti* (*karissati*) al., *arahatam* (*arahantànam*), *sabbhi* (*santehi*), *vaddha* (*vuddha*), *klesa* (*kilesa*), *cetya* (*cetiya*) etc.

* See Asiatic Journal, xvii. p. 763.

† Pritchard's Physical History of Mankind, iv. 22.

The weightiest and most conclusive authority on the subject, however, to which I wish to call attention, is contained in the following observations of Dr. Weber, and which I have only seen through the medium of the valuable translations in Dr. Muir's Sanskrit Texts, since these sheets were prepared for the press.

Speaking of the way in which he conceives the Prakrits* to have risen, Dr. Weber says :—

(v.) "I take this opportunity of declaring myself distinctly against a commonly received error. It has been concluded from the existence (in inscriptions) of Prakrit dialects in the centuries immediately preceding our era, that the Sanskrit language had died out before these dialects were formed; whereas we must, on the contrary, regard the development of both the Sanskrit and the Prakrit dialects from one common source, viz. the Indo-Arian speech, as entirely contemporaneous. . . . . For a fuller statement of this view I refer to my 'Vajasaneyi Sanhitæ specimen,' ii. 204-6; and, in proof of what I have urged there, I adduce here the fact that the principal laws of Prakrit speech, viz. assimilation, hiatus, and a fondness for cerebrals and aspirates are prominent in the Vedas, of which the following are examples: ku*t*a=k*r*ita, R. V. i. 46, 4.; kāta=karta, (above, p. 30); geha=g*r*iha, (above, p. 40); guggulu=gungulu, Kātyāy., 5, 4, 17; vivi*tt*yai =vivish*t*yai, Taitt. Arany. x. 58; krikalāsa, Vrih. Ar. Mā. i. 3. 22.=krikadāsu, Rik. i. 29. 7; purodāsa,=purolāsa (comp. dasru=lacryma); pa*d*bhih=padbhih; kshullaka= kshudraka; bhallāksha=bhadrāksha, Chhandogya, 6. 1. (gloss); vikirida=vikiridra (above p. 31); gabhasti=grabhasti, or garbhasti; nighantu=nigranthu; ghas=gras; bhanj=bhranj=bhuj=bhruj; bhas=bras. . . . . . Comparative philology exhibits similar phonetic *prakriti-*

* "I once conjectured" says Mr. Colebrook, "the Prakrit to have been formerly the colloquial dialect of the Sarasvata Brahmans [see his Essays Vol. ii p. 21]; but this conjecture has not been confirmed by further researches. I believe it to be the same language with the Pali of Ceylon."—Miscellaneous Essays, ii. p. 213.

zings within the circle of the Indo-germanic languages as compared the one with the other." The same writer says in his Vajas. Sanh. specimen ii. 203. ff.; [101] "I incline to the opinion of those who deny that the Sanskrit Bhāshā, properly so called, was ever the common spoken language of the whole Arian people, and assign it to the learned alone. Just as our modern high German, arising out of the ancient dialects of the Germans, reduced what was common to all to universal rules and laws, and by the power of analogy obliterated all recollection of varieties; and just as, on the other hand these dialects, while they gradually degenerated, often preserved at the same time fuller and more ancient forms; so also the Vedic dialects, became partly combined in one stream, in which their individual existence was lost, and so formed the regular Sanskrit Bhāshā, and partly flowed on individually in their own original (Prākrita) irregular force, and continued to be the idioms of different provinces, in the corruption of which they participated. The Sanskrit language and the Prakrit dialects had, therefore, a common and a simultaneous origin: the latter did not spring out of the former, but rather, being connected by a natural bond with the ancient language, have often a more antique fashion than the Sanskrit, which, being shaped and circumscribed by the rules of grammarians, has sacrificed the truth of analogy for the sake of regularity. The Prakrit tongues are nothing else than ancient Vedic dialects in a state of degeneracy; while the Sanskrit (or Epic) *bhāshā* is the sum of the Vedic dialects constructed by the labour and zeal of grammarians, and polished by the skill of learned men. In this way we obtain an explanation of two facts: 1st, That the very same exceptions which are conceded by grammarians to the Vedic language (*chhandas*) are often found in the Prakrit dialects, being in fact nothing but original forms; and 2nd, That in

---

101 Reprinted in Indische Studien. ii. pp. 110, 111.

the Vedic writings, forms and words occur which are more irregular than any *Sanskrit* word could ever be; for as yet no fixed rules of euphony, orthography, or formation existed, —rules which were eventually deducted in part from those very irregularities. All the irregular forms which prevail in the Prakrit tongues are to be found throughout the Vedas. In the latter, the faculty which creates language is seen exuberant in its early power, while in the former (the Prakrits) it is seen in the degeneracy of full blown license, luxuriating wantonness, and at last of senile weakness. Assimilation, the hiatus, and a fondness for cerebrals and aspirates, play an important part in the Vedas, not so much in those portions which are peculiar to the Yajur-veda (which, as forming a transition from the Vedic to the Epic period, or rather itself initiating the Epic period, has also a style of language of a more modern cast, and adapted to a grammatical rule), as in the older forms and words of the Rig-veda, many of which were difficult to understand in the age of the Aitareya and Satapatha Brāhmanas (*paroxavrittayah* : comp. Roth. p. li. Nighantavah.) There occur moreover in the Epic poems many words which, however corrupted, have been received into the Sanskrit sometimes with no change, sometimes with very little, from the Prakrit languages in use among the greater part of the people."

I have thus laid before the reader, the facts stated by eminent philologists,—men who enter quite as fully into a comparison of the Grammars, as of the system of words in the two languages,—to shew the difference between the *Pali* and the *Sanskrit*; and those statements, it would seem, go the length merely of establishing the theory with which we have set out, viz., that the Pali, like the Sanskrit, is the offspring of an unknown language; and, whether the cultivation of both commenced at one and the same time or not, that "the former stands in fraternal connection with the latter—not in the relation of descent from it."

Before however dismissing this part of the subject, it may not be out of place here to advert to a few circumstances which point out that the Màgadhì (Pali) had its origin in the Punjab, or Bactria.

Dr. Stevenson remarks that "it seems highly probable that the ruder dialect from which the present Sanskrit has been formed was the spoken tongue of the tribe, who, under Bharat, as they themselves relate, settled in upper India, and afterwards gave the name of their Sovereign to the whole country, which extends from Cape Comorin to the Himalaya mountain."* The Magadhas, whose language was the Pali, also trace their origin to Bharat. It is hence probable (for, in questions relating to languages we can only deal with *probabilities*†,) that both the Pali and Sanskrit branched off from the same parent stem,—the latter taking a lead in a comparatively civilized country, attaining its present high refinement, so as to tempt men to mix it with their non-Sanskrit tongues on the South of the Vindhya; whilst the former was banished from the land from whence it arose, to different Indian countries, where it assumed the various forms exhibited by the Jaina dialects and the Maharàstri‡ of the Grammarians, and to our own "utmost Indian Isle, Taprobane," where alone it has become a dead language.

Another circumstance is deserving of attention. Tradition, which is after all the best evidence on these matters, says that the Màgadhì was the language of Saurasena,§ on the banks of the Yamunà, close upon *Mathura*.¶ The

---

* Kalpa Sutra, pp. 132—3.

† "There are no data from which the original formation of any one language can be ascertained; and consequently all opinion on the subject must rest entirely on conjecture."—Asiatic Journal, xxi., p. 653.

‡ "There is so close an affinity between the primary dramatic dialect, and the Pali, as to leave scarcely any doubt of their being originally identical."—*Professor Lassen's Institutiones Prakriticæ*.

§ Prakrit Prakasa, Sec. xi. § 2.

¶ Lassen's Int. Prakrit, § 3.

language of Saurasena* is also called Pràkrit by the Brahmans; and they treat *Màgadhì* under the same name, and place it in the same class with *Panchàla*, or the language of Punjab,† by which we understand the Zend. It is also clear that the Sanskrit Brahmans had als come from Bactria,‡ and that several languages found in that locality, for instance the Persian, the Phelevi, and the Zend,§ are more nearly related to the Sanskrit than her Indo-European sisters. On this subject, the erudite editor of the Bengal Asiatic Society's Journal (see vii. p. x.) remarks: "The history of India had been traced back to the period before the invasion of Alexander, and had been verified at each step by coins and by inscriptions; but the language of *Bactria* and of Persia, at the period of that Conquest, was still insufficiently ascertained. The Bactrian alphabet was already more than half discovered through the comparison of letters upon coins with bilingual superscriptions. Several inscriptions, as obtained from the Topes excavated, or as forwarded by travellers from within the ancient limits of Bactria, were nearly deciphered, so that very little remained to perfect the discovery also [by Mr. Prinsep], and to establish, that the *ancient Pali* language, or something very closely resembling it, prevailed over all those countries."¶ It would hence seem that the Pali, which approaches closely to the Sanskrit even in some of its

---

* "These two (Sauraseni and Maharashtri) dialects stand the nearest to the Pali, though it (the Pali) is decidedly older th an they are."—*Lassen's Indian Antiquities.*

† See Note, ante p. lxxix.

‡ "The oldest seats of the Indians, of which we find any mention made, are to be placed in the Punjab"—*Spiegel's Avesta*, i. p. 5. "The earliest seat of the Hindus within the confines of Hindustan was undoub tedly the Eastern Confines of Punjab"—Professor H. H. Wilson.

§ See Professor Spiegel's Discourse referred to in the last note.

¶ "We learn that Pali not only pervaded India, but Bactria and Persia; and tha this is no wild theory or hazardous speculation is attested by the very high authority oi the Pali Scholar, Professor Lassen, of Bonn, * * * who says, "the legends upon the Bactrian Coins are in Pali or Pracrit."—*Col. Sykes in the Journal of the Royal Asiatic Society*, vi. p. 425.

oldest forms, had originally started from the same country in which the cradle of the Sanskrit Brahmans is placed, "in or near Bactria."

VII. That the Pali was, at least, in the time of Gotama Buddha, 628-543. B. C., a highly cultivated language of Magadha and several adjacent countries, does not admit of reasonable doubt. We find from numerous works extant in Ceylon, that in grammatical structure and precision at least, it is but very little inferior to the Sanskrit. A language too, which is capable of enunciating discourses so varied and abstruse as the Pitakattàya and the voluminous Commentaries thereon, cannot but be deemed copious. It is rich in expression; and its force and harmony are but one degree removed from the idiom that has been *Sanskritized.*

Professor Wilson in his Introduction to Vikrama and Urvasi, thus speaks of the Pràkrit, regarding it as an exhibition of the Màgadhì. "The richness of the Prakrit in this play, both in structure and in its metrical code, is very remarkable. A very great portion, especially of the fourth act, is in this language, and in that act a considerable variety of metre is introduced. It is clear therefore that this form of Sanskrit must have been highly cultivated long before the play was written."

If such is the case as respects the Pràkrit of a period nearly three centuries after the Buddhist era, a higher refinement ought certainly to be accorded to the Pàli, the language of the time of Gotama.* The presumption is therefore irresistible, that it had been highly cultivated very long before the age of Gotama.

I have already adverted to the dynasty of the Màgadha kings, which commenced from the war of the "Maha Baharata," an event involved in the Mythological obscurity of the past; and it is also therefore to be presumed, that their

* The Rev. F. Mason of Burmah says:—" I do not think that the Pali is quite understood yet. * * Pali is much more copious than the *Savans* are aware though not to be compared with the Sanskrit."—*Amer. Or. Journal*, ii. p. 336.

language is of as great an antiquity as their kingdom is certainly older than the written Vedas.

"But in very truth," says Hodgson, "the extant records of Buddhism, whether Sanskrit or Pràkrit, exhibit both languages in a high state of refinement."* If this be true of the Pràkrit, it is undoubtedly so of the Pali,—"a rich, refined, and poetical language of the land in which Buddhism as promulgated by Sàkya or Gotama had its origin, at which period it was a highly refined and classical language."†

When therefore we consider the high state of refinement, to which the Pali had in very early times attained as a language,—its copiousness, elegance, and harmony, combined with its high antiquity, and its comparative simplicity, both verbally and grammatically,—its relationship to the oldest language of the Brahmans, from which their present dialect has been *Sanskritized*,—its claims to be considered the Vyavahàrika vàk of the Brahmans to which the Rig Veda refers,—its concurrence with some of the Indo-European languages, in some forms which differ from the Sanskrit,—its identification with the only original Pràkrita dialect, which was "similar to the Sanskrit",—the absence of any statement in old Brahman writers to the effect that that Pràkrita dialect was a derivative of the Sanskrit,—the great improbability of a derivative being denominated the [prakriti] Pràkrita,—the palpable inaccuracy of the definition by which in modern times, it is called "the derived, the vulgar, or the ungrammatical"—the absence in it of many a peculiarity which distinguishes derivative tongues,—and the probability that it had issued from the same ancient seat (Bactria or Punjab) from whence the Sanskrit itself had taken an easterly direction,—I believe it may be concluded that the Pali and the Sanskrit are, at least, two dialects of high antiquity, contemporaneously derived from a source, of which few, if any, traces can be discovered at the present day.

---

* Bengal Asiatic Journal, vi., p. 686.

† Turnour's Mahavansa.

To the above remarks on the relationship of the Pali to the Sanskrit, I had originally intended to add a brief sketch of the progress of Buddhism in the East, along with the Pali language, with which the former is inseparably connected. But the great difficulties which I have experienced in printing, have compelled me to reserve the subject for a future publication. For the same reason I have given the Text in Sinhalese characters. If, however, I should be permitted to complete the translation of the remaining seven books of Kachchàyana's Grammar, with which I am now engaged, I hope to be able to forward to my publishers in England, a complete edition, including the matter which has been reserved, together with the Text, in Roman characters.

Of the work now submitted, with great diffidence, to the European public, I have little to say, beyond expressing a hope that they will not severely judge of this my first attempt at translating from the Pali into English, and transferring, what may be termed "algebraic aphorisms" into intelligible phraseology. I am sensible that there are many errors, of omission and commission, in the translation; but they are such as I could not avoid. For, though living at "the very fountains of Pali literature," I have, nevertheless, been unable to consult a single friend, either as to the choice of my language or the correctness of my renderings into English. I have indeed had much assistance from native Pandits, of whom I shall have occasion to speak hereafter, but none of them possess a sufficient knowledge of the English language to be able to rectify an incorrect translation. The numerous Tìkàs and Comments, again, to which I have had access, being entirely in Sinhalese, could not afford any greater help than I have derived from the Pandits. The only European Pali Scholar in this Island, I mean the Rev. D. J. GOGERLY of the Wesleyan Mission, who had "cheerfully" promised to assist me in my labours, and to revise my translation, was, unfortunately, removed by death, at the very period when I desired to avail myself of his invaluable advice.

As to the deficiencies of my language, I believe it is unnecessary to offer any apologies,—for, I have no doubt, the European reader will make great allowances for the shortcomings of one who cannot claim the English as his native tongue.

The errors of the press are far too numerous to be passed over in silence. I believe few persons in this Island are ignorant of the difficulties which an Author has to contend with in publishing his works on Oriental literature in Ceylon.—Witness the Mahavansa, whose learned translator was obliged to append no less than thirty-five closely printed quarto pages of corrections. Referring to my own work, I may be permitted to remark, that the Compositors in Ceylon entertain an aversion to handling a MS. containing Pali or Sanskrit passages written in Roman characters, and especially with diacritical marks. Indeed it was with great difficulty that the men in one of our printing establishments could be induced to undertake this work, or, when undertaken, to continue it. From the universal inattention in Ceylon to the orthography of Oriental words and names, they sometimes took it upon themselves to set aside my spelling, and to adopt their own: and this, I need hardly remark, has entailed much labour in the correction of the press. It will scarcely be credited, that for the correction of these errors, I have often had to revise six or seven proofs of one and the same sheet. Even with such labour, and with all the vigilance I could bestow, it has been impossible to avoid a great many errors, which have rendered it necessary to add rather a copious list of Errata. My absence too, from Colombo, and from my library, during the whole of the period during which this work was going through the press, has added not a little to my difficulties.

These remarks, however, apply to the Introduction. The Grammar, which is comparatively free from errors, has been printed in the Wesleyan Mission Press, whilst its Translation, and the Appendix, have received the invaluable supervision of Mr. SKEEN, the Government Printer, at whose establishment they were printed.

In the Introduction and the Translation, I have adopted the following scheme of orthography, which will be found to approach closely the system adopted by Sir WILLIAM JONES.

VOWELS.

අ	ආ	ඉ	ඊ	උ	ඌ	එ	ඔ
a	à;	i	ì;	u	ù;	e	o

CONSONANTS.

Gutturals—	ක	k	ඛ	kh;	ග	g	ඝ	gh;	ඞ	ṅ
Palatals —	ච	ch	ඡ	chh;	ජ	j	ඣ	jh;	ඤ	ñ
Linguals —	ට	ṭ	ඨ	ṭh;	ඩ	ḍ	ඪ	ḍh;	ණ	ṇ
Dentals —	ත	t	ථ	th;	ද	d	ධ	dh;	න	n
Labials —	ප	p	ඵ	ph;	බ	b	භ	bh;	ම	m

ය y, ර r, ල l, ව v, ස s, හ h, ළ ḷ, ං ṃ

Owing however to the absence of some of the accented letters, such as ṭ, ḍ, ḷ, &c., I have been obliged in printing this work to deviate from the above system; and to adopt *italics* in their stead. This substitution again, has not been uniformly attended to by the printer; whilst I myself have failed to pay any attention to the difference of ṅ ṇ n and ṃ, all which will be found expressed by an unaccented ṇ.

It only remains for me to acknowledge the assistance which I have received in the course of this publication; and here I cannot adequately express the sense of my obligations to my Pandit, BATUVANTUDAVE, who has assisted me during a considerable period of time which has been devoted to the translation of the following sheets, and the extracts in the Introduction. I have, with his permission, given expression to a few opinions of my own, upon which, from religious differences and the dissimilarity of our education, and other causes, agreement was found impossible. But, whenever we differed, it is but right to state that I did not hastily reject his views without first devoting my best and most serious attention to them.

In the collection of materials for this rather lengthy introduction, the reader will perceive from the Notes and Annotations, the extent of assistance which I have received from the published works of Colebrooke, Wilson, Max Muller, Ballentyn, Muir, Burnouf, Lassen, Weber, Spiegel, Goldstucker, Fausboll, &c.; and I must not omit also to state that I have been greatly assisted by several learned Buddhist priests, especially SUMANGALA of Hickkaduwa, to whom my best thanks are due.

It is impossible to pass over, without due acknowledgement the useful hints and information I have obtained from Mr. J. R. BLAKE, in the course of frequent conferences on the subject of Oriental literature, and also the still more valuable translations which he has made for me from several German and French writers.

I cannot conclude more appropriately than with the words of one* in the same field of labour in which I am engaged, and who has less reason than myself to say, "et nunc haec folia non sine justo timore in lucem emitto, quæ, si non omnino displicuerint viris doctis, jam operae pretium factum esse censebo."

JAMES ALWIS.

* Professor Spiegel's Kammavacha.

KACHCHÀYANA'S GRAMMAR.

LIB. VI.—On Verbs.*

Learned sages, by the ship of comprehensive wisdom, cross the ocean of verbs (filled with) the water of radicals; (abounding with) the fishes of Vikarana,† Augment, and Tenses; (having) the current of Elision, and Anubandhas;‡ (foaming with) the billows of Ajjatanì;§ (and bounded by) the shore of Investigation.||

Hear ye my comprehensive words on Verbs, which, diffused with beautiful adornments, I, after saluting the perfect Buddha of infinite knowledge, do declare so that they may be easily mastered.

---

* In the Grammatical systems of the East, the Verb constitutes the most important as well as the most difficult section. I have, therefore, selected this for translation; and have occasionally added a few notes shewing the relation in which the Pali Verb stands to the Sanskrit, and the Pràkrit.

† The vowel or syllable intervening between the base and the Affix in the several conjugational classes in the Pàli.

‡ Certain supernumerary letters which denote the class or conjugation in which the verb is inflected, or intimate the peculiarities to which each single verb is subject in its inflections.

§ Ajjatanì—See note at the end of this Chapter. As the present tense is more frequently used than the past; so, of the past tenses, the *present-perfect* (Ajjatanì) is of more frequent occurrence in the Pali. It is thence denominated, 'a wave in the ocean of verbs.'—See Clough's Bàlavatàra, p. 106.

|| Lit. Attha vibhàga—'investigations of sense.'

CAP: I.

---

1. Now,* of the terminations the first six are Parassapada.

a. Now of all the terminations, every first six terminations are named Parassapada.†

Ex. ti, anti; si, tha; mi, ma.

Q. Wherefore the term Parassapada? 'The Parassapada [mark]‡ the Agent.'§

2. The last are Attanopada.

a. Of all the terminations every last six terminations are named Attanopada;‖ that is to say:—

Ex. te, ante; se, vhe; e, mhe.

Q. Wherefore the term Attanopada? 1 'The Attanopada (mark) the action and the object.' ¶

---

* The stanza given in the text, as a note to 'atha,' is supposed by some to be the interpolation of a Commentator to explain the force of that particle with which this chapter opens. It would also seem that Kâtyâyana has also given a similar explanation—'*Om* and *atha* are both used in the beginning of Chapter, &c.,' Indische Studien, iv. p. 103. In the words of the Pàli text: '*atha* is used in the beginning of a Chapter, and as a word of benediction, completion, emphasis, and as an inceptive particle.'

† 'Words for another.'

‡ The words within brackets have been supplied from Commentaries and other sources.

§ *S*eshàt kartari parasmaipadan—Pànini, lib. 1, Cap. iii. § 78.

‖ 'Words for one's self.'

¶ The two systems of inflection—the first conveying a transitive sense, and the action passing parassa 'to another;' and the second bearing a reflexive sense, and the action reverting attano 'to one's self'—may be regarded as Voices. Although the Pàli, like the Pràkrit, does not preserve this distinction to the same extent that the modern Sanskrit does; yet the former agrees in this respect with the *Vedic*-Sanskrit, wherein one Voice is used for another: as, brahmachàrina michchhate (for *ti.*) 'He wishes for the religious student.' In the Pàli the above change is also admissible, and the foregoing sentence equally serves as an example. Again in the àtmanepada the initial *ta* of a termination is rejected in the Vedas, as dakshinatah *s*aye (*s*ete) 'He sleeps on his right side.' So likewise in the Pàli, wherein the last sentence may be thus rendered—dakkhinato saye (sayeyya or sayetha.) See Bàlavatàra, p. 104.

3. Each two, the Pa*th*ama,* Majjhima, and Uttama.†

a. Of all the above terminations, both in the Parassapada and Attanopada, each (set of) two is named the third, second, and first person (respectively.) That is to say;

Ex. ti, anti—Third persons.
si, tha—Second persons.
mi, ma—First persons.

In the Attanopada likewise, [thus:]
te, ante—Third persons.
se, vhe—Second persons.
e, mhe—First persons.

So likewise every where.

Q. Wherefore the terms 'third, second, and first persons'?

(To shew that the affixes of) the third person should be used, when a nàma,‡ [whether] expressed (or not), agrees with the verb; (the affixes of) the second persons, when tumha; and (those of) the first, when amha.§

4. In speaking of all by one, the first person.

a. In speaking of all the three persons, viz., the first, second, and third by one (verb) the highest (or first) person should be adopted.‖

---

* Eastern writers begin with the third person, and therefore call it the pa*th*ama or 'first;' they treat of the second next, and name it the majjhima or 'the middle,' and the first they designate uttama 'the highest or chief.' In the above translation, to avoid confusion, I have used the terms ordinarily employed in European systems, viz., the third, second, and first persons.

† In Pànini, this same rule is merely adapted to the Sanskrit which has a dual number; thus, Tinas trìni trìni prathama maddhyamottamàh.—Lib. 1. c. 4. § 101.

‡ Here *nàma* is used as a generic term for a noun of the third person, as opposed to *tumha* (2 p.) and *amha* (1 p.)

§ Vide infra. note to rule 5.

‖ This may be thus explained:—When one verb governs two or more nominatives of different persons, the former takes the [plural] termination proper to the first person; but if there be no nominative of the first person, the verb should be made to agree with the second:—as,

1. So cha tvan ahan pachàma = 'we cook.'
2. So cha ahan pachàma = 'we cook.'
3. Tvan cha ahan pachàma = 'we cook.'
4. So cha tvan pachatha = 'ye cook.'

This is also the case in the Muràthi. See Dr. Stevenson's Grammar, p. 140.

Ex. Socha pa*t*hati
'He reads—and'
techa pa*t*hanti
'They read—and'
tvancha pa*t*hasi
'Thou readest—and'
tumhecha pa*t*hatha
'Ye read—and'
ahancha pa*t*hàmi
'also I read.'
} = Mayan pa*t*hàma, 'We read.'

So pachati
te pachanti
tvan pachasi
tumhe pachatha
ahan pachàmi.
} = Mayan pachàma, 'We cook.'

In like manner the highest person should be used in the other tenses.

5. The third person when a nàma, which agrees [with the verb,] is expressed, &.*

a. (A termination proper to) third person is used when the noun (nominative), which exercises government,† is either expressed or not.

Ex. So gachchhati, 'He goes.'
Te gachchhanti, 'They go.'
} [When expressed.]

Gachchhati, '(he) goes.'
Gachchhanti, '(they) go.'
} When not expressed.

Q. Wherefore 'the Nominative'?

[To distinguish it from the agent or the Instrumental in a

---

* Pànini lays down the same rule; but by changing the order of persons from the third to the first, thus;—Yushmadyupapade samànàdhikarane sthàninyapi madhyamah—Lib. 1. Cap. 4 § 105. Asmadyuttamah—ib. § 107. Seshe prathamah § 108.

† Tulyàdhikarana—lit. 'that which has common property, or agrees with one another.' I have rendered this 'the Nominative.'

sentence like] Tena haññase tvan Devadattena. 'By that Devadatta thou art killed.'

6. The second when tumha.

a. (A termination proper to) the second person, is used when the nominative tumha is either expressed or not.

Ex. Tvan yàsi, 'Thou goest.'
Tumhe yàtha, 'Ye go.' } [When expressed.]

Yàsi, '(thou) goest.'
Yàtha, '(ye) go.' } When not expressed.

Q. Wherefore 'the Nominative'?

(To mark the difference between it and the Instrumental as) Tayà pachchate odano. 'By thee is rice cooked.'

7. The first, when amha.

a. (A termination proper to) the first person is used when the nominative amha is either expressed or not.

Ex. Ahan yajàmi, 'I worship.'
Mayan yajàma, 'We worship.' } [When expressed.]

Yajàmi, '(I) worship.'
Yajàma, '(we) worship.' } When not expressed.

Q. Wherefore 'the Nominative'?

[To mark the difference between it and the Instrumental, as in a sentence like] Mayà ijjate Buddho, 'By me Buddha is worshipped.'

8. As to time.

a. Know that this 'time' exercises an authority (adhikàra.)*

9. Vattamànà (are) the present.

a. The Vattamànà affixes are in the present Tense.

Ex. Pá*t*aliputtan gachchhati, 'He goes to Pá*t*aliputta.'
Sàvatthin pavisati, 'He enters Sàvatthi.'
Viharati Jetavane, 'He dwells in Jetavana.'

* This Sutta is supposed to exercise an authority over the succeeding Suttàni.

10. In commanding and blessing, in undefined* time, the Panchamì.†

a. In the sense of both commanding and blessing‡ without any distinction of time, the terminations are Panchamì.

Ex. Karotu kusalan, 'Let him do meritorious acts.'

Sukhan te hotu, 'Be happiness to thee.'

11. The Sattamì, in the sense of assent and inclination.§

a. In the sense of assent and inclination the terminations are Sattamì, where the time is undefined.‖

Ex. Tvan gachchheyyàsi, 'Thou mayest go.'

Kimahan kareyyámi, 'What may I do.'

12. In the unperceived past, Parokkhà.

a. The terminations (which signify) time past,¶ unperceived (by the narrator) are Parokkhá.

Ex. Supine kila** eva máha, '[He,] it is reported, said so in a dream.'

---

* "Since these moods do not comprehend other tenses under them, but are susceptible of all times,—present, past, and future, it can lead to no embarrassment to consider them as tenses."—William's S. Gr. p. 56.

† This answers to the Imperative and the Benedictive Moods, of the Sanskrit Grammarians.

‡ There is great misapprehension as to the origin of the name Panchamì for the Imperative and Benedictive Moods. The Bàlavatàra says, [Panchamì (Sattamì) tyàyan pubbà chariya saññà] that it is a name given by former teachers. But the Mahà Sadda Nìti, in reference to this passage, says, that the Panchamì is so named after some of the Sanskrit Grammarians, such as the Kàtantra, &c., which place the Imperative as a fifth tense of the verb. In Pànini likewise Let, the Scriptural Imperative, which Professor Bopp says, is confined to the Vedas, and is wanting in the Classic Sanskrit [Comp. Gr. II. p. 951] takes a fifth place in the list of tenses; and, if the appellation of Panchamì has been thence coined, it is reasonable to believe that Sattamì has had a similar origin. But such is not the case, for Lin., the Potential, which is identical with the Pàli Sattamì, occupies an eighth, and not a seventh, place in Pànini's List.

§ This is the Potential Mood of the Sanskrit Grammarians.

‖ See Bàlavatàra, p. 104.

¶ Apachchakkha is interpreted to mean that which the senses cannot discern, 'the unperceived,' or 'the indefinite.'

** This aptate answers to the Singhalese la or lu; see my Sidatsangarà, p. 171, § 12. Also my Introduction to Singhalese Grammar, §§ 316-17.

Evan kila poràná àhu, 'Thus, it is reported, the ancients said.'

13. In the perceived from yesterday, Hìyattanì.

a. In [the sense of] time past from yesterday, whether (the same be) perceived or unperceived, the terminations are Hìyăttanì.

Ex. So maggan agamá, 'He went to the road.'
Te agamù maggan, 'They went to the road.'

14. In approximate, Ajjatanì.

a. In [the sense of] time approximately (or recently) past from this day, whether (the same be) perceived or unperceived, the terminations are Ajjatanì. *

Ex. So maggan agamì, 'He has gone to the road.'
Te maggan agamun, 'They have gone to the road.'

15. When mà combined, all times, &.

a. Hìyattanì and Ajjatanì terminations, when combined with mà, are in all the tenses.

Ex. Màgamà or Màgamì, 'Let him not go.'
Màvachà or Màvachì, 'Let him not say.'

Note.—By the combination of an 'and' [to the Sutta] the Panchamì terminations [are also understood.]

Ex. Mà gachchhàhi, 'Go thou not.'

16. In the future, Bhavissantì.

a. In the future tense the terminations are Bhavissantì.

Ex. So gachchhissati, 'He will go.'
Sá karissati, 'She will do.'
Te gachchhissanti, 'They will go.'
Te karissanti, 'They will do.'

17. Kàlàtipatti in an action past going beyond.

* See note at the end of Chapter First.

a. Kálátipatti* only in an action past going beyond.

Ex. So che tan yànan alabhissà agachchhissà, 'If he had that vehicle, he would have gone.'

Te che tan yànan alabhissansu agachchhissansu, 'If they had that vehicle they would have gone.

18. The Vattamànà ti, anti; si, tha; mi, ma;—te, ante; se, vhe; e, mhe.

a. This appellation Vattamànà is for these twelve terminations;—ti, anti; si, tha; mi, ma;—te, ante; se, vhe; e, mhe.

Q. What does Vattamànà imply? 'Vattamànà [express] the present time.'

19. The Panchamì tu, antu; hi, tha: mi, ma;—tan, antan; ssu, vho; e, àmase.

a. This appellation Panchamì is for these twelve terminations—tu, antu; hi, tha; mi, ma;—tan, antan; ssu, vho; e, àmase.

Q. What does Panchamì signify? 'Panchamì [expresses] command and blessing in undefined time.' †

20. The Sattamì eyya, eyyun; eyyàsi, eyyàtha; eyyàmi, eyyàma;—etha, eran; etho, eyyavho,; eyyan, eyyàmhe.

a. The appellation Sattamì is for these twelve terminations;—eyya, eyyun; eyyàsi, eyyàtha; eyyàmi, eyyàma;—etha, eran; etho, eyyavho; eyyan, eyyàmhe.

Q. What does Sattamì signify? 'The Sattamì conveys the sense of assent and inclination.'

---

* Kiriyàtipanne = kriyàtipattau. Pànini lib. 3. Cap. 3. § 139. In the Sinhalese Commentary to the Bàlavatàra, this is defined to be 'the uncertain or the doubtful assertion of an action.' It may be translated the 'Conditional.'—See Laghukaumudi, p. 161-2.

† i. e., without any distinction of time.

21. The Parokkhà; a, u; e, ttha; a, mha; —ttha, re; ttho, vho; i, mhe.

a. The appellation Parokkhà is for these twelve terminations;—a, u; e, ttha; a, mha;—ttha, re; ttho, vho; i, mhe.

Q. What does Parokkhà signify? 'Parokkhà (implies) the unperceived past.'

22. The Hìyattanì; à, ù; o, ttha; a, mhà; —ttha, tthun; se, vhan; in, mhase.

a. The appellation Hìyattanì is for these twelve terminations—à, ù; o, ttha; a, mhà;—ttha, tthun; se, vhan; in, mhase.

Q. What does Hìyattanì signify? 'Hìyattanì (expresses) the perceived [past] from yesterday.'

23. The Ajjatanì; ì, un; o, ttha; in, mhà; — à, ù; se, vhan; a, mhe.

a. The appellation Ajjatanì is for these twelve terminations;—ì, un; o, ttha; in, mhà; à, ù; se, vhan; a, mhe.

Q. What does Ajjatanì imply? 'Ajjatanì (expresses) approximate* [time.]'

24. The Bhavissanti; ssati, ssanti; ssasi, ssatha; ssàmi, ssàma;—ssate, ssante; ssase, ssavhe; ssan, ssàmhe.

a. The appellation Bhavissanti is for these twelve terminations; ssati, ssanti; ssasi, ssatha; ssàmi, ssàma;—ssate, ssante; ssase, ssavhe; ssan, ssàmhe.

Q. What does Bhavissanti signify? 'Bhavissanti (expresses) the future.'

25. The Kàlàtipatti; ssà, ssansu; sse, ssatha; ssan, ssamhà; ssatha, ssinsu; ssase, ssavhe; ssan, ssàmhase.

---

* i.e.—The nearest past.

a. The appellation Kàlàtipatti is for these twelve terminations; ssà, ssansu; sse, ssatha; ssan, ssamhà; ssatha, ssinsu; ssase, ssavhe; ssan, ssàmhase.

Q. What does Kàlàtipatti imply? 'Kàlàtipatti (expresses) an action past, going beyond.'

26. Hìyattanì, Sattamì, Panchamì, (and) Vattamànà, (are) Sabbadhàtuka.*

a. Sabbadhàtuka is the appellation for the four, Hìyattanì, &c.

Ex. A'gamà, 'He went.'
Gachchheyya, 'He may go.'
Gachchhatu, 'Let him go.'
Gachchhati, 'He goes.'

Q. Wherefore Sabbadhàtuka? '[To distinguish them from] the Asabbadhàtuka [which take] i as an augment.'†

End of the First Chapter on Verbs.

NOTES.

Whilst in the Pràkrit "the only tenses of the active voice which remain, seem to be the present, the second future, and the Imperative" [Cowell's Pràkrit Prakàsa, p. xxix]; the Pàli has nearly all the tenses known to the Sanskrit, viz: 1 Vattamànà, 2 Panchamì, 3 Sattamì, 4 Parokkhà, 5 Hiyattanì, 6 Ajjatanì, 7 Bhavissantì, and 8 Kàlàtipatti. The first answers to the Present Tense; the fourth, fifth, and sixth to the Past; and the seventh to the Future. The second is the Imperative; the third is the Potential; and the eighth, the Conditional. Thus, the Pàli differs from the Sanskrit merely in the absence of those elaborations, by which the Imperative is distinguished into "commanding" and "blessing," and by

---

* Pànini, III. 4. 113. Sàrvadhàtuka 'applicable to all the radicals.'

† For the coincidences between the Rules, &c., of this chapter, and those in Pànini; compare Pànini, III. 1. 1—30.

which also the Future is divided into the "definite" and the "indefinite." There is, however, some difficulty in reconciling the Sanskrit Præterites with the three past Tenses in the Pàli. This arises from the promiscuous use of two, at least, of the three præterites, both in the Pàli and Sanskrit; and also from the confused definitions of Grammarians.

One of these Tenses, Lit. is defined [see Pànini, III. 2. 115.] to be, 'what took place before the current day, and unperceived (by the narrator.)' [Dr. Ballentyn's Laghu Kaumudì, § 417.] The introduction of the words, "before the current day," which we do not find in the Pàli definition, adds not a little to this confusion. The Parokkhà (paroksha, Sans.) as 'the past of any period,' and from its agreement in purport, as well as in its construction by re-duplication, may, however, be identified with the Second Præterite of Dr. Wilkins, and Professor Wilson.

Another Præterite, Lang, which is defined to be "the past before the commencement of the current day" [Pànini III. 2. 111; Laghu Kaumudì, § 450] agrees with the First Præterite of Dr. Wilkins and Professor Wilson; and is identical with the Pàli Hìyattanì [hyastana, Sans.]; although, I must observe, it does not seem to convey, as remarked by several European Grammarians, and amongst them by Pr. Wilson, "action past, but not perfected." See Wilson's Grammar, p. 112.

The remaining Præterite, Lung, which is the Third in European Sanskrit Grammars, can only refer to the Pàli Ajjatanì; but its definition in Sanskrit Grammars as 'what is past (indefinitely)' [Pànini III. 2, 110; Laghu Kaumudì, § 462] does not accord with the Pàli definition, nor with the adyatana bhùta kàla, given by Dr. Wilkins, as 'the past time of to-day'—p. 651.

According to Pàli Grammarians, the three past tenses in the Pàli, have a clear syntactical distinction, which does not appear to exist in the modern Sanskrit. [See Bopp's Comp. Grammar, II. p. 729.] Although in the former, all the three tenses express the past; yet they are for three different periods of the past, that is to say;—The Ajjatanì is 'time past within the current day.' The Hìyattanì is for 'time recently past before yesterday.' And the Parokkhà, or the re-duplicate præterite, is 'for time past unperceived (by the narrator)' i.e. an action past at a time, of which the senses have no perception; or, in other words, action indefinitely past. See note ¶ at p. 6, supra.

As the Pàli, like the Sanskrit, loves the use of the present tense; so likewise in using the past the former prefers, what is called 'a wave in the ocean of verbs,' the Ajjatanì, which has a *present*-perfect sense. The Bàlavatàra lays down the farthest limit of this past time as follows:—

Pachchhimo' tìta rattiyà yàmo addham'amussa và
Kàlo siyà tvajjatano Veyyàkarana dassinan.

'The Ajjatanì tense of the Grammarians is [commences from] the last Yàma [from 3 A.M.] of the previous night, or, its half [from 5 A.M.]'

Thus the Pàli Ajjatanì (adyatana, Sans.) which is regarded as 'the præterite of to-day' or 'action which *has taken* place during the current day,' appears to me to be the "present-perfect," (amavi), in the Latin; and I have accordingly rendered it into English in my translation: and, in view of the other distinctions to which I have adverted, I believe, I am justified in regarding the Hìyattani as "the definite past;" and the Parokkhà as "the indefinite past."

CAP: II.

1. At the end of verbal, and nominal roots, Affixes.

a. The affixes are at the end of these, (viz.) verbal and nominal roots.

Ex. Karo-ti, 'He does.'

Gachchhati, 'He goes.'

[But] kàreti, 'He causes to do' [where] one does, and another bids the doer, *do;* or. [where one] causes the doer.

Pabbatàyati—[as where] 'the Sangha conducts himself-as-a mountain.'

Samuddayati—[as where one] 'acts-himself-like-the-ocean.'

Likewise Chichchi*tà*-yati [as where] 'the Sea (roars) acts-like* chichchi*ta*.'

Vàsi*tt*ho--[to express] 'the-son of Vasi*tt*ha.'† In like manner other affixes should be employed.

2. Kh, chh, s, optionally after tija, gupa, kita, màna.‡

a. The radicals tija, gupa, kita, màna, optionally take after them the affixes kh chh and s.

Ex. Titikkhati, 'He endures.'

Jiguchchhati, 'He reproaches.'

Tikichchhati, 'He cures.'

Vìmansati, 'He investigates.'

Q. Wherefore 'optionally'? [Because the roots sometimes take other affixes, e. g.] Tejati, 'He sharpens'; Gopati, 'He protects'; Màneti, 'He offers.'§

---

* 'Making the noise indicated by chichchi*ta*.'

† Gotama mentions Vasi*tt*ha as a Rishi who composed the Vedas.

‡ Tija, 'to endure;' gupa, 'to conceal;' kita, 'to cure;' and màna, 'to investigate.'

§ To words with these exceptional inflections, the writer of Rùpasiddhi assigns different meanings. In the above translation I have adopted his explanations.

3. Also after bhuja ghasa hara supa, &c., in desideratives with tun.*

a. The radicals bhuja, ghasa, hara, supa, &c., optionally take after them, in desideratives with tun, the affixes kh, chh, and s.

Ex. Bhottu michchhati = Bubhukkhati.

[In the sense of] 'He-wishes-to-eat,' = Bubhukkhati.

Ghasitu michchhati = Jighachchhati.

[In the sense of] 'He-wishes-to-eat,' = Jighachchhati.

Haritu michchhati = Jiginsati.†

[In the sense of] 'He-wishes-to-take,' = Jiginsati.

Supitu michchhati = Sussùsati.

[In the sense of] 'He-wishes-to-sleep,' = Sussùsati.

Pàtu michchhati = pivàsati.

[In the sense of] 'He-wishes-to-drink,' = pivàsati.

1st *Q.* Wherefore 'optionally'? [Because the same words are used in an infinitive form, thus] Bhottu'michchhati, 'He wishes to eat.'

2nd *Q.* Wherefore 'in desideratives with tun?' [To shew that primitives do not take those affixes, as in] Bhunjati, 'He eats.'

4. After a nominal root denoting comparison to the nominative, àya in the sense of treatment.

a. The affix àya (in the sense of) treatment comes after the nominal root, when it denotes a comparison to the Nominative.‡

Ex. Pabbatàyati, 'He conducts himself as a mountain.'

Chichchi*t*àyati, 'It roars like chichchi*t*a.'

Note.—In like manner should others be employed.

5. And ìya denoting comparison.§

---

* The sign of the Infinitive.

† This word is written in all the Pali works Jiginsati, also see Clough's Bàlàvatàra, p. 111. *Qy.*—Shonld it not be Ji*h*insati?

‡ Pànini, III. 1, 11.

§ Pànini, III. 1, 10.

n. And the affix íya (in the sense of) treatment, comes after a nominal root which denotes a comparison.*

Ex. Achhattan chhattamiva àcharati=chattìyati, 'He treats that which is not an umbrella, like an umbrella =chattìyati.'

Aputtan putta miva àcharati=puttìyati, 'He treats as a son, him who is not a son = puttìyati.'

1st *Q.* Wherefore 'that which denotes comparison?' (To mark the difference between exact likeness and mere conformation to a model, in which latter case the rule does not apply; as) Dhammamàcharati, 'He practises dhamma.' †

2nd *Q.* Wherefore 'treatment'? (To shew that although the verb may denote an identical likeness; yet if it does not convey a continuance of the action, or usage, the rule does not apply; as) Chatta miva rakkhati, 'He preserves (it) like an umbrella.'

In like manner should other (affixes) be used.

6. After a nominal root implying self-desire.

a. After a nominal root, implying desire for one's self, the affix becomes ìya.‡

Ex. Attano pattamichchhatì·ti = pattìyati.

'He desires a vessel for himself' = pattìyati.

So likewise; vatthìyati, 'He desires raiment for himself.'

Parikkhàrìyati, 'He desires Parikkhàra§ for himself.'

Chìvarìyati, 'He desires yellow robes for himself.'

Dhanìyati, 'He desires wealth for himself.'

Pañyati, 'He desires clothes for himself.'

Q. Wherefore the words 'desire for one's self?' [To shew that where the desire expressed is not for one's self, the rule

---

* In the Bàlàvatàra this is explained to be a nominal root which denotes camparison to [dutìyantan nàman] 'a noun in the second case' or the Accusative.

† i.e.—'He conforms himself to the duties of religion.'

‡ See Laghu Kaumudì, p. 297.

§ Parikkhàra—theologically, the necessaries of life for an ascetic.

does not apply; as] Aññassa pattamichchhati, 'He desires a vessel for another.'

So likewise should others be used.

7. In the sense of the Causal Agent the Causal (affixes) ne naya nàpe nàpayà after the radical.

a. In the sense of the Causal Agent* all roots take the affixes, ne, naya, nàpe, nàpayà; and they receive the appellation of Kàrita 'the Causal.'

Ex. Kàreti, kàrayati, kàràpeti, [or] kàràpayati, 'He causes to do'—[where] one does, and another bids the doer 'do'; or [where one] causes the doer.

Kàrenti, kàrayanti, kàràpenti, (or) kàràpayanti, 'They cause to do'—[where] some do, and others bid the doers 'do, do.'

Pàcheti, pàchayati, pàchàpeti (or) pàchàpayati, 'He causes to cook'—[where] one cooks, and another bids him 'cook'; or [where one] causes the cook.

Pàchenti, pàchayanti, pàchàpenti (or) pàchàpayanti, 'They cause to cook'—[where] some cook, and others bid those who cook, thus 'cook-cook.'

So likewise,

Haneti, hanayati, hanàpeti, (or) hanàpayati, 'He causes to kill.'

Bhaneti, bhanayati, bhanàpeti, (or) bhanàpayati, 'He causes to utter.'

In like manner should also others be used.

Q. Wherefore 'in the sense of the Causal Agent'? [To exclude primitives, such as] karoti, 'He does'; pachati, 'He cooks.'

Note—By the insertion of 'the sense,' the affix *la* may be (understood; as) Jotalati, 'He causes to glitter.'

* Hetu 'the cause'; but it means here [yo kàreti so hetu] 'He who does the act—the agent.' Also see Pànini, 1, 4, 55. Clough's version of Bàlavatàra throws no light whatever on the subject. He translates pàcheti, 'He cooks.' See p. 108 § 149.

8. After a crude noun with the sense of a verb, naya, &.

a. After a nominal root with the sense of a verb, the affix is naya; and it is named Kàrita.*

Ex. atihatthayati = hattinà atikkamati maggan, 'By means-of-the-elephant he-goes-beyond-† the way.

upavìnayati = vìnàya upagàyati, 'He plays music with a lute.'

dalha yati = dalhan karoti vinayan, 'He excels in vinaya.

visuddhayati = visuddhà hoti ratti, 'The evening is bright.'

Note.—By the addition of the 'and' such affixes as àra, àla are admissible; as antaràrati, 'He incurs danger;' upakkamàlati, 'He devises a plan.'

9. Yá in the substantive and passive voices.

a. In the substantive and passive voices, the affix ya comes after all the radicals.

Ex. *th*ìyate, '(it is) standing.'
bujjhìyate, 'is known.'
pachchate, 'is cooked.'
labbhate, 'is acquired.'
karìyate, 'is done.'
ijjate,' is sacrificed.'
uchchate, 'is spoken.'

Q. What is the force of 'the substantive and passive voices'? [By that expression the active voice is excluded; as in the following examples] karoti, 'he does'; pachati, 'he cooks'; pa*th*ati, 'he reads.'

Note.—By the insertion of yo [in the rule] the affix ya is admissible in other than the substantive and passive voices; as daddallati, 'it illumines intensely.'‡

---

* See preceding rule.

† i.e.—Completes his journey.

‡ This exception so far as our observation extends, is confined to verbs indicating the repetition of an act, or its intensity. See Pànini, VII. 4, 82.

10. A substitution of y. v and the letters of the ch. class for it, and the final letter of the radical.

a. As exigency may require the letters of the ch class, y. (or) v. may be substituted for it i.e. [see preceding rule] the affix ya, joined to the final letter of the radical.

Ex. vuchchate, 'is said'; vuchchante, 'are said.'
uchchate, 'is said'; uchchante, 'are said.'
majjate, 'is intoxicated'; majjante, 'are intoxicated.'
pachchate, 'is cooked'; pachchante, 'are cooked.'
bujjhate, 'is known'; bujjhante, 'are known.'
yujjhate, 'is fought'; yujjhante, 'are fought.'
kujjhate, 'is provoked'; kujjhante, 'are provoked.'
ujjhate, 'is abandoned'; ujjhante, 'are abandoned.'
haññate, 'is killed'; haññante, 'are killed.'
kayyate, 'is done'; kayyante, 'are done.'
dibbate, 'is played'; dibbante, 'are played.'*

11. Optionally the augment of i class.

a. When the affix ya comes after a radical, the vowels of the i class are optionally augmented.

Ex. kariyyate 'is done,' kariyanti 'are done'; gachchhiyate 'is gone,' gachchhiyyanti 'are gone.'

Q. Wherefore 'optionally'? [To shew that the augment is not inserted in a word like the following] kayyate 'is done.'

12. And assumes the previous letter.

a. When the affix ya comes after a radical, the same is optionally changed into the letter preceding it.

Ex. vu*dd*hate, 'is increased'; 'phallate, 'is fructified'; dammate, 'is subjugated'; labbhate, 'is acquired'; sakkate, 'is abled;' dissate 'is seen.'

Q. Wherefore 'optionally'? [To mark the exception as in] damyate, 'is subjugated.'

---

* This example is put in to shew the promiscuous use of b and v.

13. And likewise in the active voice.

a. As (different) substitutions take place [according to previous rules] to the affix ya, in the substantive and passive voices; so likewise the same substitutions for the affix ya may be adopted in the active voice.

Ex. bujjhati, 'he knows'; vijjhati, 'he pierces,' maññati 'he thinks,' sibbati 'he stitches.'

14. A (after) bhu, &c.*

a. In the active voice the affix *a* comes after the radicals of the bhu, &c. class.

Ex. bhavati 'is'; paṭhati 'reads'; pachati 'cooks'; yajati 'sacrifices.'

15. After rudh &c, with a niggahìta† before, &.

a. In the active voice the affix *a* comes after the radicals of rudha, &c. class, with a niggahìta augment before [the final letter of the root.]

Ex. rundhati 'obstructs'; bhindati 'breaks'; chhindati 'cuts.'

Note.—By the insertion of 'and' [to the rule, other] affixes such as i, ì, e, and o, are admissible with a niggahìta before the [final letter of the root]; as rundhiti, rundhìti, or rundheti, 'obstructs'; sumbhoti, 'shines.'

16. Ya after div, &c.

a. In the active voice the affix ya comes after the radicals of the diva, &c. class.

Ex. dibbati 'sports'; sibbati 'stitches'; yujjhati 'fights'; vijjhati 'pierces'; bujjhati 'knows.'

17. And nu, nà,‡ and unà, after su, &c.

---

* This and the following rules are in reference to the several classes of verbal roots.

† Name for the Sanskrit anusvàra.

‡ Some Pali writers use this na short.

a. In the active voice the affixes nu, nà, and unà come after the radicals, of su, &c. class.

Ex. abhisunoti or abhisunàti 'well-hears'; sanvunoti or sanvunàti 'obstructs'; àvunoti or àvunàti 'strings'; pàpunoti or pàpunàti 'obtains.'

18. Nà after ki, &c.

a. In the active voice, the affix nà comes after the radicals, of ki, &c. class.

Ex. kinàti 'buys'; jinàti 'conquers'; dhunàti 'shakes'; lunàti 'cuts'; punàti 'purifies.'

19. And ppa and nhà, after gah, &c.

a. In the active voice, the affixes ppa and nhà come after the radicals of gaha, &c. class.*

Ex. gheppati or ganhàti 'takes.'

20. O, and yirà after tan, &c.

a. In the active voice, the affixes o and yirà come after the radicals of tanu, &c. class.

Ex. tanoti 'stretches'; tanohi 'stretch (thou)'; karoti 'does'; karohi 'do [thou]'; kayirati 'does'; kayiràhi 'do [thou].'

21. Ne, naya after chur, &c.

a. In the active voice, the affixes ne and naya come after the radicals of chura, &c. class.

Ex. choreti or chorayati 'steals'; chinteti or chintayati 'thinks'; manteti or mantayati 'deliberates.'

22. Attanopada (mark) the action and the object.†

a. The attanopada (affixes) are used to mark the action and the object.‡

---

* Although by the appendix, '&c.' a class is meant; I have not been able to ascertain that such is the case. Some grammarians dispute the correctness of the &c. here; and they limit the rule to gaha.

† See ante Cap. 1 § 2 Q.

‡ In the substantive and passive voices, vide ante §§ 9, 10.

Ex. uchchate 'is spoken'; uchchante 'are spoken.'
labbhate 'is acquired'; labbhante 'are acquired.'
majjate 'is intoxicated'; majjante 'are intoxicated.'
yujjhate 'is fought'; yujjhante 'are fought.'
kayyate 'is done'; kayyante 'are done.'

23. Also the agent.

a. The attanopada (affixes) also mark the agent [in the active voice.]

Ex. maññate 'he respects' [himself.]
rochate 'it brightens' [of itself.]
sochate 'it grieves.'
sobhate 'it illumines.'
bujjhate 'he understands' [by himself.]
jàyate 'he produces' [by his own effort.]

24. Verbal terminations after radicals and affixes.

a. Verbal terminations come after the radicals ending with affixes [beginning] from kh, &c., and ending with the kàrita.*

Ex. titikkhati 'he endures'; jiguchchhati 'he reproaches'; vìmansati 'he investigates.'

Ta*t*àkan samudda miva attànam'àcharati = samuddàyati 'the lake conducts itself like the sea.'

Puttìyati 'he treats (him) as a son of his own'; pàchayati 'he causes to cook.'

25. Parassapada, the agent.

a. The parassapada mark the agent.†

Ex. karoti 'he does,' pachati 'he cooks,' pa*t*hati 'he reads,' gachchhati 'he goes.'

26. Bhû, &c., are radicals.

---

* See ante § 7.
† See Cap. 1 § 1.

a. Classes of words such as bhû, &c., receive the appellation of radicals.

Ex. bhavati 'is'; bhavanti 'are.'
pachati 'cooks'; pachanti 'cook.'
charati 'walks.'
chintayati 'thinks.'
gachchhati 'goes.'

End of the Second Chapter on Verbs.

Notes.

In the Pàli, the roots dhàtu) are nearly identical with those in the Sanskrit; and are distinguished into different conjugations, the same as in the Sanskrit, by anubandhas, or characteristic letters affixed to them.

The Pràkrit verb seems to be far less complete than the Pàli; for the former has but one Conjugation, equal to the first in the Sanskrit, though fragments of forms belonging to other Conjugations frequently occur in the Dramatic works. (Pr. Cowell's Pràkrit Prakàsa, p. xxix.)

The Pali forms of verbs and participles, generally, depart less from the Sanskrit than the Pràkrit ones do (see Tables in Dr. Muir's Sanskrit Texts, II. p 97, et seq.) In the Sanskrit there are ten Conjugations. To the Pali are unknown three of them, answering to the 2nd, 3rd, and 6th in the Sanskrit.

True it is that Kachchàyana gives (see § 19 supra) another class, at the head of which he places *gah*. But, not only is the existence in the Pàli, of this [eighth] class ignored in the Dhàtu Manjusa, but the writer of the Mahà Saddanìti says, that the *àdi* (by which a 'class' is indicated) in the Sutta above noticed, is a mistake,—which is indeed probable: since, except *gah* it is difficult to discover any other Pali radical which comes under this class, and since also *gah* itself may be conjugated as a verb of the *ki* class.

The seven Conjugations known to the Pali, answer to the first, fourth, fifth, seventh, eighth, ninth, and tenth classes of the Sanskrit verb; thus:

Pali class.		Affixes.	Place in Sanskrit.
1.	bhû	a	1
2.	rudh	a	7
3.	div	ya	4
4.	su	nu, na, una.	5
5.	ki	nâ	9
6.	tan	o, yirâ	8
7.	chur	ne, naya	10

The writer of the Dhàtu Manjusa remarks that the second, third, and sixth Conjugations of Sanskrit Grammarians are comprehended in the first of the Pali verbs, which also occupies the same place in the Sanskrit classes. It may indeed be readily believed that the three classes which the Sanskrit possesses over the Pali, are merely the elaborations of Grammarians. For, although in the Sanskrit, primitive verbs may belong to any one of the first nine classes; yet it is a significant fact that by far the greatest number do not belong to the second and third: and the third is only distinguished from the second by a syllable of reduplication in the special tenses. [Bopp's Comp. Gram. p. 107.]

In considering the characteristics of the Sanskrit classes, it is also remarkable that the sixth, like the first, adds *a* to the root, "the difference between the first class of nearly one thousand roots (almost the half of the entire number), and the sixth class which contains about 130 roots," being, as remarked by Bopp in his Comp. Gram. p. 104, that "the former raise the vowel of the root by Guna, while the latter retain it pure." "As *a* has no Guna," adds the same writer, "no discrimination can take place through this vowel between the classes 1 and 6; but nearly all the roots which belong to either, having *a* as the radical vowel, are reckoned in the first class."

I may also here observe that in the Vedas some verbs, e.g. *mri*, of the sixth conjugation, are inflected as if belonging to the first—a circumstance from which it may be inferred that the Sanskrit roots were not originally divided into ten classes.

The correspondence between the Pali and Sanskrit affixes in the remaining Conjugations will be readily seen, the differences being indeed very slight. The distinction, however, between the two first Conjugations in the Pali, is, that in the second the root takes an augment of a niggahìta before the final consonant [Bopp, p. 108.] In the affixes the Cerebral *n* is an anubandha, which however is not very frequent in the Pàli. The *n* in the affixes of the seventh class denotes the substitution of vriddhi [see Bàlavatàra, p. 88] for the radical element.

Although the Grammar before us does not distinctly name all the derivative verbs known to the Sanskrit, and has not shewn the peculiarities of the *Frequentative* form of the verb; (see note at p. 17,) yet the existence of them in the Pali is undoubted. More on this subject hereafter. See notes to the third Chapter infra.

CAP: III.

1. Sometimes the primary letter of a monosyllabic radical* is reduplicated.

a. The primary letter of a monosyllabic radical is sometimes reduplicated.

Ex. titikkhati 'forbears.'
jiguchchhati 'reproaches.'
tikichchhati 'cures.'
vìmansati 'investigates.'
bubhukkhati 'wishes to eat.'
pivàsati 'wishes to drink.'
daddallati 'illumines intensely.'
jahàti 'abandons.'
chankamati 'walks repeatedly.'

Q. Wherefore 'sometimes'? [To mark the exceptions; such as] kamati 'walks'; chalati 'shakes.'

2. The first abbhàsa †

a. The first [letter] of a reduplicate root is named abbhàsa.

Ex. dadhàti 'holds.'
dadàti 'gives.'
babhùva 'became.'

3. Is short. ‡

a. The (first) vowel in the abbhàsa is short.

Ex. dadàti 'gives'; dadhàti 'holds'; jahàti 'abandons.'

4. The second and fourth become first and third.

a. When the abbhàsa is either the second or fourth [letter

---

* Lit.—a root having one single vowel.
† Same in Pànini—see vi. 1-4.
‡ Same in Pànini, vii. 4-59.

E

in a class] they are (respectively) changed into the first, and third [letters of that class.]*

Ex. chichchheda 'He (it is reported) cut.'
bubhukkhati 'wishes to eat.'
babhùva 'became.'
dadhàti 'holds.'

5. Ch. class for k class.

a. When the abbhàsa is a k [or another of that] class, the same is changed into [its corresponding letter in the] ch class.

Ex. chikichchhati, 'cures'; jiguchchhati, 'reproaches'; jighachchhati, 'wishes to eat'; chankamati, 'walks repeatedly'; jiginsati, 'wishes to take'; jangamati, 'frequently goes.

6. Optionally v. and t. for màna and kita.

a. Optionally the abbhàsà of the radicals màna and kita are respectively changed into v. and t.

Ex. vìmansati 'investigates'; tikichchhati 'cures.'

Q. Wherefore 'optionally'? [To mark the exception as in the example] chikichchhati 'cures.'

7. J for h.

a. The h in the abbhàsa is changed into j.

Ex. jahàti 'abandons'; juvhati† or juhoti 'sacrifices'; jahàra '(it is said) he abandoned.'

8. Optionally i‡ and a for the last.

a. The last§ of the abbhàsa becomes, i; optionally a.

Ex. jiguchchhati 'reproaches'; pivàsati 'wishes to drink'; vìmansati 'investigates'; jighachchhati 'wishes to eat'; babhùva 'became'; dadhàti 'holds.'

---

* Or in other words 'when the abbhàsa is an aspirate, it is changed into a non-aspirate.' This rule too accords with Pànini; but with a slight verbal difference—See Pànini, viii. 4-54.

† In the Pali the v and h change positions in composition.

‡ Whenever the word vanna is mentioned with a short vowel, as in the text (ivanna) the long vowel is included. The Bàlàvatàra says: vannaggahanan sabbattha rassa dìgha sangahanatthan.

§ By the 'last' is meant the inherent vowel: e. g. the u in ju-guchchhati is the last in the abbhàsa.

Q. Wherefore 'optionally'? [To mark the exception, as in the example] bubhukkhati 'wishes to eat.'

9. And a niggahìta.

a. Optionally an augment of niggahìta (anusvàra) after the abbhàsa.

Ex. chankamati 'walks repeatedly'; chañchalati 'frequently shakes'; jangamati 'frequently goes.'

Q. Wherefore 'optionally'? [To mark the exceptions as in the instances] pivàsati 'wishes to drink'; daddallati 'illumines intensely.'

10. After pà and mà, và and man [before the affix] sa.

a. When the roots pà and mà take the affix sa, optionally they receive after the abbhàsa, the substitutions và and man respectively.

Ex. pivàsati 'wishes to drink'; vìmansati 'investigates.'

11. Ti*tt*ha for *th*à.

a. Optionally ti*tt*ha is substituted for a root such as *th*à.

Ex. ti*tt*hati 'stands'; ti*tt*hatu 'let him stand'; ti*tt*heyya 'he may stand'; ti*tt*heyyun 'they may stand.'

Q. Wherefore 'optionally'? [To mark the exception as in the example] *th*àti 'stands.'

12. Piba for pà.

a. Optionally piba is substituted for the root pà.

Ex. pibati 'drinks'; pibatu 'let him drink'; pibeyya 'he may drink.'

Q. Wherefore 'optionally'? [To mark the exception as in the example] pàti 'he drinks.'

13. Jà jan and nà for ñà.

a. Optionally jà jan and nà are substituted for the root ñà.

Ex. jànàti 'knows'; jàneyya 'may know'; jàniyà 'may know'; jaññà 'know thou'; nàyati 'he knows.'

Q. Wherefore 'optionally'? [To mark the exception] viññàyati 'is well-known.'

14. Optionally passa, dissa, and dakkha for disa.

a. Optionally passa, dissa and dakkha are substituted for the root disa.

Ex. passati 'sees'; dissati 'sees'; dakkhati 'sees.'

Q. Wherefore 'optionally'? [To mark the exception] addasa* 'he saw.'

15. Ch for the final consonant, [when followed by the] affixes chh., &.†

a. The final consonant of the radical becomes ch, when it (the root) takes the affix chh.

Ex. jiguchchhati 'reproaches'; tikichchhati 'cures'; jighachchhati 'wishes to eat.'

16. And ka, when kha.

a. The final consonant of the radical becomes ka, when it takes the affix kha.

Ex. titikkhati 'forbears'; bubhukkhati 'wishes to eat.'

17. Gin for hara, when sa.

a. Gin is substituted for the entire root hara, when it takes the affix sa.

Ex. jiginsati 'wishes to take.'

18. àha and bhùva, for brù and bhù (before) parokkhà.

a. Aha and bhùva are (respectively) substituted for the radicals brù and bhù, before parokkhà terminations.‡

Ex. àha '(it is reported) he said.'
àhu '(it is reported) they said.'
babhùva '(it is reported) it became.'
babhùvu '(it is reported) they became.'

---

* This is sometimes written addasà.
† The Vutti is deficient in explaining the &c.
‡ See Cap. i. § 12.

Q. Wherefore parokkhà? [To mark the exception as in the Ajjatanì, see Cap. 1. § 14] abruvun 'they have said.'

19. Optionally, before all, chchh. for the final of gami.

a. Optionally the final m in the root gamu, becomes chchh before all the affixes and terminations.

Ex.	
gachchhamàno gachchhanto	'going.'
gachchhati gameti *	'he goes.
gachchhatu gametu	'let him go.'
gachchheyya gameyya	'he may go.'
agachchha agamà	'he went.'
agachchhi agami	'he has gone.'
gachchhissati gamissati	'he will go.'
agachchhissà agamissà	'he would have gone.'
agachchhìyati agamìyati	'he is gone.'†

Q. Wherefore 'of gami'? [To shew that the rule is limited to the given verb;‡ and that it does not apply to is] ichchhati 'he wishes.'

20. The a in vach [becomes] o before Ajjatanì.

---

* Gameti, gametu, and gameyya my be also the causatives of the forms given with them within brackets.

† It will be seen that these examples do not illustrate the parokkhà.

‡ Even were there no express statement to the effect that this Pali writer had a previous knowledge of Sanskrit Grammar, the above vutti would clearly establish the fact. For obviously the object here was to shew the difference between the Pali and the Sanskrit in which latter ish and gam come under the same rule. See Pànini vii. 3, 77; and Laghu kaumudi, No. 533.

a. Before Ajjatanì terminations, the a in the root vach becomes o.

Ex. avocha 'he has said'; avochun 'they have said.'

Q. Wherefore 'before Ajjatanì'? [Witness the examples in the hìyattani, as] avachà 'he spoke; avachu 'they spoke.'

21. Before hi mi and ma, the a is long.

a. Before the terminations hi, mi, and ma, the a is long.

Ex. gachchhàhi 'go thou'; gachchhàmi 'I go'; gachchhàma 'we go'; gachchhàmhe 'we go.'

Note.—By reason of the insertion of 'mi'* (in the rule) the a is sometimes short before the termination hi; as gachchhahi go thou.'

22. Optionally hi is elided.

a. The termination hi is optionally elided.

Ex. gachchha for gachchhàhi 'go thou.'
gama for gamehi 'go thou.'
gamaya for gamayàhi 'go thou.'

Q. Wherefore 'hi'? [To limit the rule to that particular termination; as] gachchhati, 'he goes'; gamiyati 'he is gone.'

23. And ssa, in bhavissanti; [when] the vowel in hoti† [becomes] eha, oha, e.

a. Optionally the ssa in bhavissanti terminations is elided, when the vowel in the radical‡ hu is changed into eha, oha, e.

Ex. hehiti	'he will be.'	hehinti	'they will be.'
hohiti		hohinti	
heti		henti	
hehissati		hehissanti	
hohissati		hohissanti	
hessati		hessanti	

* I am not sure whether I have correctly rendered the above note. It is not intelligible.

† Eastern Grammarians frequently give the inflected verb in the third person when strictly the root should be given.

‡ See my observations on this radical at the end of Chapter Fourth.

Q. 1st. Wherefore hù? To exclude the radical bhù of the same import, to which the rule does not apply; as] bhavissati 'he will be'; bhavissanti 'they will be.'

Q 2nd. Wherefore 'in bhavissanti'? [To shew that the rule is limited to the future tense, as in] hoti 'he is' honti 'they are.'

24. Kàha for kara including its affix.

a. Before bhavissanti terminations optionally kàha is substituted for the radical kara including its affix, [when] always the ssa is elided.

Ex. kàhati, kàhiti 'he will do'; kàhasi, kàhisi 'thou wilt do'; kàhàmi 'I will do'; kàhàma 'we will do.'

Q. Wherefore 'optionally'? [Witness] karissati 'he will do' karissanti 'they will do.'

Note—that by the force of the words 'including its affix' [the rule may be extended] to other roots before bhavissanti terminations, when the radicals take the substitutions khàmi, khàma, and chhàmi, chhàma, e. g., the radical vas, vakkhàmi 'I shall relate'; vakkhàma 'we shall relate'; the radical vasa—vachchhàmi 'I shall dwell'; vachchhàma 'we shall dwell.'

End of the Third Chapter on Verbs.

NOTES.

Although the Grammar before us has not distinctly defined the derivative verbal forms known to the Sanskrit; yet, it will be observed (see examples to the very first rule with which this Chapter commences), that the Pali is not deficient in any of them. It has the Passive, the Causal, the Nominal, the Desiderative, and the Intensive forms.

The Pali, like the Sanskrit Passive, receives the syllable ya to the root, Cap. ii. § 9. Although y is frequently lost by assimilation, as in pachchate 'is cooked'; bhujjate 'is known'; it is, nevertheless, retained in words like karìyate 'is done.' The Pali is, in this respect, different from the Pràkrit, which, in the formation of the Passive, generally takes ìa or ijja; as, pa*d*hìai or pa*d*hijjai [Vararuchi vii. 8, 9,] for the Pali pa*tt*hate 'is recited.' In the Pràkrit ai, we clearly see the Dravidian termination ei, which runs through the entire body of its principal dialect, the Tamil; e. g. avei 'those'; talei 'head'; videi 'to sow'; irukkei (the verbal nouns for) 'being.' In the termination ijja, however, may be discovered the representative of the Sanskrit y, viz., g or j, into which the y passes in different forms of the Pràkrit and the Indo-European languages. See Bopp's Comp. Grammar, pp. 17, 110.

In the Pali there are four forms of the Causal verb, viz, e, aya, àpe, and àpayà; [Cap. ii. § 7,] whilst, of these, two alone are generally found in the Pràkrit, e. g. kàredi or kàràvedi. The first answers to the Pali kàreti, and the second (in which, as in the Dravidian, the p is changed into v) to kàràpeti. These again may be regarded as the vernacular forms of kàrayati and kàràpayati, which are known to the Sanskrit, in which, it is moreover remarkable, the first aya is the prevailing affix, the second payà being confined to 'those roots which ending in à, or in a diphthong to be changed into à, receive before aya the affix of a p,' as in sthàpayàmi 'I make to stand.' Bopp's. Comp. Gram. p. 1002. The difference between the Pali, Pràkrit, and Sanskrit causal affixes may be thus exhibited:—

(i.)	kareti	—	kàrayati	—	kàràpeti	—	kàràpayati.
(ii.)	kare*d*i	—	....	—	kàràve*d*i	—	....
(iii.)	....	—	kàryati	—	....	—	sthàpayati

It is indeed very remarkable, as stated by Professor Bopp, that the contraction of aya into e, as in the Pali and Pràkrit manemi, is also to be found in 'the Old-High German, and the Latin of the second conj.' Comp. Gram. p. 109.

With regard to the Pràkrit form of the Causative, Professor Lassen has the following observations.* "From the Sanskrit form of the Causative roots in à, which insert a servile p between the termination of the root and the addition ay, arises another form of the Pràkrit Causative which adds àp to the root, or to the theme of the present active. The Causative inflects this dissyllable in àp (whence àb; Comp. sec. 37) entirely like that which has just been mentioned. This form is derived from the Sanskrit discourse of one of the lower orders; for, in the Vetàlapanchavinsati, and in other Milesian tales we read jìvàpayati, mochàpayati, and others of the kind. Vararuchi observes, vii. 17, that kàràbeyi is also called karàbeyi, i.e., if àp be added, the vowel of the Sanskrit Causative is now and then shortened. Examples of this are thàbehi Vik. 6, 10; lohàbedi Sak. 58, 5 from lubh; tuaràbedu Màl. Vik. 44, 10; marisàbedha Sak. 55, 9; mo (ch) àbehi Sak. 153, 6; Vik. 13, 14; 14, 3. Fut. moàbissam &c."

I may here refer to a peculiarity of the Pali Causal verb, which has been noticed by the writer of the Bàlavatàra, viz., that Intransitive verbs with a causal affix, convey a transitive signification; e g., bhikkhu ràgàdi dùsakan maggan bhàveti, 'the priest contemplates the defiling path of the passions.'†

> Akammakàpi hetvatthappachchayantà sakammakà
> Tan yathà bhikkhu bhàveti maggan ràgàdi dùsakan.

The affinity between, what I conceive to be, the cultivated forms of the Causal affixes and the Passive, is obvious. The same relationship which exists between these forms exists also between them and the affixes of the Nominal verb, which

* Lassen's Inst. Pràk. p. 360.
† See Clough's Bàlavatàra, p. 108.

takes àya and ìya in several different senses, as in the Sanskrit. [Laghu Kawmudhi 297.] Thus,

karì ......(ya)	......ya-te	.........Passive.				
kàra ......(ya)	......ya-ti	.........Causal.				
pabbat ...(àya)	......àya-ti	.........(i.)	Nominal,	Cap. ii.	§ 4.
chatt......(ìya)	......ìya-ti	.........(ii.)	do.	do.	§ 5.
chatt......(ìya)	......ìya-ti	.........(iii.)	do.	do.	§ 6.
upavìn ...(aya)	......aya-ti	.........(iv.)	do.	do.	§ 8.
dad-dal...(ya)	......l (y)a-ti	...... Intensive.				

Of the Intensive and Desiderative forms in the Pràkrit, Professor Lassen remarks that "reliques only of these verbs are extant, and, in truth, these kinds of derivative verbs rarely pass over into common conversation. Jugutsa, whence the Pràkrit jugutcha. It is extant in M. M. 36, 11, etc." Pràk. Inst. p. 367.

The Desiderative and Intensive forms of the verb, are indeed no strangers in the Pali. See Cap. ii. § 3; also iii. § 1. They are both formed, as in the Sanskrit, by the reduplication of the first syllable of the root. The Intensive form appears, as in the Sanskrit, generally, in verbs signifying 'to shine,' 'to be beautiful,' 'to lament.' Where, however, the primitive verb has a reduplicated form, as in titikkhati, it does not, as we learn from Moggallàyana, undergo a reduplication in its formation into the Desiderative; as titikkhisati 'he wishes to endure,' jiguchchhisati 'he wishes to reproach.' In these examples the affix *s*,* is the same as in the Sanskrit. But this is sometimes changed in the Pali into kh, or chh. See Cap. ii. §§ 2, 3. The Desiderative verb may also be formed into a Causal, e. g., bubukkhàpeti. See Moggallàyana's Pali Grammar.

---

* ish = is 'to desire.'

CAP: IV.

1. Before mi, ma, an for the final of dà.

a. Before mi, and ma, an is substituted for the final letter of the root dà.

Ex. dammi 'I give'; damma 'we give.'

2. Before a causal affix, (the radical) when not ending with a compound consonant, is subject to vuddhi.

a. The root, when not ending with a compound consonant, is subject to vuddhi[*] before a causal affix.

Ex. kàreti kàrayati kàràpeti kàràpayati	'he causes to do.'	kàrenti kàrayanti kàràpenti kàràpayanti	'they cause to do.'

Q. Wherefore 'when not ending with a compound consonant'? [Witness] chintayati[†] 'he reflects'; mantayati 'he causes to deliberate.'

3. Optionally Ghata, &c.[‡]

a. When not ending with a compound consonant the roots ghata, &c., optionally receive vuddhi substitutions before causal affixes.

Ex. ghàteti ghateti ghàtayati ghàtàpeti ghàtàpayati ghatàpayati	'he causes to unite.'

---

[*] Vuddhi is the change or substitution to which the vowels are subject. Thus à for a; e for i and ì; and o for u and ù.

[†] Can this be the causal form? I have not seen this word used in such a sense.

[‡] See Pànini, vi. 4, 92.

gàmeti
gameti
gàmayati
gamayati
} 'he causes to go.'

Q. Wherefore 'ghata, &c.'? [To exclude roots such as kara e. g.] kàreti 'he causes to do.'

4. And others.

a. When not ending with compound consonants all roots receive vuddhi substitutions before other affixes.

Ex. jayati 'he conquers'; bhavati or hoti 'is.'

Note—by the insertion of an 'and' [to the sutta it may be laid down that,] the affix nu also takes the vuddhi substitutions; as abhisunoti 'he hears well'; sanvunoti 'he closes.'

5. Guha dusa long.

a. Before causal affixes, the vowel of the roots guha dusa, becomes long.

Ex. gùhayati 'he causes to conceal'; dùsayati 'he causes to pollute.'

6. Before ya, u for (v)a in vacha, vasa, vaha, &c.

a. Before the affix ya the (v)a in the roots vacha, vasa, vaha, &c., becomes u.

Ex. uchchate
vuchchati } 'is said.'
vussati 'is inhabited.'
vuyhati 'is borne.'

7. Before y, h is transposed; (and) optionally (changed into) l.

a. Before the affix ya, the letter h is transposed; and the affix ya is optionally changed into l.

Ex. vuyhati or vulhati 'is borne.'

8. Before ppa, ghe for gaha.

a. Before the affix ppa, ghe is substituted for the entire root gaha.

Ex. gheppati 'he takes.'

9. Before nhà, ha is elided.

a. Before the affix nhà, the ha in the root gaha is elided.

Ex. ganhàti 'he takes.'

10. Before Ajjatanì, kàsa for kara.

a. Before Ajjatanì terminations, the form of kàsa is substituted for the entire root kara.

Ex. akàsi or akari 'he has done.'

akàsun or akarun 'they have done.'

*Note**—by the expression atta 'the form,' sa may be augmented in others, e. g., ahosi 'has been'; adàsi 'has given.'

11. The mi mà of asa (become) mhi, mhà; and the last is elided.

a. The terminations mi and mà, which come after the root asa, are optionally changed into mhi and mhà; when the final letter of the root is elided.

Ex. amhi, or asmi 'I am.'

amha, or asma 'we are.'

12. Ttha for tha.

a. The termination tha of the root asa is changed into ttha, when [as before] the final letter of the root is elided.

Ex. attha 'you are.'

13. Tthi for ti.

a. Ti, the termination of the root asa is changed into tthi; when the final letter of the root is also elided.

Ex. atthi 'he is.'

---

* This note like several others is not intelligible to my mind. By the expression 'form of kàsa,' a substitution of sa may be implied; but how an augment can be understood, I do not perceive. Again aññatthàpi 'in other places' can according to the text, only refer to terminations other than Ajjatani; yet from the examples given to the note, which are in the Ajjatani tense, it would seem that something else was meant.

14. Tthu for tu.

a. Tu, the termination of the root asa is changed into tthu; when the final letter of the root is also elided.

Ex. atthu 'let him be.'

15. Also [when] si.

a. Also when si is the termination of the root asa, its final letter is elided.

Ex. ko nu tvam'asi 'who art thou'?

16. Ttha tthan, for ì im, after labha.

a. When the terminations ì and im, come after the root labha, the same are changed into ttha and tthan; and the final letter of the root is elided.

Ex. alattha 'he has got'; alattham 'I have got.'

17. Chchhi for i, after kudha.

a. When the termination i comes after the root kudha, the same is changed into chchhi; and the final letter of the root is elided.

Ex. akkochchhi 'he has angered.' *

18. Optionally dajja for the root dà.

a. Dajja is optionally substituted for the entire root dà.

Ex. dajjàmi or dadàmi 'I give'; dajjeyya or dadeyya 'he may give.'

19. Vajja for vada.

a. Vajja is optionally substituted for the entire root vada.

Ex. vajjàmi or vadàmi 'I speak'; vajjeyya or vadeyya 'he may speak.'

20. Ghamma for gamu.

a. Ghamma is optionally substituted for the entire root gamu.

---

* In the Dhammapada this word is used to signify 'abused,' (see Gogerley's Trans: in The Friend iv. p. 21.) When it means 'abused,' or 'reviled,' akkochchhi is derived from kunsa, and not from kudha.

Ex. ghammatu 'let him go'; ghammàhi 'go thou'; ghammàmi 'let me go.'

Q. Wherefore 'optionally'? [To shew the regular forms] gachchhatu 'let him go'; gachchhàhi 'go thou'; gachchhàmi 'let me go.'

21. Before ya, ì for dà, dhà, mà, *th*à, hà, pà, maha, matha, &c.

a. Before the affix ya, the final vowel of dà, dhà, mà, *th*à, hà, pà, maha, matha, &c., becomes ì.

Ex. dìyati 'is given'; dhìyati 'is holden'; mìyati 'is measured'; *th*ìyati 'is stationed'; hìyati 'is reduced'; pìyati 'is drunk'; mahìyati 'is adored'; mathìyati 'is churned.'

22. I for the first of yaja.

a. Before the affix ya, i is substituted for the first letter of the root yaja.

Ex. ijjate mayà Buddho 'Buddha is worshipped by me.'

23. Imsu for um of all.

a. The termination um of all radicals, is changed into imsu.

Ex. upasamkamimsu 'they have approached'; nisìdimsu 'they have sat down.'

24. Optionally jìra (or) jìyya, and mìyya for jara and mara.

a. Optionally the roots jara, and mara take the substitutions jìra or jìyya, and mìyya.

Ex. jìrati or jìyyati 'he becomes decrepid': jìranti or jìyyanti 'they become decrepid'; mìyati or marati 'he dies'; mìyanti or maranti 'they die.'

25. And the initial of asa is elided before all.

a. Before all terminations and affixes, the initial [vowel] of the root asa, is optionally elided.

Ex. siyà 'it may be'; santi 'they are'; santo 'being'; samàno 'being.'

Q. Wherefore 'optionally'? [To mark the exception e. g.] asi 'thou art.'

26. For asabbadhàtuka, bhù.

a. In asabbadhàtuka* terminations, the very root asa, optionally becomes bhù.

Ex. bhavissati 'he will be'; bhavissanti 'they will be.'

Q. Wherefore 'optionally'? [To mark the exception e. g.] àsum 'they have been.'

27. Optionally iyà, and aññà for eyya after ñà.

a. Iya, and aññà are optionally substituted for the termination eyya after the root ñà.

Ex. jàniyà 'he may know'; jaññà 'he may know.'

Q. Wherefore 'optionally'? [Witness] jàneyya 'he may know.'

28. Nà is rejected [or] changed into ya.

a. The affix nà of the root ñà is sometimes elided, and sometimes changed into ya.

Ex. jaññà 'he may know'; nàyati 'he knows.'

Q. Wherefore 'optionally'? [To mark the exception e. g.] jànàti 'he knows.'

29. A [becomes] e, and is rejected.

a. The affix a [see Cap. ii. § 14] is sometimes elided, and sometimes changed into e.

Ex. vajjemi or vademi } 'I speak.'
vajjàmi or vadàmi }

30. O becomes u.

a. Optionally the affix o [see Cap. ii. § 20] becomes u.

Ex. kurute or karoti 'he does.'

Q. Wherefore 'o'? [To shew the exception as in] hoti 'is.' †

---

* The asabbadhàtuka comprise all the moods and tenses except the sabbadhàtuka, see Cap. i § 26.

† This is not very intelligible.

31. And also the a of kara.

a. The a of the radical kara optionally becomes u.

Ex. kurute, karoti, kubbate, kubbati, and kairati 'he does.'

Q. Wherefore 'kara'? [To exclude other radicals, such as] sarati 'walks'; marati 'kills.'

32. Before a vowel o becomes ava.

a. Before a vowel, the final o of a radical optionally becomes ava.

Ex. chavati 'quits'; bhavati 'is.'

Q. 1st. Wherefore 'before a vowel'? [To show that the rule does not apply except before a vowel, e. g.] hoti 'is.'

Q. 2nd. Wherefore 'o'? [To limit it to the rule, e. g.] jayati 'conquers.'

33. E becomes aya.

a. Before a vowel, the final e of the radical optionally becomes aya.

Ex. nayati 'leads'; jayati 'conquers.'

Q. Wherefore 'before a vowel'? [To shew that the rule does not apply except before a vowel, e. g.] neti 'leads.'

34. Before a causative, they become âva and âya.

a. Before a causative they, viz., o and e, take the substitutions âva and âya.

Ex. lâveti 'he causes to cut'; nâyeti 'he causes to lead.'

Note.—By analyzing the suttan, âya is admissible before other affixes, e. g., gâyati 'he sings.'

35. I is augmented before asabbadhâtuka.

a. Before asabbadhâtuka terminations, i is augmented.

Ex. gamissati 'he will go'; karissati 'he will do'; labhissati 'he will acquire'; pachissati 'he will cook.'

Q. Wherefore 'before asabbadhâtuka'? [To shew that

the rule does not apply to sabbadhâtuka terminations, e. g.] gachchhati 'goes'; karoti 'does'; labhati 'acquires'; pachati 'cooks.'

36. In certain instances, radicals, terminations, and affixes become long, take transformations, substitutions, and receive elision and augment, &c.

a. In certain instances, which are not here treated of, under the different voices of the verb, the elongation, transformation, substitution, elision, and augment, which radicals, terminations, and affixes receive [or undergo] should be adopted according to [the models furnished in] the word of Buddha.

Ex. jàyati * 'is born.'
kareyya 'he may do.'
jàniyà 'he may know.'
siyà 'may be.'
kare 'he may do.'
gachchhe 'he may go.'
jaññà 'he may know'; or 'know thou.'
vakkhetha 'you speak.'
dakkhetha 'you see.'
dichchhati 'he sees.'
àgachchhun 'they have come.'
ahosi 'has been.'
ahesun 'have been.'

Note.—In this wise should others be used.

37. The attanopadàni [become] the very parassapada.

a. Sometimes the attanopada (terminations) are changed into parassapada.

Ex. vuchchati 'is spoken'; labbhati 'is acquired'; pachchati 'is cooked'; karìyati 'is done'; sijjhati 'is accomplished.'

Q. Wherefore 'sometimes'? [To shew that the change

* The commentator deduces this from the root ji 'to conquer.'

is optional; as] vuchchate, labbhate, pachchate, kariyate, sijjhate.

38. A is augmented in the hiyattanì, ajjatanì, and kàlàtipattì.

a. Sometimes when the terminations are the Hìyattanì, Ajjatanì, [or] Kàlàtipattì, a is augmented [before the root.]

Ex. agamà 'he went'; agami 'he has gone'; agamissà 'he would go.'

Q. Wherefore 'sometimes'? [To indicate that the change is optional; as] gamà, gamì, gamissà.

39. ì after brù, when tì.

a. ì is augmented after the root brù, when the termination is tì.

Ex. bravìti 'he speaks.'

40. The final of a root of many vowels is elided.

a. Sometimes the final [vowel] of a root of many vowels is elided.

Ex. gachchhati 'goes'; pachati 'cooks'; sarati 'remembers'; marati 'kills [or dies]'; charati 'walks.'

1st *Q.* Wherefore 'of many vowels'? [To exclude monosyllabic roots, as] pàti 'drinks'; yàti 'goes'; dàti 'gives'; bhàti 'shines'; vàti 'wafts.'

2nd *Q.* Wherefore 'sometimes'? [To mark the exceptions, such as] mahìyati 'adores'; matìyati 'churns.'

41. Optionally the finals of isu and yama [are changed into] ichchha.

a. Optionally the finals of isu and yama are changed into ichchha.

Ex. ichchhati 'wishes'; niyachchhati 'regulates.'

Q. Wherefore 'optionally'? [To mark the exceptions such as] esati 'searches'; niyamati 'determines.'

42. The n of kàrita is elided.

a The n of kàrita affixes is elided.

Ex. kàreti
kàrayati
kàràpeti
kàràpayati
} 'causes to do.'

For the advancement of religion, the verb has been (thus) briefly illustrated by me: may the learned, according to their own respective attainments, reflect, (hereon.)

End of the Fourth Chapter on Verbs.

NOTES.

Some modern writers on Pali Grammar follow, in their illustrations, the principles of Sanskrit Grammar. E. g., the eight conjugations of Pali verbs are classed by Moggallàyana differently from Kachchàyana; and the classification by the former seems to be nearly in accordance with that adopted by Sanskrit writers. He also, like Vararuchi, refers the student in certain parts of his Grammar 'to the Sanskrit,' for the explication of 'that which has been omitted.' But it is very remarkable that the older the grammarian, the less he has identified the Pali with the Sanskrit. Kachchàyana is, certainly, one of the latter class. Although he has borrowed a few technical terms from Sanskrit Grammarians* (see Introduction, p. xxv.), and has even adopted the language of Pànini, as we have shown in the notes, and in the Introduction (p. xvii.); yet he has referred us for all that has not been

* This merely proves the superior culture of the Sanskrit, at this time.

treated of, in his work, to the Text-books of Buddhism—not, to the Sanskrit. This indicates clearly that he, at least, did not regard the Pali as an emanation of the Sanskrit. It is also clear from the whole tenor of his work that he wished to treat of the Pali as a dialect distinct from the Sanskrit. Confining my observations to the portion of Grammar which is published, two circumstances may be here adduced in support of this.

(i.) That where the Sanskrit takes the substitute chha for the finals of these, viz., ish 'to wish,' gam 'to go,' and yam 'to restrain,' when an affix follows having an indicatory s, as gachchhati 'he goes.' [Laghu Kawmudhi, p. 187]; the Pali receives it only in the verb gam 'to go.' It is clearly to show this difference that Kachchàyana gives us the Vutti in Cap. iii. § 19.

(ii.) It is indeed with the same object that a little farther on he calls attention (§ 23) to the existence in the Pali of a verb *Substantive* unknown to the Sanskrit. This is *hù;* on which a few remarks may not be out of place here.

Vararuchi, in his Pràkrit Prakàsa (vii. § 3) states that *ho* and *huva* are the substituted forms of the verbal root bhû. If this were so, the substitution would indeed be invariably found in all the variations of the root. But such is not the fact. When both Vararuchi cap xii. § 12 and Hemachandra § 269, speaking of the Saurasenì, give *bhuvo bhah,* a commentator, adds *vâ* with ex. *bhodi, hodi; bhuvadi, huvadi; bhavadi, havadi;* showing clearly the existence of both forms in the Pràkrit. This is the case in several Pràkrit languages, e. g., in the Maràthà, which also possesses the Pali *hû,* the Sanskrit *as* is used to supply the deficiences of the paradigm of the root *hû.* The Pali likewise takes in *bhû* to fill up the deficiencies of the uncultivated root *hù,* and the indiscriminate use of *bhû, hû,* and *as* disproves the alleged substitution. It is also disproved by the fact that in the Conjugation of hû it takes different modifications which are not found in the forms of bhû; e. g. bhavati is not havati, but hoti; abhava is not ahava, but ahuvà. So likewise the other forms of hû, not one of which is identical with the forms of bhù. Take, for instance, the principal Ajjatani forms in bhù and hù; and their difference is manifest:—

abhavi	ahu / ahosi	abhavinsu	ahavun / ahesun
abhavo	ahosi	abhavattha	ahosittha
abhavin	ahosin / ahun	abhavamhâ	ahosimha / ahumha

Again, if we regard hû as the substituted form of bhû, how is it that the former, like *as*, is so irregular? wherefore have we not as many forms without a *b* as with it? why is it deprived of Attanopada forms in all Tenses except the Hìyattanì? why indeed does it take so many forms as six in the future, when without the alleged substitution of h for bh, it has but one single form, bhavissati? For the illustration of other differences I subjoin the following

COMPARATIVE TABLES

OF BHU, AS, HU.

Present Tense.

Parassa-pada.

	Singular.			Plural.	
3 bhavati	atthi	hoti	bhavanti	santi	honti
2 bhavasi	asi	hosi	bhavatha	attha	hotha
1 bhavâmi	asmi / amhi	homi	bhavâma	asma / amha	homa

Attanopada.

3 bhavate	......	......	bhavante	......	......
2 bhavase	......	......	bhavavhe	......	......
1 bhave	......	......	bhavâmhe	......	......

Definite Past.

Parassapada.

3 abhava	......	ahuvà	abhavù	......	ahuvu
2 abhavo	......	ahuvo	abhavattha	......	ahuvattha
1 abhava	......	ahuvan / ahuva	abhavamhà	......	ahuvamha

Attanopada.

Singular.			Plural.		
3 abhavattha	......	ahuvattha	abhavatthun......		ahuvatthun
2 abhavase	......	ahuvase	abhavavhan		ahuvavhan
1 abhavin	......	ahuvin	abhavamhase ...		ahuvamhase*

Present Perfect.

Parassapada.

3 abhavi	àsi	ahu ahosi	abhavinsu	àsinsu àsun	ahavun ahesun
2 obhavo	ási	ahosi	abhavattha	àsittha	ahosittha
1 abhavin	ásin	ahosin ahun	abhavamhà	àsimha	ahosimha ahumha

Attanopada.

3 abhavà	......	......	abhavû	.....	......
2 abhavase	......	......	abhavavhan		......
1 abhava	......	......	abhavamhe		......

Indefinite Past.

Parassapada.

3 babhûva	......	......	babhûvu	......	......
2 babhûve	......	......	babhûvittha		......
1 babhûva	......	......	babhûvamha......		......

Attanopada.

3 babhùvittha		......	babhûvive	......	......
2 babhùvittho		......	babhùvivho		......
1 babhùvi	......	......	babhùvimhe		......

Future Tense.

Parassapada.

3 bhavissati	......	heti hehiti hohiti hessati hehissati hohissati†	bhavissanti	......	henti hehinti hohinti hessanti hehissanti hohissanti
2 bhavissasi	......	hesi hehisi hohisi hessasi hehissasi hohissasi	bhavissatha	......	hetha hehitha hohitha hessatha hehissatha hohissatha

---

* The Attanopada forms of the radical hû, so far as my observation goes, are confined to this Hiyattani Tense.

† The forms with ho, such as hohissati; hohissasi, hohissami &c., are given by the Rev. F. Mason of the Baptist Union, as those of 'the Second Future Tense.' See Am. Or. Journal iv., p. 280. But I can find no authority for this. For some of the changes of this verb in the Future Tense, see Rule in cap. iii. § 20.

1 bhavissàmi	......	hemi hehàmi hohàmi hessàmi hehissàmi hohissàmi	bhavissàma	......	hema hehàma hohàma hessàma hehissàma hohissàma

Attonopada

3 bhavissate	......	......	bhivissante	......	......
2 bhavissase	......	......	bhavissavhe	......	......
1 bhavissan	......	......	bhavissàmhe	......	......

The Imperative.

Parassapada.

3 bhavatu	atthu	hotu	bhavantu	santu	hontu
2 bhavàhi	àhi	hohi	bhavatha	attha	hotha
1 bhavàmi	asmi	homi	bhavàma	asma	homa

Attanopada.

3 bhavatan	......	.....	bhavantan	......	......
2 bhavassu	......	......	bhavavho	......	......
1 bhave	......	......	bhavàmase	......	......

The Potential.

Parassapada.

3 bhave bhaveyya	siyà assa	heyya	bhaveyyun	siyun assu	heyyun
2 bhaveyyàsi	assa	heyyàsi	bhaveyyàtha	assatha	heyyàtha
1 bhaveyyàmi	assan	heyyàmi	bhàyeyyàma	assàma	heyyàma heyyan

Attanopada.

3 bhavetha	......	......	bhaveran	......	......
2 bhavetho	......	......	bhaveyyavho	......	......
1 bhaveyyam	......	......	bhaveyyàmhe	......	......

For the forms of hû in the Potential, the Rûpasiddhi gives the above; but we have not met with any of them in the text books of Buddhism. We have, however, found a different form huveyya in Mahà Vagga lib i., 'huveyya pàvuso.'* In accordance with this the other persons should be formed as follows:—

......	......	huveyya	......	......	huveyyun
......	......	huveyyàsi	......	......	huveyyàtha
......	......	huveyàmi	......	......	huveyyàma

* avuso—a term of address. This is, I believe, not found in the Sanskrit; see y observations thereon in the C. B., A. S. J. for 1856—8., p. 247.

THE CONDITIONAL.

Parassapada.

3 abhavissa	......	ahavissa	abhavissansu	ahavissansu
2 abhavisse	......	ahavisse	abhavissatha	ahavissatha
1 abhavissam	......	ahavissam	abhavissamha	ahavisamha*

Attanopada.

3 abhavissatha	......	......	abhavissante	......
2 abhavissase	......	......	abhavissavhe	......
1 abhavissam	......	......	abhavissamhe	......

PARTICIPLES.

Present.

Decl. { bhavamàna, bhavanta } { santa, samàna }

Passive.—bhûyamàna

Past.

Decl.— bhûta, huto, hutàvi ....

Indec.— hutvà or hutvàna ....

Future.

Decl.— bhàvi ....
bhavissanta ....
bhavissamàna ....

From the above differences; and the confused mode in which the Pràkrit Grammarians treat of bhavadi havadi, &c., it may be inferred that they were indebted to little beyond their own observations for the elucidation of the laws of the Pràkrit; and that they consequently mistook a distinct radical for the modified form of another.

The Rev. Henry Ballantine of the American Board in India remarks, with reference to this radical in the Maràthà, "The substantive verb, especially, exhibits the most striking dissimilarity between the Sanskrit and the Maràthà languages. In Maràthà, we have the following forms of the substantive verb.

* For these forms of hû in the Conditional, I am indebted to the writer of the Rûpasiddhi.

	Singular.			Plural.		
	1st per.	2nd per.	3rd per.	1st per.	2nd per.	3rd per.
Pr. Ind.	— àhe	...àhes	...àhe	àho	.. àhà	.. àhet
Sd. form	— hoya	...hos	...hoya	hwo	...hwà	. .hot
H ndu fm	— hò	...hai	...hai	hai	...ho	...hai
Im.In.mas	— hoto	...hotàs	...hotà	hoto	...hotà	...hote

"The root of this verb is evidently *ho* or *he,* reminding us of the Hebrew *hàvàh* or *hàyàh.** The Sanskrit root of the substantive verb *as,* is employed in Maràthà to fill up the deficiencies of the paradigm of the original root; being used in the formation of the present habitual tense, and of the past habitual, and also of the conditional mood, e. g.; *asato* 'he is habitually;' *ase* 'he was habitually,' *asalà* 'if he were;' but these are evidently later introductions, required and employed only when the language had been considerably cultivated." †

That *hû* is a radical distinct from *bhû* appears not only from the express mention of it, as such (cap. iii § 23) by Kachchàyana, and other Pàli Grammarians; but also from its existence both in the Indo-European languages and in the Pràkrit.

Although, of the Sanskrit auxiliaries as 'to be' bhû 'to become,' and kri 'to do,' all which exist in the Pali,—the German idioms alone substitute for the third, a verb signifying 'to do' [Bopp's Comp. Gr., p. 843]; and although some of the other European dialects possess the two first, both separately and conjointly [e. g. *es* Lat. *is* Teut., *esti* Gr., *ist* Germ., *is* Eng., and *be* and *is* Eng. &c.,]; it is, nevertheless, remarkable that in the last we find another form *have,* which renders the same assistance to the principal verb that *be* (bhû) and *is* ('as') do. There is, therefore, I conceive, no objection to its ('have') being regarded as a *verb substantive* of that language from whence the Pràkrits and their Indo-European sisters have

* 'Some would derive this root from the Sanskrit bhû 'to be,' and others from the Sanskrit as, but either of these derivations is far-fetched and unsatisfactory."

† Amer. Oriental Journal, iii., p. 380.

sprung up. Moreover, the difference between 'have' and 'be' is simply that which exists between 'possession' and 'existence.' Possession itself conveys, as the Muràthì *honen* does, 'the entrance on the state of existence.' Dr. Stevenson's Muràthi Grammar, p. 86. The signification of existence is again not far removed from the idea of possession. The power of the one has clearly grown out of the other. The two auxiliary verbs *have* and *be*, which play a most important part in English Syntax, are indeed not more different in signification than the *as*, *bhû* and *kri*, which Sanskrit writers employ both in the Reduplicate Præterite, and in composition with nouns (Wilson's San. Gr., p. 350.)*

The auxiliary verb which has *h* for its radical consonant in the Indo-European languages; e. g. *habeo* Lat., *haban* Goth., *have* Eng., is intimately related to *hu* (va) Pràk., *ho* (na) Murà.,† and is therefore clearly traceable to the Pali *hû*, of which the inflexions, [*ve* Eng, *beo* Lat., *ban* Goth., *va* Pràk., *va* Sin.,] are found in the præterite.

Neither Vararuchi nor the other Pràkrit Grammarians seem to have been struck by coincidences such as the following; or, they would not, I apprehend, have traced the Pràkrit *hû* to *bhû*:

Pàli.	Pràk.	Mur.	Lat.	Goth.	Eng.
homi	———	hoya	habeo	haba	have
hosi	hosi	hos	habes	habais	hast
hoti	{ hoi	hoya	habet	habai*p*	has
homa	{ huvai	hvo	habemus	habam	have
hotha	———	hvà	habetes	habai*p*	have
honti	{ honti huvant	hot	habent	habant	have

* e. g. sukli-karoti=seti-karoti; sukli-bhavati=seti-bhavati; sukli-syàt=seti-siyà.

† "At Cuttack we have hoti, atthi, as in the modern Pali."—American Oriental Journal, vol. ii., p. 336.

On the supposition, however, that "the simpler the form the older is its origin", my Pandit is inclined to believe that the Pàli form *hû*, is even more ancient than its fuller form assumed by the Pràkrit in common with some of her Indo-European sisters; and for this belief confirmatory proof may be found in the fact that the simple Pàli *hû* is found in the radical elements of such a different class of languages as the Chinese [(s)hec], the Burmese [(s)hi], and the Tavoy dialect [hi.]* Be this however as it may, the existence of *hû* in some of the European dialects is manifest; and its absence in some others, as in the Sanskrit, furnishes no valid objection to its being regarded as a radical; for we have satisfactory proof that the Sanskrit has not only lost several roots, which are to be found in the Vedas, [e. g. kan, ink, ubj, sav, ven, sach, myaksh, thsar, dhraj, maud, ves, vaksh, turv, bharv, &c.,] but that some primitive radicals had also disappeared from the Vedic Sanskrit.† The absence of *hû* in the Sanskrit is, moreover, not more surprising than that the Greek, Latin, and the old Slavonic which possess the defective *as*, have not borrowed the fuller *bhû*.

* Am. Oriental Journal, vol. iv., p. 279.
‡ See Dr. Muir's Sanskirt Texts, p. 272.

APPENDIX.

Note at page xxxii.

Scarcely a century* had elapsed from the death of Gotama, when, in the tenth year of Susinàga's successor, Kàlàsoka, the teachings of Gotama were disregarded in the strongholds of Buddhism, and usages contrary to his doctrines prevailed even amongst the priesthood. The Sovereign himself "extended his protection" to those who deviated from the orthodox doctrines.

It is therefore not surprising that many thousands of priests who had been doubtless much inconvenienced by the rigid rules of discipline in the Buddhist Church, openly introduced certain innovations, of which the following is a condensed account.

The order by which priests were prevented from keeping *salt* for more than seven days, was construed not to extend to the case where salt was preserved in a horn. The allotted time for their morning meals, was extended to "two inches of shadow" *after* the meridian sun. The general prohibition against enjoyments was restricted to the *Vihàras*. Certain ceremonies, which were permitted only in the *Uposatha* hall, were extended to the monasteries. Consent, which was made the condition precedent upon which certain religious acts could be performed, was considered dispensable, where the act was confirmed after its completion. The doctrines of

---

* Dasa dasaka vassamhi Sambuddhe parinibbute
Vesàliyan Vajjiputtà dìpenti dasavatthuke.
That is—"when a century had elapsed from the date of Buddha's *parinibban*, the Vajjians of Vesàli declared the ten innovations."—*Dìpàvansa.*

Buddhism, for which Gotama exacted implicit obedience, were set at naught upon the example of preceptors, or the authority of the fathers of the Church. Substantial food, which was forbidden after mid day, was thought not to extend to whey, "a component part of *milk.*" Fermented liquor, the drinking whereof was totally prohibited, did not in their opinion include *toddy,* resembling water. Costly coverlets, against the use of which Gotama laid his Canon, were considered to comprise only fringed cloth. All precious metals, which they were inhibited from receiving, were construed to mean all metals *besides gold and silver.** Such were the innovations of a body of ten thousand priests which led to the *Dùtiya Sangìti* or second Convocation.

1.—Uddhamman ubbinayancha
Apagatan Satthu Sàsane;
Atthan dammancha bhinditvà.
Viloman dìpayinsute.

2.—Tesan niggaha natthàya
Bahûbuddhassa sàvakà;
Dvà dasa sata sahassàni
Jina puttà samàgatà.

3.—Etasmin sannipàtasmin
Pàmokkhà a*tt*ha bhikkhavo;
Satthu kappà mahà nàgà
Durà sadà mahà ganì.

4.—Sabbakàmì cha Sàlho cha
Revato Kujja Sobhito;
Vàsabhagàmi Sumano
Sàna vàsecha Sambhuto;

5.—Yaso Kàkanda puttocha
Jinan di*tt*hà ime isì;
Pàpànan nigga hatthàya
Vesàliyan samàgatà;

* See Chùlavagga, lib. 4 of the Vinaya.

6.—Vàsabhagàmì cha Sumano
Anuruddhassànu vattakà;
Avasesà ànandassa
Di*tt*ha pubbà tathàgatan.

7.—Susuṇàgassa putto
Asoko àsi mahìpatì;
Pà*t*aliputta nagaramhi
Rajjan kàresi khattiyo.

8.—Tancha pakkhan labhitvàna
A*tt*ha therà mahiddhikà;
Dasavatthunan ninditvà
Pàpe nimmaddayinsute.

9.—Niddha metvà pàpa bhikkhû
Madditvà vàda pàpakan;
Saka vàda sodhanatthàya
A*tt*ha therà mahiddhikà.

10.—Arahantànan satta satan
Uchchinitvàna bhikkhavo;
Varan varan gahetvàna
Akansu dhamma sangahan.

11.—Kù*t*àgàra sàlàyan
Vesàliyan puruttame;
A*tt*ha màschi ni*tt*hàsì
Dutìyo sangaho ayan.

'They (the sinful priests) made a melange by departing from the sense and phraseology of the dhamma and Vinaya, the doctrines of Buddhà.(1)

'With a view (therefore), to degrade them, many priests, disciples of Buddha, (in all) twelve hundred thousand, assembled together.(2) In this congregation' there were eight preeminent principal bhikkhus, who had a large retinue, who were (unapproachable, i. e.) without their equals, and not inferior to Buddha (himself; viz.)(3) Sabbakàmi, Sàlha,

Revata, Kujjasobhita, Vàsabhagàmi, Sumana, Sambhûta of Sàna,(4) and Yasa, son of Kakanda, all who had seen Buddha. They assembled at Vesàli with a view to reproach the sinful priests.(5)

'Vàsabhagàmi and Sumana were the disciples of Anuruddha, and the rest of Ananda. They had all seen Buddà.(6)

'[At this time] Asoka, the son of Susinàga, a Khattiya prince, reigned in Pàtaliputta.(7)

'The (abovenamed) eight pre-eminent theras, having gained (this prince) to their side, censured the ten indulgences, and (oppressed) inflicted pains and penalties on the sinful innovators.(8) Having (thus) overcome the sinful bhikkhus, and suppressed their heresies; these illustrious eight priests, with the object of purifying their own discourses,(9) assembled seven hundred arahats—pre-eminent *bhikkhus;* and held a Council of dhamma.(10)

'This second Sangìti was brought to a close in eight months, at the *Kùtàgùra Hall,* in the renowned city of *Vesàli.*(11)

The account given of this convocation in the Tibetan Annals* does not precisely accord with that in the Mahàvansa. Both the accounts indeed agree as to the number of convocations,—as to their having been holden at three different places,—as to the first having been immediately after the death of Gotama,—and as to the second having been 110†

* See Asiatic Researches, xx., p. 41.

† Here too, there is a slight difference of ten years, which is too trivial to be noticed; and it is probable that the mistake arose by confounding the numbers 100, and 10, which may have occurred in a passage such as the following, conveying information as to the date of the second Convocation.

Atìte dasame vasse Kàlàsokassa ràjino;
Sambuddha parinibbànà evan vassa satangatan.

years from the last date. The difference between the two, however, consists in that the Tibetan writers allege the second to have taken place in the reign of the celebrated Asoka of Patàliputta, and the third during the reign of one Kanishka on the North of India, upwards of 400 years A. B.; whereas the Sinhalese version represents that the second occurred in the reign of Kalàsoka, and the third in the 17th year of the reign of Asoka, which would be 325 B. C.

Prof. Max Muller in commenting upon this point,* intimates as his opinion, that the Ceylonese, by a stretch of their imagination, introduced into their history an intermediate Asoka, and an intermediate Council. But there is no solid ground for such a supposition. That a Council was held about the close of the first century of the Buddhist era, is clear enough from all the accounts on the subject; and this could not have been, as stated in the Tibetan Annals, during the reign of Asoka the Great, for the best evidence which History furnishes us, proves that that monarch commenced to reign 325 B. C., or 218 after Buddha. In whose reign, then, was the Second Council held, which sat about a century after Buddha? The Sinhalese affirm that it was in the reign of one '*Kàlàsoka*, son of Susinàga.' The *Vishnu Purâna*,† and other Indian traditions, fully support this statement. It is clear indeed, that according to the latter, the king who agrees with the Kàlàsoka of the Ceylonese

---

* See his History of Ancient Sanskrit, p. 271, et seq.

† Compare Mahawansa with the following account in the *Vishnu Purána*.

'The next Prince will be Sisunàga; his son will be *Kákavarna* (36 years V. and M.); his son will be Kshemadharman, (Kshemakharman 20 years V. Kshemadharman 36 years M.); his son will be Kshatraujas, (40 years V.; Kshemajit or Kshemarchis, 36 years M.; Kshetrajna, Bh. P.) his son will be Vidmasàra, (Vimbisàra 28 years, V.; Vindusena or Vindhyasena 28 years, M.; Vidhisàra Bh.); his son will be Ajàtasatru, his son will be Dharbaka, (Harshaka 25 years, V.; Vansaka, 24 years, M.);

is called *Kàkavarna;* but this difference is not a sufficient objection against the correctness of the Ceylonese accounts; since both the names, as is often the case, may stand for the same person: and their identity is, moreover, established by the fact, that both historians agree as to *Kàkavarna* or *Kàlàsoka* having been the son of *Susinàga.**

It appears, therefore, that the authors of the Tibetan version of the scriptures, which were recorded after the Ceylonese, and long after the events to which they relate, mistook Asoka the Great for Asoka, surnamed *Kàlàsoka,* of whom, perhaps, they had never heard; and, having once thrown the second Council into the reign of the first mentioned Monarch, they had no alternative but to fix the third and posterior Convocation as having taken place during the reign of a subsequent celebrated sovereign. There was indeed much reason to name Kanishka. For, next to Asoka Hushka, Jushka and Kanishka † may be regarded

---

his son will be Udayàsva, (33 years v.; Udibhi or Udàsin, 33 years M.,) his son also will be Nandivardhana, and his son will be Mahànanda, 42 and 43 years, v.; 40 and 43 years, M.) These ten Saisunàgas will be kings of the earth for 362 years.

'The son of Mahananda will be born of a woman of the *Sudra* class; his name will be Nanda, called Mahapadma; for he will be exceedingly avaricious. Like another Parasuràma, he will be the annihilator of the Kshatriya race, for after him the kings of the earth will be sûdras. He will bring the whole earth under one umbrella, he will have eight sons Sumàlya, and others, who will reign after Mahàpadma; and he and his sons will govern for a hundred years. The Brahman Kau*t*ilya will root out the nine Nandas.

'Upon the cessation of the race of Nanda, the Mauryas will possess the earth. Kau*t*ilya will place Chandragupta on the throne; his son will be Vindusàra; his son will be Asokavardhana; his son will be Suyasas; his son will be Dasaratha; his son will be Sangata; his son will be Sàlisûka, his son will be Somasarman; his son will be Sasadharman, and his successor will be Vrihadratha. These are the ten Mauryas, who will reign over the earth for 137 years.'

* Susunágassa putto, Asoko àsi mahîpatí, Pàtaliputta nagaramhi, rajjankàresi Khattiyo.—*Dipàvansa.*

† See Ràja Tarangani in the Asiatic Researches, xv.

as the only 'Asiatic princes who were imbued with the virtue of merit, who founded Colleges and Chetiyas, and during whose reign the regions in the North of India were greatly under the spiritual control of Buddhist ascetics preeminent for their rigid piety.'* Perhaps too, the Tibetan account is in this respect correct; and there was, in point of fact, a fourth Council held in the territories of *Kanishka*, of which the Ceylonese knew nothing, and the Tibetans had but a confused notion of the second and third *Sangítis*, which they jumbled together, taking the date of the one, and the name of the Sovereign who reigned at the other.

The above supposition derives great support from the fact noticed by Pr. Muller himself,—that 'the Buddhists of Ceylon did not borrow the outlines of their history either from the Brahmans or from the Buddhists of Magadha;' and also from the pecularitics of language and style which distinguish the Tibetan from the Pali digests of the Sinhalese.

From a paper entitled '*the Peculiarities of the Gàthà style,*' in the Bengal A. S. Journal,† we gather that the Buddhist literature of Nepal, from which the sacred scriptures of Tibet, Tartary, and China have been compiled,‡ is in an ugly Sanskrit dialect, destitute of the niceties of the Sanskrit Grammatical forms of declension and conjugation, &c.; that the authors have sacrificed Grammar to the exigencies of metre; that it is in a mixed style of prose and Gàthàs; that it bears a strong resemblance to the Tantras of the 4-7th centuries of the Christian era, and that it appears to be the production of men to whom the task of compilation was assigned without

* Journal of the Ceylon Branch of the Asiatic Society for 1856-8, p. 199.

† By Babu Regendralal Mittra; volume for 1854, p. 604.

‡ Mons. Burnouf regards this as a fact conclusively demonstrated. See his Introduction to the History of Buddhism.

sufficient materials at their disposal. In view of these peculiarities Mons. Burnouf has pronounced the Nepal sacred scriptures to be a barbarous Sanskrit, in which the forms of all ages, Sanskrita, Pali, and Pràkrita, appear to be confounded.* Referring to the difference of language of the different parts of the *Mahàvaipulya* or 'the highly developed-sutras,' the same distinguished Orientalist remarks, that it indicates in the clearest manner, that there was *another digest* besides the compilations of the three great ecumenical convocations of the Buddhists, and that in his opinion the Nepal scriptures comprise a *fourth digest*, which he regards as the crude composition of writers to whom the Sanskrit was no longer familiar, and who endeavoured to write in the learned language they ill understood with the freedom which is imparted by the habitual use of a popular but imperfectly determined dialect. This appears to be exceedingly probable; and, assuming the compilation in the reign of Kanishka to be a fact, there seems to be no reason to doubt, but many circumstances to confirm, the conjecture of Mons. Burnouf—that these sutras were committed to writing out of India in countries on the west of the Indus, or, for example, *Cashmir*,—countries where the learned language of Brahmanism and Buddhism would be cultivated with less success than in Central India. (p. 105.)

Mons. Burnouf's critical observations, and the doubts expressed by Babu Rajendralal, demand a few remarks. In the first place it is necessary to know how the discourses of Buddha were originally written—whether altogether in prose or in verse. They are thus described by Buddhagosa;—

'The whole of the foregoing, comprising in it the nine divisions, are, the *Sûttan*, *Geyyan*, *Weyyàkarana*, *Gàthà*, *Udànan*, *Itivuttakan*, *Jàtakan*, *Abbhûtadhamma* and the *Wedattan*.

---

* L'Histoire du Buddhisme, p. 164.

'The *Sûttan,* be it understood, contains, the two *Vibhangà* and (two) *Niddesà,* the *Khandaka* and *Parivàra,* and in the Suttanipàta, the *Mangala suttan; Ratana suttan, Nàlaka suttan* as well as the *Tuwataka suttan,* and all the other discourses of Tathàgata bearing the signification of *Suttan.*

'Be it understood further, that the *Geyyan* contains every *suttan* composed in Gàthà (metre) together with (its prose portions.) The whole of the Sanguttaka consists throughout of that description (of composition *being Gàthà together with prose.*)

'The *Weyyàkarana,* be it understood, consists of the whole of *Abhidhamma Pitaka,* the *Suttantà* not composed in *Gàthà,* and the words of *Buddha* which are not classified under any of the other eight *Angàni.*

'Be it known the *Gàthà* consists of the *Dhammapadàni Theragàthà, Therigàthà,* and those unmixed (detached) *Gàthà* not comprehended in any of the above named *Suttantà.*

'The *Udànan,* be it known, consists of the eighty two *Sûttantà,* delivered (by Buddha) in the form of hymns of joyous inspiration.

'The *Itiwuttakan,* be it understood, comprises the one hundred and ten *suttantà* which commence with the words, 'It was thus said by Bhagavà.'

'The *Jàtakan,* be it understood, comprises the five hundred and fifty *Jàtakas* (incarnations of Buddha) commencing with the Appanakajàtakan.

'The *Abbhûtadhamma,* be it understood, comprises all the Sûttantà, containing the miracles and wonders, commencing with such expressions as *bhikkhus.* These miraculous and wondrous *dhammà* (powers) are vouchsafed to Ananda.'

'The *Vedattan,* be it understood, consists of the *Chûlavedattan,* the *Mahàwedattan,* the *Sammàdhitthi,* the *Sakkapanhà* the *Sankhàrabhajaniyà* the *Màhàpunnàman,* as well as the whole of those *Suttantà* which have conferred wisdom and joy on those who heard them.'*

The foregoing extract shews that the sacred compilation of the Buddhists, like the compositions of the Brahmanical *Sûtra* period, which is indeed identical with the date of the Buddhist writings, was partly in prose and partly in *Gàthà* or verse; and that some of the suttans are in *Gâthâ* (metre) together with prose. This is a peculiarity in eastern compositions, especially the Pali, to which I wish to invite attention here. Of this the fifth chapter of the Attanagaluwansa presents a complete illustration. Where, indeed, poetry is immediately followed by prose, the latter is intended to express something more than the writer has been enabled to do in verse, owing to the restraints of versification. Again, from the nature of the subjects which are treated of in Gàthàs, it would also seem that poetry was selected for 'joyous hymns,' and also with a view to create a better impression of certain matters than of others, or to render their study easier. This alone, therefore, furnishes no argument against the genuineness of the Nepal works. But the various other traits to which Mons. Burnouf refers, taken in connection with the following extracts from the Dìpàvansa, satisfactorily explain away the difficulties raised by Babu Rajendralal, whilst at the same time they conclusively prove the correctness of the conjecture that the Nepal collection owes its origin to another digest of the Buddhist literature besides those of the three Convocations, or in the words Pr. Benfey, 'it consists of merely translations from Buddhist sources, which were originally composed in Pali.'† The Dipàvansa says:—

* Translated from Buddhagosa's Atthakathà entitled the Sumangala Vilàsini, by the Hon'ble Geo. Turnour, and published in the Bl. A. S. J., vol. vi. p. 526.

† See his Indien, p. 194.

1.—Nikkaddhità pàpa bhikkhù
Therehi Vajji puttakà;
Aññan pakkhan labhitvàna
Adhammavàdi bahù janà;
2.—Dasa sahassà samàgantvà
Akansu dhamma sangahan.
Tasmàyan dhamma sangìtì
Mahà sangìtì vuchchatì.
3.—Mahà sangìtikà bhikkhû
Viloman akansu sàsanan;
Bhinditvà mûla sangahan
Aññan akansu sangahan.
4.—Aññattha sangahìtan suttan
Aññattha akarinsute—
Atthan dhammañcha bhindinsù
Nikàyesu cha panchasù.
5.—Pariyàyadesi tan vàpì
Attho nippariyàya desitan;
Nitatthancheva neyyatthan
Ajànitvàna bhikkhavo.
6.—Aññan sandhàya bhanitan
Aññattha *t*hapayinsute;
Vyanjana chhàyàya te bhikkhú
Bahun atthan vinàsayun.
7.—Chha*dd*etvà eka desancha
Suttan vinaya gambìran;
Patirúpan sutta vinayan
Tantin cha akarinsute.
8.—Parivàran atthuddhàran
Abhidhamman chhappakaranan;
Pa*t*isambhidancha niddesan
Eka desancha Játakan
Etta kan vissajitvàna
Aññan na akarinsute.

9.—Nàma linga parikkhàran
'Akappakaranànicha;
Pakatibhàvan vijahitvà
Tañcha aññan akansute.

10.—Pubbangamà bhinnavàdà
Mahà sangítí kàrakà;
Tesancha anukàrena
Bhinna vàdà bahû ahû.

11.—Tato aparu kàlamhì
Tasmin bhedo ajàyatha;
Gokuliko Ekabbohàrì
Dvidhà bhijjittha bhikkhavo

12.—Gokulikànan dveva bhedà
Apara kàlamhi jàyatha;
Bahussutikà cha Paññattì
Dvidhà bhijjittha bhikkhavo.

13.—Chetiyàcha puna vàdì
Mahà sangìti bhedakà;
Pancha vàdà ime sabbe
Mahà sangìti múlakà.

14.—Atthan dhammancha bhindinsu
Eka desancha sangahan;
Ganthancha eka desanhì
Chha*dd*etvaññan akansute.

15.—Nàmalingan parikkhàran
'Akappakaranànicha;
Pakatibhàvan vijahitvà
Tancha aññan akansute.

16.—Visuddha thera vàdamhì
Puna bhedo ajàyatha;
Mahinsàsakà Vajjiputtà
Dvidhà bhijjittha bhikkhavo.

17.—Vajjiputtaka vàdamhì
Chatudhà bhedo ajàyatha;
Dhammuttarikà Bhadrayànì
Chànnàgàrikàcha Sammitì.
18.—Mahinsakànan dve bhedà
Apara kàlamhi jàyatha;
Sabbatthi vàdà Dhammaguttà
Dvidhà bhijjittha bhikkhavo.
19.—Sabbatthivàda Kassapikà
Kassapikenapi Sankantikà;
Sankantito Suttavàdì
Anupubbena bhijjatha.
20.—Ime ekà dasa vàdà
Pabhinnà thera vàdato,
Atthandhammancha bhindinsu
Eka desancha sangahan;
Ganthan cha eka desamhi
Chha*dd*etvàna akansute.
21.—Nàmalingan parikkhàran
'Akappakaranà nicha;
Pakatibhàvan vijahetvà
Tañcha aññan akansute.*
22.—Sattarasa bhinnavàdà
Eko vàdo abhinnako;
Sabbe va*tt*hà dasa hontì
Bhinnavàdena tesaha.
23.—Nigrodhova mahà rukkho
Therovàdàna muttamo,
Anùnà'n adhikancheva

* It is remarkable that the repetition of an act is conveyed by a repetition of the same stanza—a circumstance which proves the truth of the tradition, that the Dipàvansa was compiled by royal chroniclers, to whom it was assigned as a task.

Kevalan Jina sàsanan;
Kan*t*akà viya rukkhamhì
Nibbuttà vàda sesakà.

24.—Pa*t*hame vassa sate natthì
Dutìye vassa satantare;
Bhinnà sattarasa vàdà
Uppannà Jina Sàsane.

'Many individuals (viz.) ten thousand sinful Vajjian* *bhikkhûs* who had been expelled by the *theras*, assembled together; and, having formed another party, held a council of *Dhamma*. This is thence called *Mahà Sangìti*.

'The bhikkhus who held the *Mahà Sangìti* reduced the religion into confusion,† set aside‡ the first compilation,§ and made another.¶ They placed in different places the *Suttans* which occurred in different other places, and distorted the sense and the words‖ of the five *nikàya*. They did so, ignorant of (the difference between) the general discourses, and those (delivered) on particular occasions, and also (between) their natural and implied significations. They expressed** in a different sense that which was otherwise declared, and set aside various significations under the unwarranted authority (shadow of) words.†† They omitted one portion of the *Suttan*,

* *Vajji*—a portion of Behar in which the Lichchavi Princes were settled. It is however not stated where the Council was held. Doubtless it was at a distance from the principal seat of Government and Buddhism, which at this period was at *Vesàli* or modern Allahabad.

† *Viloman akansu* 'made to bristle,' 'ruffled,' 'crossed,' 'reversed,' 'confused.'

‡ *bhinditvà*—'having broken,' 'split,' 'set aside.'

§ *Sangahan*—from the context I would render this word 'compilation' and not 'rehearsal.' The acts here related, taken in connection with the original import of the word, can only refer to a *written* and not a *mental* collection.

¶ *Akarinsu* 'made,' 'done,' 'effected.' The same word is used in the following sentence, wherein I have rendered it 'placed.'

‖ *Dhamma* here means phraseology of the Scriptures, as opposed to their *attha* 'the sense' or 'import.'

** T*hpayinsu*—'They made to stand.'

†† *Vyanjana* 'letters,' and in some of the Buddhist writings, 'words' or 'sentences.'

and *Vinaya* of deep import, and substituted* (their own) version† of them and the text.‡ They left out the *Parivàran* annotations,§ six books|| of the Abhidhamma, the *Patisambhidà*, the *Niddesa*, and a portion of the *Jàtakas*¶ without replacing any thing in their stead. They, moreover, disregarded** the nature of nouns, their gender, and (other) accidents,†† as well as the (various) requirements of style,‡‡ and corrupted the same by different forms.

'The originators of the Mahà Sangìti were the first seceders. Many followed their example. Since then, there was a breach in that association and the Priests were divided into two sections—the *Gokulika* and *Ekabbohàri*. Subsequently the Gokulikas branched off into two others, viz., *Bahusutikà* and *Paññati*. Subsequently still, there arose a schism (called) the *Chetiya*. Then there were altogether five schisms which had sprung up from the *Mahà Sangìti*—the same which was the first (being a sixth).

---

* *Patirûpa*—placed another figure or 'counterpart.'

† From a comparison of the Ceylon and Nepal Versions of the sacred writings I find the latter has three sections, the *Vaipulya*, the *Nidan*, and the *Upadesa*; all which are additions to the original discourses. Compare the following list taken from *Hodgson's Illustrations*, with the list from Buddhagosa's *atthakathà*, ante p. 61. Hodgson says; The Bauddha scriptures are of twelve kinds known by the following twelve names, 1 Sutra; 2 Geya; 3 *Vyàkarana;* 4 Gàtha; 5 Udan; 6 Nidan; 7 Ityyukta; 8 Jàtaka; 9 Vaipulaya; 10 Adbhuta dharma; 11 Avadan; and 12 Upadesa.'

‡ *Tantin.* The text; see my remarks hereon in the Introduction.

§ *Atthuddhàran* 'explanatory discourses.'

|| *Pakarana* 'compilation,' 'something made methodically,' 'an original composition.'

¶ The version of the Jàtakas in Ceylon is, I believe, deficient.

** 'Akappakarani—also 'decorations, embellishments, niceties of style or composition, or figures of speech.'

†† The peculiarities here noticed, when compared with those of the *Gàthà dialect* of the Nepal Scriptures (See Essay thereon by *Babu Rajendralal Mitra* in the Bl. A. S. J. for 1854, p. 604, et seq.) there can be no doubt of the identity between this *fourth code* of the Buddhists and the Nepal version. The differences of style therein illustrated by Mr. Mittra exactly correspond with the defects of composition here described.

‡‡ *Parikkàran*—'attributes,' 'decorations,' 'accidents.'

'These heretics (also) distorted the sense and the phraseology (of the scriptures); omitted a portion of the (original) compilation, and of the *gàthàs,* and substituted others (in lieu of them). They (further) disregarded the nature of nouns, their gender, and other accidents, as well as the various requisites of style, and corrupted the same by different substitutions.*

'In the doctrines of the orthodox priests there was again a breach (which resulted in the establishment) of two sects called the *Mahìnsaka* and *Vajjiputtà.* From the latter arose four sects, called *Dhammuttarikà, Bhadrayàni, Channàgàrika,* and *Sammiti.* Afterwards, two (more) schisms, the *Sabbatthivàda* and *Dhammagutta* arose out of the *Mahìnsaka;* and from the *Sabbattikà* gradually sprung up the *Kassapikà,* and from the latter the *Sankantika,* and from it the *Saltavàdì* schism. These eleven emanated from the orthodox party.

'They (likewise) made a compilation by distorting the sense, and the phraseology of the sacred discourses; and by omitting a portion of the text and of the *gàthàs.* They too disregarded the forms of nouns, their gender, and other accidents, as well as the various requirements of style, and corrupted the same by different substitutions.

'The schisms of the seceders were (thus) seventeen, the *vàda*† of those who had not seceded, was one; and with it there were altogether eighteen sects.

'Like the great Nigrodha (among) trees, the orthodox discourses alone are supreme among doctrines; and they are moreover the pure (very) word of Buddhà, without retrenchment or addition. The doctrines which have arisen from it are like the thorns of a tree.

---

* "In the Gathà, says Mr. Mittra, we find the old forms of the Sanskrit Grammar gradually losing their impressive power, and prepositions and periphrastic expressions supplying their places, and time-hallowed verbs and conjugations juxtaposed to vulgar slangs and uncouth provincialisms."

† The word *vàda* which we have differently translated at different places to convey *heresy, schism,* &c., means simply as in this place, 'discourse,' 'discussion,' 'demonstrated conclusion,' 'doctrine,' 'principle.'

'There were no (heresies) in the first century (anno Buddhæ) but in the second, seventeen sprung up in the religion of Buddha.'

Whilst the above passage clearly indicates that there were several codes, different from the orthodox version of the sacred writings, which were authenticated at three different convocations; and that the Nepal version is one of those codes; it would also seem that the compilation in question was made,—not in the *Tantra* period above referred to—not in the age of *Kanishka,* but—in the early part of the second century of the Buddhist era.* The difference of style is, however, to be accounted for; and it is easily done. The Nepal version is by one century later than the orthodox version; but it is not stated where the unauthorized council of the heretics was held. Those who originated it being priests, who were 'expelled' and 'degraded,' it may be reasonably inferred that they went out of the *Vajjian* country, which was a part of the Magadha kingdom subject to the Lichchavi princes, and held their *Sangiti* in a distant country, (as it would seem from the writings themselves,†) then subject to the influence of the Brahmans; and M. Burnouf himself, who has examined a portion of the Pali Digha Nikàya and its parallel passage in the Nepal scriptures, thinks, that 'it is quite possible that these two versions may have been nearly contemporaneous in India, and have been current there from the

* I find Prof. Max Muller agrees with me in believing that although the Nepal works have been referred by Oriental Scholars to a much more modern period of Indian Literature, yet it can now safely be ascribed to an ante-Christian era. *Buddhism and Buddhist Pilgrims, p.* 24.

† Some of the Nepal Scriptures appear to be unauthorized additions from a Brahmanical source; and, as remarked by Hodgson, Upadesa treats of the esoteric doctrines equivalent to tantra, the rites and ceremonies being almost identical with those of the Hindoo tantras, but the chief object of worship, different, though many of the inferior ones are the same.—*Hodgson's Illustrations.*

earliest period of Buddhism, before the events occurred which transported them to Ceylon. The Pali version (he adds) would be popular among the inferior castes and the bulk of the people of Magadha and Oude, while the Sanskrit version was used by the Brahmans.*

The Vajjian code was not, therefore, as it was once supposed by M. Burnouf, 'the work of a period when Buddhism ceased to flourish in Hindustan;' and, from the facts stated in the Dìpàvansa, it may fairly be concluded that the anomalies in composition were the result of ignorance, and 'the consequence of haste and inattention,' of Sanskrit and Pali speaking men, who had not a sufficient acquaintance with either for the purposes of compilation, and who therefore amplified the Pali gàthàs with a Sanskrit paraphrase. It may thence also be inferred, that the code which they then compiled was the basis of the subsequent compilation in the reign of *Kanishka*, which has *since travelled* into Nepal, and from thence into Tibet and China. This appears very clear to my mind, from the circumstance that the third Indian compilation of the third century is altogether ignored in the Tibetan writings. For, if it went to Nepal directly after its authentication in the reign of *Kàlasoka*, the Nepalese could not make a mistake as to the name of the *Sovereign*; and, if it was taken upon the termination of the third Convocation, in the reign of Asoka the Great, they were not likely to commit an error as to *date*. And again, if the former were the case, the Nepalese were not likely to know any thing of the Cashmirian code, and could not, on the other hand, fail to know of the Convocation in the reign of Asoka. In other words, the facts of the Nepalese, at no great distance from Hindustan, only recognizing the two Sangìtìs, which were held up to the time of the compilation of

---

* Extracted from Dr. Muir's Sanskrit Texts, p. 75.

the hereties, as recorded in the Dìpàwansa; of their altogether omitting that which took place in the reign of the subsequent Asoka in *Central India;* and of their recording a fourth (as the third) which took place in *the west of India;*—taken in connection with the philological peculiarities already noticed, lead to the inference that the Nepalese did not receive their version until after it had left Hindustan, between the first and fourth centuries, and had travelled on to Cashmire in the reign of Kanishka, when the orthodox doctrines were partly lost, and partly mutilated in Central India.*

The inferences contained in the preceding notes are not altogether without confirmatory proof. The Chinese traveller Hiouenthsang mentions "eighteen sects;" and it is important to bear in mind that one of them is called *Sarvästivadas,* which is clearly the *Sabbattavàda* of the Pali *Dìpàvansa.* The language of the Buddhists, which is called the *Fan,* is the Brahmanical language (the Sanskrit) and not the *Màgadhi,* which we call the *Pali.* For apart from other evidence, such as the existence of a dual number in the language here spoken of, the same word *Fan* is used to designate *Brahmà.* The god Fan (Brahma) and the king of heaven (Indra) established rules and conformed to the times. "Le dieu *Fan* (Brahma) et le roi du ciel (Indra) établirent des règles et se conformèrent au temps."† Although the Chinese have confounded Dharmàsoka with Kalàsoka, yet the time too at which these sectarians flourished, was about the period indicated in the Pali annals, viz., three hundred years after the death of Gotama, when a Kàtyàyana of Sarvastivàda sect is said to have composed a work Abhidharma jñàna Prasthàna.

---

* Vide the discourse of Revata thera in the Mahawansa, p. 251.

† Hiouen-thsang's Travels, by M. Reinaud.

As an exercise for the student, and in support of the facts advanced at p. xxvii., the following extracts are here presented:

1.

MAHA VAGGA.

Tena khopana samayena añña-taro puriso chorikan katvà palàyitvà bhikkhusu pabbajito hoti. Socha ante pure *likhito* hotì—'yattha passitabbo tattha hantabbo' ti. Manussà passitvà evam'ahansu—'ayan so likhitako choro handa nan hanàmà—ti. • Ekachche evam'àhansu—"màyyà evanavachuttha; anuññàtan raññà Màgadhena sàniyena Bimbisàrena, 'ye samanesu Sàkyaputtiyesu pabbajanti na te labbhà kinchi kàtun; Svàkkhàto dhammo, charantu brahmachariyan sammà dukkhassa anta kiriyàyà'"—tì. Manussà ujjhàyanti khìyante vipàchenti—'Abhayuvarà ime samanà Sàkya-puttikà nayime labbhà kinchi kàtun, kathan hi nàma likhita choran pabbàjessantì'—ti. Bhagavato etam' attan àrochesun—'Na bhikkhave likhita choro pabbaje tabbo; yo pabbàjeyya àpatti dukkatassa.'

'At that time a certain person having committed theft, fled, and became a recluse amongst the priests. It was *written** of him at the Royal precincts—'that he shall be punished wherever found.' People who saw him said (to each other) thus—'This is that (*recorded*) proclaimed thief,—let us therefore kill him.' Some said, "Sirs, say not so; it has been decreed by the powerful Bimbisàra king of Magadha,—'If any person be ordained amongst the priests of the Sàkya fraternity, he shall be exempt from all acts (of punishment). (For) the *dhamma* has been well defined by Gotama: (wherefore) let them, with a view to the total extinction of trouble

---

* From the following extract which speaks of a 'leaf pin' or *stile*, it may be inferred that the writing *material* was the Talipot leaf. *Vide infra*, Sà kira pubbe bhikkhunì hutvà panna-sùchiyà saddhin pattkancha padìpiyatelancha datvà jatissarà bhaveyyanti patthanan *t*hapesi—'She having been a female ascetic, and having given a *panna-sùchiya* [a leaf-pin] or stile together with a [blank] book, and also oil for the lamp, aspired to a knowledge of what had transpired in previous births.—*Rasavàhini*, p. 42.

pursue (unmolested) the duties incumbent on Religious students." People thence began to enlarge (upon the subject) and speak contemptuously and disparagingly (of the priesthood, saying)—'These Priests of the Sakya fraternity are fearless—they are exempt from the infliction (of punishment.) But, how is it that they admit into the priesthood a (recorded) proclaimed thief! This, they (the priests) reported to Bhagavà, (who thereupon decreed:) 'Priests no (likhita) proclaimed thief shall be admitted into the Priesthood: if any should do so, he shall commit *dukkuta* or an offence.

II.

Papancha sudani.

(vol. iii. p. 482.)

Majjhima dese kira Ràjagaha nagare Bimbisàre rajjan-kàrente pachchante Takkasilà nagare Pukkusàti rajjan kàresi. Atha Takkasilàto bhan*d*an gahetvà vànijà Ràjagahan àgatà, pannàkàran gahetvà ràjànan addasansu; ràjà te vanditvà *th*ite 'kattha vàsino tumhe'ti puchchhi 'Takkasilà vàsino devà'ti— 'Atha te ràjà janapadassa khemasubhikkhatàdìni nagarassa cha pavattin puchchhitvà 'ko nàma tumhàkan ràjà'ti puchchi'—'Pukkusàti nàma devà'ti—'Dhammiko'ti? àma deva dhammiko chatuhi sangahavatthùhi janan sanganhàti, lokassa màtà-pitu*tt*hàne *th*ito, anke nipanna dàrakan viya janan tosetì-ti. 'Katarasmin vaye vattatìti?'—Athassa vayan àchikkhinsu. Bimbisàrena sama vayo jàto. Atha te ràjà àha 'tàtà tumhàkan ràjà dhammikocha vayenacha me samàno sakkuneyyàtha tumhàkan ràjànan mama mittan kàtun'ti;' 'sakkoma devà-ti.' Ràjà tesan sunkan vissajjetvà gehan dàpetva 'gachchhatha bhan*d*an vikkinitvà gamanakàle man disvà gachchheyyàthà'ti àha. Tathà katvà gamanakàle ràjànan addasansu; ràjà "gachchhatha tumhàkan ràjànan mama vachanena punappuna àrogyan puchchhitvà 'ràjà tumhehi saddhin mittabhàvan ichchhatì'ti vadathàti àha. Te sàdhùti pa*t*isunitvà gantvà bhan*d*an pa*t*isàmetvà bhuttapàtaràsà ràjànan upasankamitvà vandinsu. Ràjà 'kahan *bhane** tumhe ime divase nadissathà'ti puchchi; te sabban pavattin àrochesun Ràjà 'sàdhu tàtà tumhe nissàya mayà majjhima dese ràjà mitto laddhoti attamano ahosi.

Aparabhàge Ràjagaha vàsinopi vànijà Takkasilan agamansu. Te pannàkàran gahetvà àgate Pukkusàti ràjà kuto àgatatthàti puchchhitvà Ràjagahatoti sutvà 'mayhan sahàyassa nagarato àgatà tumhe'ti. àma devàti; 'arogyan me sahàyassà'ti; àrogyan puchchitvà 'ajja pa*tt*hàya mayhan sahayassa nagarato janghasatthena và saka*ta* satthena và vànijà àgachchhanti sabbesan mama visayan pavi*tt*ha kàlato pa*tt*hàya vasanatthànesu gehàni ràja ko*tt*hàgàrato nivàpan dentu sunkan vissajjentu kinchi upaddavan mà karontù'ti bherincharàpesi. Bimbisàropi attano nagare tatheva bherincharàpesi. Atha Bimbisàro Pukkusàtissa *pannan*† pahini, 'Pachchanta dese nàma mani muttàdìni ratanàni uppajjanti, yan mayhan sahayassa rajje dassanìyan và ratanan uppajjati tattha me màmachchharàyatù'ti, Pukkusàtìpi 'Majjhima deso nàma mahà jana pado yan tattha eva rùpan ratanan uppajjati tattha me sahàyo mà machchharàyatù'ti pannan pahini. 'Evan te gachchhante kàle añña maññan adisvà dalha mittà ahesun. Evan tesan kathikan katvà vasantànanva pa*t*hama taran Pukkusàtissa pannàkàro uppajji,—ràjà kira a*tt*ha pancha vanne anaggha kambale labhi, so 'atisundarà ime kambalà sahàyassa me pesissàmì'ti làkhàgulama*tt*e a*tt*ha karandake likhàpetvà tesu te kambale pakkhipitvà làkhàya va*tt*àpetvà, setavatthena ve*t*hetvà samugge pakkhipitvà vatthena ve*t*hetvà ràja muddikàya lanchhetvà 'mayhan sahàyassa dethà'ti amachche pesesi. Sàsananncha adàsi, 'ayan pannàkàro nagaramajjhe amachchàdi parivutena da*tt*habbo'ti. Te gantvà Bimbisàrassa adansu; so sàsanan sutvà amachchàdayo sannipatantùti bherin charàpetvà;

---

* A vocative particle or term of address by a superior to inferiors; or by a King to his subjects.

† Probably a letter written on the Talipot leaf.

nagara majjhe amachchàdi parivuto setachchhattena dhàriyamànena pallanka vare nisinno lanchhan bhinditvà vatthan apanetvà samuggan vivaritvà anto bhan*d*ikan munchitvà làkhàgule disvà, 'mayhan sahàyo Pukkusàti ùna vittako me sahàyoti maññamàno maññe iman pannàkàran pahinì'ti: ekangulan gahetvà hatthena va*tt*etvà tulayanto anto dussa bhan*d*an atthìti aññàsi. Atha nan pallankapàde paharì. Tàvadeva làkhà paripatì; so nakhena karan*d*akan vivaritvà anto kambala ratanan disvà itarepi vivaràpesi: sabbesu kambalà ahesun. Atha ne pasàràpesi, te vanna sampannà phassa sampannà dìghato solasa hatthà tiriyan a*tt*ha hatthà ahesun. Mahà jano disvà anguliyo pho*t*hesi chelukkhepan akàsi 'amhàkan rañño adi*tt*ha sahàyo Pukkusàti adisvàva eva rùpan pannàkàran pesesi;—Yuttan eva rùpan mittan kàtun'ti attamano ahosi. Ràjà eka mekan kambalan agghàpesi, sabbe anagghà ahesun. Tesu chattàro sammà sambuddhassa pesitvà chattàro attano ghare akàsi. Tato chintesi pachchhà pesentena pa*t*haman pesita pannàkàrato atirekan pesitun va*tt*ati; sahàyena cha me anaggho pannàkàro pesito, kinnukho pesemìti kinpana Ràjagahe tato adhikan ratanan natthì'ti. No natthi, mahà puñño ràjà api kho panassa sotàpanna kàlato pa*tt*hàya *t*hapetvà tìni ratanàni aññan ratanan somanassan janetun samatthan nàma natthì. So ratanan vichinitun àraddho. Ratanan nàma saviññànakan aviññànakanti duvidhan tattha aviññànakan suvanna rajatàdi saviññànakan indriya baddhan. Aviññànakan saviññànakasseva alankàràdi vasena paribhogan hoti, iti imesu dvìsu ratanesu saviññànakan se*tt*han. Saviññànakampi duvidhan tirachchhàna gata ratanan manussa ratananti, tattha tirachchhàna gatan hatthi assàdi tampi manussànan upabhogattha meva nibbattati. Iti imesu dvìsu manussaratanan se*tt*han. Manussa ratanampi duvidhan, itthi ratanan purisa ratananti, tattha chakkavatti rañño uppanna itthi ratanampi purisasseva upabhoggan; iti imesu dvìsu purisa ratana meva se*tt*han. Purisa ratanampi duvidhan, agàriya ratanan anagàriya ratanancha; tattha agàriya ratane apichakkavatti ràjà ajjapabbajita sàmaneran panchapati*tt*hitena vandati, iti imesu dvìsu anagàriya ratanam'eva se*tt*han. Anagàriya ratanampi duvidhan sekha ratanan asekha ratanancha, tattha sata sahassampi sekhànan asekhassa padesan napàpunàti iti imesu dvìsu asekharatana'meva se*tt*han. Tampi duvidhan Buddha ratanan sàvaka ratananti; tattha sata sahassampi sàvaka ratanànan Buddha ratanassa padesan napàpunàti, iti imesu dvìsu Buddha ratana meva se*tt*han. Buddha ratanampi duvidhan, pachcheka buddha ratanan sabbaññu buddha ratananti: tattha sata sahassampi pachcheka buddhànan sabbaññu buddhassa padesan na pàpunàti, iti imesu dvìsu sabbaññu buddha ratanan yeva se*tt*han. Sadeva kasmin hi loke buddha ratana saman ratanan nàma natthi, tasmà asadisameva ratanan mayhan sahàyassa pesessàmìti chintetvà Takkasila vàsino puchchi, 'tàtà tumhàkan janapade buddho dhammo sangho-ti imàni tìni ratanàni dissantì-ti,' 'ghosopi so mahà ràja tattha natthi dassanan pana kuto-ti. Sundaran tàtàti, ràjà tu*tt*ho chintesi—' Sakkà bhaveyya jana sanga-hatthàya mayhan sahàyassa vasanatthànan sammà sambuddhan pesetun. Buddhà pana pachchantimesu jana padesu na arunan u*tt*hapenti, tasmà satthàrà gantun nasakkà, Sàriputta Moggallànàdayo mahà sàvake pesetun sakkà bhaveyya, mayà pana therà pachchante vasantìti sutvàpi manusse pesetvà te attano samìpan ànàpetvà upa*tt*hàtu meva yuttan, tasmà therehipi nasakkà gantun; yena pan'àkàrena sàsane pesite satthàcha mahà sàvakàcha gatàviya hont', tenà kàrena sàsanan pahinissàmì'ti chintetvà chaturatan'àyàman vidatthi matta puthulan nàti tanu nàti bahalan suvanna pa*tt*an kàràpetvà tattha ajja akkharàni likhissàmìti pàtova sìsan nahàyitvà uposathangàni adhi*tt*hàya bhuttapàtaràso apanìta gandha màlàbharano suvanna sarakena jàti hingulakan* àdàya he*tt*hato pa*tt*hàya dvàràni pidahanto pàsàdan àruyha disàmukhan sìha-

* Vermilion used as a writing material.

panjaran vivaritvà àkàsa tale nisìditvà suvanna pa*tt*e akkharàni likhanto: 'Idha Tathàgato loke uppanno arahan sammà sambuddho vijjà charana sampanno sugato loka vidù anuttaro purisa damma sàrathi satthà deva manussànan buddho bhagavà'ti; buddhagune tàva eka pade sena likhi. Tato evan dasa pàramiyo pùretvà Tusita bhavanato chavitvà màtu kuchchhismin pa*t*isandhimganhi; evan loka vivaranan ahosi; màtu kuchchhiyan vasamàne idan nàma ahosi; agàra majjhe vasamàne idan nàma; evan mahà bhinikkhamanan nikkhanto; evan mahà padhànan padahi; evan dukkara kàrikan katvà mahà bodhi man*d*an àruyha aparàjita pallanke nisinno sabbaññuta ñànan pa*t*ivijjhi; sabbaññutan pativijjhantassa evan loka vivaranan ahosi; sadevake loke aññan eva rùpan ratanan nàma natthì-ti.

Yankinchi vittan idhavà huranvà
Saggesu và yan ratanan panìtan
Nano saman atthi Tathàgatena
Idampi buddhe ratanan panìtan
Etena sachchena suvatthi hotu—

Evan eka desena buddha gune likhitvà, dutiyan dhamma ratanan thomento, 'svàkkhàto bhagavatà dhammo sandi*tt*hiko akàliko ehipassiko opanaiko pachchattan veditabbo viññùhi,' chattàro satipa*tt*hànà chattàro sammappadhànà, chattàro iddhi pàdà panchindriyàni panchabalàni satta bojjhangà ariyo a*t*-*t*hangiko maggoti satthàrà desita dhammo nàma evarùpocha eva rùpochàti sattatinsa bodhapakkhiye eka desena likhitvà;

Yam buddha se*tt*ho parivannayì suchin
Samàdhimà'nan tarikaññamàhu
Samàdhinà tena samù navijjatì
Idampi dhamme ratanan panìtan
Etena sachchena suvatthi hotu—

Evan eka desena dhamma gune likhi. Tato tatiyan sangha ratanan thomento 'supa*t*ipanno bhagavato sàvaka sangho ujupa*t*ipanno bhagavato sàvaka sangho ñàyapa*t*ipanno bhagavato sàvaka sangho sàmìchipa*t*ipanno bhagavato sàvaka sangho yadidan chattàri purisa yugàni a*tt*ha purisa puggalà esa bhagavato sàvaka sangho àhuneyyo pàhuneyyo dakkhineyyo anjalikaranìyo anuttaran puññakkhettan lokassa,'—kulaputtà nàma satthu dhamma kathan sutvà evan nikkhamitvà pabbajantì, kechi setachchhattan pahàya pabbajanti, kechi uparajjan; kechi senàpati*tt*hànàdìni pahàya pabbajanti, pabbajitvà pana imancha pa*t*ipattin pùrentìti chulla sìla majjhima sìla mahà sìlàdìni eka desena likhitvà chhadvàra sanvaran satisampajaññan chatupachchayasantosan navavidha senàsanan nìvaranappahàna parikam-majjhànàbhiññà a*tt*huppattin kamma*tt*hànàni yàva àsavakkhayà eka desena likhi. Solasakkhattukan ànàpàna sati kamma*tt*hànà vitthàreneva likhitvà satthu sàvaka sangho nàma eva rùpehi cha gunehi samannàgato;

Ye puggalà a*tt*ha satan* pasatthà
Chattàri etàni yugàni hontì
Te dakkhineyyà sugatassa sàvakà
Etesu dinnàni mahapphalàni
Idampi sanghe ratanan panìtan
Etena sachchena suvatthi hotu—

Eka desena sangha gune likhitvà 'bhagavato sàsanan svàkkhàtan nìyyànikan sache mayhan sahàyo sakkoti nikkhamitvà pabbajatù'ti--likhitvà suvanna pa*tt*an sanharitvà sukhuma kambalena ve*t*hetvà sàra samugge pakkhipitvà tan samuggan suvanna samugge suvannamayan rajatamaye rajatamayan manimaye† manimayan pavàlamaye‡ pavàlamayan lohitankamaye§ lohitankamayan masàragallamaye‖ masàra gallamayan phalikamaye¶ phalikamayan dantamaye** dantamayan sabba ratanamaye sabba ratanamayan kilanjamaye kilanjamayan samuggan sàrakaran*d*e *t*hapesì. Puna sàraka-

---

* *Attha satan* is also defined as 108.

† This is probably glass. ‡ coral. § ruby. ‖ emerald. ¶ crystal. ** lit. teeth—ivory.

ran*d*akan suvanna karan*d*ake ti purimanayeneva haritvà, sabba ratana maya karan*d*akan kilanjamaye karan*d*ake *t*hapesi. Tato kilanjamayan sàramaye pelàyà'ti; puna vuttanayeneva haritvà sabba ratanamayapelan kilanjamayapelàya *t*hapetvà bahi vatthe nivàsetvà ràjamuddikàya lanchhetvà amachche ànàpesi: 'Mama ànà pavattita*tt*hàne maggan alankàràpetha maggo a*tt*hùsabha vitthato hotu, chatùsabha*tt*hànan sodhita mattakameva hotu majjhe chatùsabhan ràjànubhàvena pa*t*iyàdethàti. Tato mangala hatthin alankàràpetvà tassa upari pallankan paññàpetvà setachchhattan ussàpetvà nagara vìthiyo sitta samma*tt*hà samussitadhaja-patàka-kadali-punnaghata-gandha-dhùpa-pupphà-dìhi-supari-man*d*ità kàretvà, attano attano visayappadese eva rùpan pùjan karontùti, antara bhogikànan javana dùte pesetvà sayan sabbàkàrena alankaritvà sabba tàlàvachara-sammissa-balakàya-parivuto pannàkàran pesemìti attano visaya pariyantan gantvà amachchassa mukhasàsanan adàsì; 'tàta mayham sahàyo Pukkusàti iman pannàkàran pa*t*ichchhanto orodhà majjhe apa*t*ichchhitvà pàsàdan àruyha pa*t*ichchhatù'ti. Evan sàsanan datvà pachchanta desan satthà gachchhatìti panchapati*tt*hitena vanditvà nivatti. Antara bhogì teneva niyàmena maggan patiyàdetvà pannàkàran nayinsù. Pukkusàtipi attano rajjasìmato pa*tt*hàya teneva niyàmena maggan patiàdetva nagaran alankàràpetvà pannàkàrassa pachchuggamanan akàsì. Pannàkàro Takkasilan pàpunanto uposatha-divase pàpuni pannàkàran gahetvà gata amachchopi raññà vutta sàsanan àrochesi ràjà tan sutvà pannàkàrena saddhin àgatànan kattabba-kichchan vichàretvà pannàkàran àdàya pàsàdan àruyha 'mà idha kochi pàvisì'ti dvàra-rakkhan kàretvà sìhapanjaran vivaritvà pannàkàran uchchàsane *t*hapetvà sayan nìchàsane nisinno lanchanan chhinditvà vàsan apanetvà kilanja pelato pa*tt*hàya anupubbena vivaranto sàramaya samuggan disvà chintesì. 'Mahà parihàro nàyan aññassa ratanassa bhavissatì addhà majjhima dese sotabbayuttakan ratanan uppannan'ti. Athanan samuggan vivaritvà ràja lanchhanan bhinditvà sukhuma-kambalan ubhato viyùhitvà suvanna pa*tt*an addasa. So tan pasàritvà 'manàpàni vata akkharàni samasìsàni samapantìni chaturassànìtì àdito pa*tt*hàya vàchetun àrabhi; tassa idha Tathàgato loke uppannoti buddhagune vàchentassa balava somanassan uppajji. Nava navuti loma kùpa sahassàni uddhaggalomàni ahesun. Attano *t*hitabhàvan và nisinna bhàvan và najànàti: athassa kappako*t*i-sata-sahassehipi evan dullabha sàsanan sahàyan nissàya sotun labhintì bhìyo balavapìti udapàdì. So upari vàchetun asakkonto yàva pìtivegapassaddhiyà nisìditvà parato 'svàkkhàto bhagavatà dhammo'ti dhamma gune àrabhì. Tatràpissa tatheva ahosi; so puna yàva pìtivegapassaddiyà nisìditvà parato 'supa*t*ipanno-ti' sangha gune àrabhì. Tatràpissa tatheva ahosi. Atha sabba pariyante ànàpàna satikamma*tt*hànan vàchetvà chatukka panchaka jhànàni nibbattesi. So jhàna sukheneva vìtinàmeti añño kochi da*tt*hun nalabati, ekova chullupa*tt*hàko pavisati evan a*dd*hamàsa mattan vìtinàmesi.

'Whilst Bìmbisàra was ruling in the city of Ràjaghà in the *Majjhimadesa,** Pukkusàti was reigning in the city of Takkasilà in the foreign regions. At this time some Traders with merchandize from Takkasilà† entered Ràjagaha, and, taking along with them presents, saw the king. He inquired of those, who stood rendering obeisance—'of what country are you?' 'We, please your Majesty, (replied they) are residents of Takkasilà.' Thereupon the king, having ques-

---

* This is the *Maddhyadesa* of Sanskrit writers—'the middle country' as distinguished from the *Dakkhinà* or the Dekhan on the south, and the *Hìmavanta* or the 'snowy region' in the Himalaya. The Hindus describe 'the celebrated Maddhya desa' to be—

Himavad Vindhyayormadhyan
Yat pràg Vinasanà dapi—*Manu.*

'that which lies midway between Himavad and Vindhya, to the east of Vinàsa, and to the west of Prayàga.' But see note at p. xxix.

† A collegiate city of great renown in the North-west of *Majjhima.*

tioned them on the affairs of (their) city, and the prosperous condition, and the favorableness, of the seasons of the country—asked 'what is the name of (your) Sovereign?' 'Sire, *Pukkusàti* (is his) name.' 'Is he virtuous?' demanded the king. 'Yes, your Majesty,' replied they; 'he is virtuous—he pleases the people with the four *Sanghavatthu*,*—occupies the position of a parent† to the world—and, like a suckling on the lap, pleases men.' 'What is his age?' They then stated his age. He was as old as Bimbisàra. Thereupon the king addressed them (and said,) 'Sons, your king is virtuous (like me), and in age too, he is equal to me; can you make your king a friend of mine?' 'We can, Sire,' replied they; (when) the king remitted their taxes, gave them a house, and said to them 'Go, and sell your merchandize; and at the time of departure you shall see me.' When all this had been accomplished, they visited the king at the time of their departure;—and the king said to them, 'Go; and, after repeated inquiry as to the health of your king in my name,‡ say to him, 'the king is desirous of your friendship.' They, (the merchants,) expressed their assent, went their way, arranged their goods, took their morning-meal,‖ and having approached their king, accosted him. The king said to them, 'Men, where (were you)? You were not seen for these (many) days.' They related all the (foregoing) matters; (to the king), when he, greatly delighted, said; 'Sons, Sàdhu! On your account I have obtained a friend (in the person of) the king of the *Majjhima desa*.'

Sometime after (some other) traders, who were residents of Ràjagaha, went to *Takkasilà*. King Pukkusàti, before whom

* The *Sangahavotthu* are the four pre-eminent virtues of kings, viz.—*dàna* 'gifts—liberality;' piya vachana 'pleasing conversation;' *attha chariyà* 'fruitful conduct—well being in law;' and *Samànatthatà* 'regarding all as one's self.'

† Lit. 'father and mother.'

‡ Lit. *mama vachanèna* 'in my language'—'in my name.'

‖ This is a bahuvrìhi compound—*bhutta pàta ràsà*. 'they-who-ate-the-food-of-early-dawn:' 'took their breakfast.'

they appeared with offerings, inquired of them from whence they had come; and, when he heard they had come from Ràjagaha, he asked them, 'Have you come from the capital of my friend?' 'Yes, your Majesty,' replied the traders. 'Is my friend in health?' demanded the Prince. Having made that inquiry the king caused to be proclaimed, by beat of drums, that 'from this day whenever traders come (hither) from the city of my friend, either with caravans of beasts, or caravans of waggons, they shall all be provided with habitations in their respective localities, and with batta from the Royal Stores from the period of their entrance into my kingdom,—that they shall also be exempted from taxes,—and that in no wise shall they be oppressed.' Bimbisàra also caused a similar proclamation in his own city. Thereafter Bimbisàra sent a leaf* to Pukkusàti to the effect, that 'precious articles such as gems, pearls, etc., are produced in the *Pachchanta*† regions. Should there be anything valuable or worth seeing in my friend's kingdom; withhold it not from me.' Pukkusàti, in like manner, forwarded a leaf to the effect, that 'the Majjhimadesa is a great country. If similar precious things are produced in it, my friend (too) should not withhold it from me.' Thus these (two) for a length of time were intimate friends without seeing each other. Of these, who had (thus) entered into terms, Pukkusàti first came by a (suitable) object for a present, that is to say;—he received eight invaluable blankets of five colours; and, thinking 'these blankets are beautiful, I shall send them to my friend'—caused eight (round) caskets to be turned, and lackered. Having deposited the blankets therein, (they were) secured round the lid with lacker. They were (then) wrapped in white cloth, and deposited in a chest, which being also covered with

* Doubtless, the Talipot leaf is meant.

† Lit. 'the barbarous—wild—unenlightened;' but here the foreign regions are meant; See ante, p. xxix.

cloth, was (stamped) sealed with the king's signet. (This done) he sent Ministers, saying, 'Give this to my friend.' A missive too, was given to the effect, that 'this present is worthy the (inspection) acceptance of him who is surrounded by Ministers in the midst of the city.'

They (the ministers) accordingly went and delivered it to Bimbisàra, who, having heard (its contents), caused by beat of drum, the ministers, etc., to be assembled. Surrounded by them, and seated on the royal* couch, under the uplifted white state-canopy, in the midst of the capital, he broke the seal, removed the wrapper,† opened the box, and released (untied) its contents; and, when he had seen the round lackered (caskets), he reflected—'my friend Pukkusàti has sent this present under the impression that his friend was (wealthless) poor.' He then took up a casket; and, feeling its weight with his hand, ascertained that it contained an article of raiment; he struck it on a pedestal of the couch, when the lacker (with which it had been seamed) dropped down. When he had opened a casket with (his) nail, he saw that it contained a valuable blanket, and caused the others also to be opened. There were blankets in all when spread, they were beautiful in colour, and soft to the touch; and they were sixteen cubits in length, and eight in width.

The multitude, seeing this, snapped their fingers, waived their garments round their heads; and, highly delighted, exclaimed, 'Pukkusàti, the unseen friend of our king, has sent such a present even without seeing him. Such a personage is indeed worthy of being made a friend.'

The king caused every one of the blankets to be appraised; and they were all found invaluable. Of these he sent four to Buddha, and kept for himself‡ four; and reflected—'One

---

* Lit. vare 'best, excellent.'
† Lit. 'cloth.'
‡ Lit. 'in his own house.'

who returns, should send a better gift than the first. An invaluable present has been sent by my friend. What shall I send (him)? What! Is there nothing more valuable in Ràjagaha? Yes, there is.* Though the king is fortunate (in precious things,) yet from the time he entered the path of *Sotàpanna*† no precious thing, save *the three Ratanas*,‡ was calculated to produce delight (to him.) He (however) commenced to find out some precious thing. A *Ratana* or precious thing, is two-fold—*Saviññàna* and *Aviññàna*.§ The latter (comprises such things) as gold, silver, etc.; and the former is that which is associated with the senses. The one (aviññàna), as an (article of) adornment, contributes to the enjoyment of the other, (Saviññàna.) Thus from among these two ratanas, Saviññànaka is chief. Saviññànaka are also two-fold, viz., *Brutes* and *Men*. Brutes are (such as) elephants, horses, etc.; and the same exist for the very enjoyment of man. Of these two, therefore, *man* is the chief ratana. The estimable man is also two-fold; that is to say, *male* and *female*. Here too, the female, though born for a universal monarch, is for the enjoyment of the male. Thus of these two also, the very male is the chief. The estimable male is also two-fold—the layman and the recluse. Here again as to the layman, though he be a universal monarch, he makes the five-membered‖ obeisance to even a *Sàmanera* of a single day's standing. Thus, of these two also, the very *Recluse* is the chief. The estimable Recluse is also two-fold—*Sèka* and *Asèka* (viz., he who has entered the paths, and he who has

---

* *No natthi*—'*not*, that there is *not*.' A double negative to intensify the affirmative. See Sakuntalà, pp. 110, and 24, note 1.

† Lit. 'entrance into the stream'—'fallen into the path,' that which is the first stage of sanctification, leading to final bliss.

‡ The three gems; the most inestimable things—objects as precious as *ratana* or 'gems'—Jàtau jàtau yad utkrishtam taddhi ratnam prachakshate, 'whatever is best of its kind, that indeed they call *ratna*.' Hence 'the three gems' is an expression for 'the triad of Buddhism.'

§ See Gogerly's Essay, in the Friend, vol. ii. 67.

‖ See my Essay on modes of Address, in C. B. A. S. J., for 1856—8.

reached the end of the paths). Of these a hundred thousand of the first cannot equal the least part of one of the latter. Thus of these, Asèka is supreme. He is also two-fold—*Buddha* and *Sàvaka*.* Of these, a hundred thousand of the Sàvakàs cannot equal the least part (atom) of Buddha. Thus, of these the very Buddha is supreme. The inestimable Buddha is again two-fold—*Pachcheka* Buddha, and *all-perfect* Buddha. Here too, a hundred thousand Pachcheka Buddhas cannot equal the least part of the all-perfect Buddha. Thus of these two, the all-perfect Buddha is alone supreme. In the world, including (that of) the devas, there is no estimable object (ratana) equal to Buddha.

Wherefore (the king) resolving, that 'he would send to his friend this very *incomparable ratana*,' asked of the inhabitants of *Takkasilà*, 'Sons, are there to be seen in your country the three most inestimable objects, *Buddha, Dhamma*, and *Sangha*?' They replied 'the very names are not known; † how (therefore) can they be seen?' Saying, 'Sons, very good,' the king with pleasure thus pondered: 'Is it possible, with a view to the people's propitiation, to send Buddha to the residence of my friend? But, Buddhas never remain till the dawn, in the most distant foreign countries. Gotama cannot, therefore, go. The great disciples, such as Sàriputta, Moggallàna, etc., cannot be sent: and, since it is my duty, on hearing that priests resided in a foreign country, to send for them hither, and to pay attentions to them; (other) priests also cannot go. Since, however, a missive sent (on the dhamma) is the same as if Buddha and his chief disciples proceeded thither, I shall send a letter.' Thus pondering, he caused to be made a plate of gold, four cubits long, and about a span wide, and neither very thick, nor very thin. Thinking that he would write the letter that very morning, he went through his bath,‡

* Lit. 'hearer'—'pupil.'

† Lit. 'there is not even that sound.'

‡ Lit. 'washed his head.'

made the *Uposatha* vows;* took his breakfast, and divested himself of all scents, flowers, and ornaments. Then taking real vermilion into a gold dish, he closed all the doors below, and entered his palace; and, moreover, opening the casements facing the cardinal points, he sat upon the upper-most story,† and wrote‡ on the gold leaf as follows:

"Tathàgata has appeared in this world. He is *(Arahan,)* a highly sanctified Saint. He is supreme Buddha. He is endowed with both *Vijjà* and *Charana.*§ He is (*Sugata*) one who has attained beatitude. He is fully acquainted with the world. He is the best charioteer (who is able to subjugate) men. He is the teacher of gods and men. He is Buddhà, or perfect intelligence. He is worthy of adoration.' These attributes of Buddha were first written on a small portion;—and (he then described how) having perfected the ten *pàramitàs*, or pre-eminent duties, he was born in *Tosita*, and was conceived in his mother's womb; how that event contributed to the world's emancipation;‖ what happened when he was yet unborn; what took place when he was a householder; how he departed forsaking the world; how he greatly exerted; how, having accomplished difficult acts, and having ascended the region of the *Bodhi*,** and having sat upon his unconquerable seat, he attained to the wisdom of *Omniscience;* how (such a result) contributed to the prosperity of the world; and that such another supreme being was not in all the universe, including the heavens—'*Yankinchi, &c.*

"Whatever wealth, or whatever most desirable object there may be in this life, or in that which is to come, or in the heavens—the same is not to be compared to Tathàgata. This

---

* These are the 'A*tth*angasìla.'
† àkàsa tale—'story nearest the sky.'
‡ Akkharàni likhanto, lit. 'writing letters.'
§ See explanation of this at p. xxxiv.
‖ Loka vivaranan.
** *Ficus religiosa*, the tree under which Gotama became Buddha.

too is a highly distinguishing characteristic of Buddha. By the power of this truth, may there be prosperity!"

Having thus briefly recorded the virtues of Buddha; the inestimable *dhamma* was secondly lauded as follows—'The *dhamma* is well defined by Bhagavà. It is attended with results immediate, and without lapse of time. It is inviting.* It is full of import. It should be acquired individually by the wise.' This done, a condensed account of the *Sattatinsa bodhapakkhiya*† delivered by Buddha were given to the effect, that they were the four *Satipatthànà*, the four *Sammappadhànà*, the four *iddhipàdà*, the five *indriya*, the five *bala*, the seven *bojjhangà*, and the eight-bodied supreme *magga.*—"*Yam buddha, &c.*

'Is there a pure thing which the supreme Buddha has enlarged upon; (or in other words, is there) any *Samàdhi*, which has been declared (to be productive of) immediate reward; with that *Samàdhi*‡ nothing can be compared. This too, is a distinguishing characteristic of the *word.*§ By the power of this truth, may there be prosperity!'

Thus briefly he wrote the character of *dhamma*; and then, thirdly, praised the inestimable *Sangha* as follows: 'The association of Bhagava's disciples‖ are well conducted. They live uprightly, prudently, and peaceably. They are (classed collectively into) four pairs; or eight individuals.¶ They are fit objects of charity, are deserving of hospitality, and are worthy of being offered unto. They (stand) to men (in the place of) a merit-productive-field.' This done he briefly wrote that respectable people who had heard the discourses

* Ehipassiko, lit. that which bids, 'come and see'—it is inviting—not hidden.

† The thirty-seven Elements of Buddhism, for an explanation of them see my *Attanagaluvansa*, note to Chap. iv. § 7.

‡ The act of confining one's mind to the contemplation of doing good.

§ The *dhamma*—'doctrines'—'the word.'

‖ The words *bhagavato sàvaka sanghò* are repeated after every phrase.

¶ See note at p. 78.

of Buddha, departed and embraced ascetism; that some did so after abandoning thrones;*—some after leaving (the high dignity of a) sub-king; and others (that of) General Commander of the Forces; and that when they had so embraced *ascetism*, they purused the prescribed duties of *chulla-sila*, *majjhima sila*, and *mahà-sila*, etc.† He also gave a brief account of the (religious observances, commencing from) *chhadvàra sanvaran*; *sati-sampajañña*; the four *pachchaya santosa*; the nine kinds of *senàsana*; and *nivaranappahàna*; together with the (prescribed) *kammatthànàni*, and the results of *parikamma*, *jhàna*, and *abhiññà*, until the extinction of distress. Having then amplified on the sixteen-fold *ànà pàna sati kammatthàna*,‡ he wrote that the Society of Buddha's disciples were also endowed with virtues like the following:—"*Ye putgalà, etc.*"

---

* Sétachchhattan—'the white umbrella;' 'the state canopy.'

† For an exposition of these duties, see the Brahmajàla suttan, translated by the Rev. D. J. Gogerly, in C. B. A. S. Journal, ii. p. 22 et seq.

‡ Some of the theological terms in the above passage, require a brief explanation. *Chhadvàra Sanvara*,—'the closing of six avenues;' 'the subjugation of six organs of sensation,' which lead to the commission of sin. *Satisampajañña*—'memory,-discretion,' 'a memorial retention of that which is ascertained by wisdom.' *Pachchaya santosa*—'contentment with the *pachchaya*,' or the requirements of an ascetic, which are four in number, viz., robes, food, habitation, and medicine. *Senàsana*—'habitations,' of which there are nine kinds adapted to the recluse. *Nivaranappahana* 'destruction of that which screens;' 'overcoming the obstacles against the leading of a religious life,' which are stated to be five, viz., 1. lust, 2. evil design, 3. apathetic indifference, 4. perturbation of the mind arising from irresolution and pride, and 5. doubt upon eight religious matters,—viz. Buddha, Dhamma, Sangha, a previous state of being, a future existence, a past-and-future state of being, the causes of continued-existence [see Ceylon Friend for 1839], and vacillation and doubt upon all matters. *Kammatthàni*—forty courses of religious action, such as devout meditation, etc. *Parikamma*, an initiatory rite of ascetism, which ought to be completed before the entrance upon *dhyàna*. It is the fixing of the mind upon one of the four elements, earth, air, fire and water, so as to impress it with the reality of the substance on which the recluse contemplates; and also the continuing to address the element repeating its name (See extract, ante p. xxii.) until the mind attains that degree of absorption, which disables the sentient faculties from discerning any other subject. *Dhyàna* is 'abstract meditation,' of which there are four degrees, each of which being considered a sanctified state or path to *nibban*, or the extinction of existence. *ànàpàna sati kammatthàna*; also sixteen modes of devout and abstract meditation by means of drawing the breath etc. See *Gunànanda Suttan*.

"Are there eight beings who have been praised by the holy, they are four couples, and are the disciples of Buddha, worthy of being offered unto. Whatever is given unto them is productive of much fruit. This too is a distinguishing characteristic of the clergy. By the power of this truth may there be prosperity!"

Having thus briefly stated the virtues of the *Sangha*, and written to the effect—that 'the religion of Buddha is well defined—it is very pure. If my friend can, let him abdicate (secular concerns) and embrace ascetism;'—he folded the gold plate, wrapped it with a soft blanket, and put it in a wooden casket. It was again deposited in a gold casket, that in a silver casket, that in a gem-set casket, that in a coral casket, that in a ruby casket, that in an emerald casket, that in a crystal casket, that in a casket made of ivory, that in another made of all sorts of gems, that in another made of mat, and that again in a wooden box. Again, the wooden box was deposited in a gold box, and that [in other boxes] according to the order above indicated, [until you come to] a box set with all sorts of gems—and that in a mat-box. This box was again deposited in a wooden chest, and the same in others in the order above indicated [until you come to] a chest set with all sorts of gems—and that again in a mat-chest. The same being then covered with cloth, and sealed with the signet of the king, he gave [the following] orders to his Ministers: 'Adorn the path within the limits of my city. Let that path be eight *usabha** in width; of which four need only be cleared. But the middle four *usabha* should be prepared (in a manner) befitting royalty.'

Thereafter (the king) caused his royal elephant to be adorned, and to place a chair upon him, and to set (over it) the white canopy of state. He also caused the streets in

* A measure of seventy yards. See *Abhidhánapadipiká*, p. 23.

the city to be purified (and cleaned) by being sprinkled (with water) and swept;—(lined) with flags and banners, plantain trees, and water vessels;* and (scented) with incense, flowers, &c. He caused running messengers to be sent to the intermediate dwellers† bidding them hold a festival as directed, within the limits of their respective abodes. Being adorned (himself) completely, and escorted by his forces, including the band of musicians, and with a view to the transmission of his gift, the king proceeded to the limits of his city, and addressed his Minister: 'Son, let not my friend Pukkusàti, in accepting this gift, receive it in the midst of his wives; but let him do so after entering his (own) palace.' So saying, and making the five-membered‡ obeisance, under the reflection that Buddha (himself) proceeded to the foreign regions, the king returned home. The intermediate dwellers prepared the way as they were bidden, and caused the progressive conveyance of the gift.

Pukkusàti observing the same formalities (which were above described) prepared the way from the limits of his rule, decorated the city, and went to meet the gift. The same reached Takkasilà on the day of *Upòsatha.*§ The minister, who was the bearer of the present, delivered the king's message. When the king had heard it he paid the necessary attentions to those who accompanied the present, ascended the palace with it, and placed a sentry at the door with orders that none should enter the palace. [This done], he opened the casement, placed the present upon a high seat, and he himself sat upon a low one. He [then] broke the seal, removed the cloth [covering], and opening each gradually from the mat chest to the wooden casket, reflected thus:—

---

* Jars or vases filled with flowers, and water.

† Residents between the two states.

‡ See my Essay on Titles of Address in the C. B. R. A. S. 1856—8. p. 261.

§ The Sabbath of the Buddhists, which is the day of the full moon, &c.

'There is nothing remarkable in this. It is (perhaps) the receptacle of a precious thing. Doubtless there has arisen in the Majjhima-desa a ratana worthy of being heard.' Thereafter he opened the casket, broke the royal seal, and, disengaging the soft blanket, saw the gold plate. When he had unfolded it, he (observed) that the characters were indeed pretty, that they were exact in (the formation) of their heads, that they were *quadrangular,** and that the lines were all uniform; and commenced to read it from the beginning. Great was his joy on reading that *Tathàgata* had appeared in the world, and of his character. The ninety-nine thousand hairs of the body stood on end in their sockets. He became unconscious as to whether he stood or sat.† Profound was his joy to reflect that he had on account of his friend, heard of the religion which it was difficult to attain even in a hundred thousand kòti of kalpas.‡ He was (thence) unable to [proceed with the] perusal [of the missive,] and therefore sat§ down; and, when his excited feelings had subsided, he resumed to read the characteristics of *dhamma,* [commencing with] *svakkhàto bhagavatà dhammò etc.* Here also the king became [intoxicated with joy] as before; and [therefore] paused (for a while): and when his excitement had again subsided, he returned to the letter, reading the characteristics of the *Sangha,* commencing from *Supatipanna, etc.* Again the king became excited as before. At last having read the *ànàpàna satikammatthànan* at the very end [of the letter] he entered upon the four and five-fold *jhànas.*‖ He (the king) was thus spending his entire time in the enjoyment of the *jhàna;* and no one was able to see him, except it were a young page who entered (his apartment.) In this manner he spent half-a month.

---

* This proves the character to have been the Nàgarí; See p. cxv.
† 'Whether he stood on his head, or his feet.'
‡ See Glossary to the Mahavansa for an explanation of these terms.
§ Paused for a while.
‖ See Hardy's Eastern Monachism, p. 253.

III.
MAHA VAGGA.

Tena kho pana samayena àyasmà mahà Kachchàyano Avantìsu viharati Kuraraghare papàte pabbate. Tena kho pana samayena Sono upàsako ku*t*ikanno àyasmato mahà Kachchàyanassa upa*tth*àko hoti: atha kho Sono upàsako Ku*t*ikanno yenà-yasmà mahà Kachchàyano tenupasankami, upasankamitvà àyasmantan mahà Kachchàyanan abhivàdetvà ekamantan nisìdi. Eka mantan nisinno kho Sono upàsako Ku*t*ikanno àyasmantan mahà Kachchàyanan etadavocha: 'Yathà yathàhan bhante ayyena mahà Kachchàyanena dhamman desitan àjànàmi nayidan sukaran àgàran ajjhàvasatà ekantaparipunnan ekantaparisuddhan sankhalikhitan brahmachariyan charitun. Ichchhàm'ahan bhante kesamassun ohàretvà kàsàyàni vatthàni achchhàdetvà agàrasmà anagàriyan pabbajitun: pabbàjetu man bhante ayyo maha Kachchàyano' ti. Dukkaran kho Sona yàvajìvan ekaseyyakan ekabhattakan brahmachariyan ingha tvan Sona tattheva agàrìbhùto buddhànan sàsanan anuyunja kàlayuktan ekaseyyan ekabhattan brahmachariyan'ti. Atha kho Sonassa upàsakassa Ku*t*ikannassa yo ahosi pabbajjàbhi sankhàro so pa*t*ippassambhi,—dutiyampi Sono upàsako Ku*t*ikanno [repeated as before from *yenà yasmà* ......to pa*t*ippassambhi.] tatiyampi [repeated as before from yenà yasmà......to bhante ayyo mahà Kachchàyano-ti. Atha kho àyasmà mahà Kachchàyano Sonan upàsakan Ku*t*ikannan pabbàjesi. Tena kho pana samayena Avanti dakkhina pato appa bhikkhuko hoti, atha kho àyasmà mahà Kachhàyano tinnan vassànan achchayena kichchhena kasirena tato tato dasa vaggan bhikkhu sanghan sannipàtàpetvà àyasmantan Sonan upasampàdesi. Atha kho àyasmato sonassa vassan vutthassa rahogatassa patisallìnassa evan chetaso pari-vitakko udapàdì sutoyeva kho me so bhagavà edisocha edisochàti nacha mayà sammukhà di*tt*ho gachchheyyàhan tan bhagavantan dassanàya arahantan sammà sambuddhan sache mam upajjhàyo anujàneyyàti. Atha kho àyasmà Sono sàyanha samayan patisallànà vutthito yenàyasmà mahà Kachchàyano tenupasamkamì; upasankamitvà àyasmantan mahà Kachchànan abhivàdetvà eka mantan nisìdì. Eka mantan nisinno kho àyasmà Sono àyasmantan mahà Kachchàyanan etada vocha. Idha maihan bhante rahogatassa patisallìnassa evan chetasoparivitakko udapàdi.—pe—.gachchheyyàhan bhante bhagavantan dassanàya arahantan sammà sambuddhan sache man upajjhàyo bhante anujàneyyàti Sadhu! Sàdhu! Sona, gachchha tvan sona tan bhagavantan dassanàya arahantan sammà sambuddhan dakkhissasi tvan Sona bhagavantan pàsàdikan pasàdanìyan santindriyan santamànasan uttamadamatha samathan anuppattan dantan guttan santindriya nàgan; tenahi tvan Sona mama vachanena bhagavato pàde sirasà vanda upajjhàyo me bhante àyasmà mahà Kachchàno bhagavato pàde sirasà vandatí'ti. Evancha vadehi Avanti dakkhinà patho bhante appabhikkhuko tinnan me vassànan achchayena kichchhena kasirena tato tato dasa vaggan bhikkhusanghan sannipàtàpetvà upasampadan alatthan. Appevanàma bhagavà Avanti dakkhinà pathe appa tarena ganena upasampadan anujàneyya; Avanti dakkhina pathe bhante kantuttarà bhùmi kharà gokantakahatà appevanàma bhagavà Avantì dakkhinà pathe ghanan ghanûpàhanan anujàneyya; Avanti dakkhinà pathe bhante nahàna garukà manussà udakasuddhikà appevanàma bhagavà Avanti dakkhinà pathe dhuvanahànan anujàneyya; Avanti dakkhinà pathe bhante chammàni attharanàni elaka chamman aja chamman miga chamman seyyatàpi bhante majjhimesu janapadesu eragu moragu majjàru jantu.—pe—.* appeva nàma bhagavà Avanti dakkhinà pathe chammàni

---

* When the same sentence is to be repeated, the mode by which the repetition is avoided by Pali and Sinhalese writers, is by writing the first and last words of the sentence that is to be repeated with a...pe...between them. This is an abbreviation of the word *peyyàla*, implying 'insert' in the sense of—'fill up the gap.' In some of our books 'p' alone occurs, and in others 'la' conveying the same signification as 'pe.'

attharanàni anujàneyya elaka-chamman aja-chamman miga-chamman. * * * *
Anujànàmì bhikkave eva rûpesu pachchanti mesu jana ɼadesu vinaya-dhara-panchamena ganena upasampadan. * * * * * * [Tatrime pachchantimà janapadà, puratthimàya disàya *Kajangalo*nàma nigamo, tassa parena *Mahà-Sàlà*, tato parà Pachchantimà janapadà, orato majjhe. Puratthimadakkhinàya disàya *Salalavatì* nàma nadì, tato parà Pachchantimà janapadà, orato majjhe. Dakkhinàya dìsàya *Setakannikan* nàma nigamo, tato parà Pachchantimà janapadà, orato majjhe. Pachchhimàya disàya *Thûnan*nàma Bràhmanagàmo, tato parà Pachchantimà janapadà, orato majjhe. Uttaràya disàya *Usìraddhajo*nàma pabbato, tato parà Pachchantimà janapadà, orato majjhe.]*

'At that time the venerable Mahà Kachchàyana lived in a cliff of the *Kuraraghara*† mountain in Avanti; and at the same time *Sona-kutikanna*‡ a lay observer of the ordinances of Buddha§ was an attendant of the venerable Mahà Kachchàyana.¶ He went to the place where Mahà Kachchàyana dwelt, and having bowed to him, took his respectable position; and addressed him as follows:—' So far as I have heard the dhamma which was propounded by the venerable Mahà Kachchàyana, it is not easy for a layman to observe *brahmachariya*‖ which is the only perfect, the only purest (state) like a turned conch-shell. I desire (therefore) to leave the laity, to enter ascetism, to divest myself of (my) hair and beard, and to put

* I have transposed the above passage which occurs a little before the paragraph before it; and I omit its translation as the same has been already given at p. xxix; vide supra note.

† Lit. 'Osprey-nest.'

‡ Kutikanna is interpreted in an Atthakathà to mean *koti-karna* 'ear of 100 lacs;' i. e. wearing an ear-ornament of that value.

§ Upàsaka.

¶ In speaking of the venerable fathers of the Church, Buddhist writers repeat *àyasmà*, which is disregarded in speaking of kings. See preceding extract. In this translation I have omitted the frequent repetition of *Sono Upàsako kutikanno*.

‖ It here means the ordinances of ascetism.

on the yellow vesture. Let his Lordship the venerable Mahà Kachchàyana admit me into (the priesthood.)' (The priest replied]—' Sona, the observance of *brahmachariya* (which confines a man) to one seat and one meal is difficult. Wherefore, Sona, be as thou art, a householder. Observe the religion of Buddha, and temporarily preserve the *brahmachariya** (which confines thee to) one seat, and one meal.' Upon which the intense desire of Sona to embrace ascetism subsided. [Yet, afterwards,] a second time [did Sona address Mahà Kachchàyana in the same language, and with the same result as before; and] a third time [did he make his application in precisely the same language;] when Mahà Kachchàyana admitted Sona into the priesthood.

At this time there were but few *bhikkhûs* in *Avanti*, the southern province. At the expiration of three years, however, Mahà Kachchàyana, having with trouble and difficulty assembled ten bhikkhûs from here and there, conferred on the venerable Sona the ordination of Upasampadà. He who held the *vassa*,† being alone, and solely intent upon [the concerns of religion]‡ pondered thus: 'I have only heard that Bhagavà was so and so. I have not seen him face to face. If my *Upajjhàya*§ will permit me I shall go to see the all-perfect Buddha, the Lord worthy of adoration.' So pondering, the venerable Sona rose up in the evening from his contemplative meditation, and proceeded to the spot where Mahà Kachchàyana dwelt; and, making his obeisance, took his respectful distance. This done, he addressed the venerable Mahà Kachchàyana as follows:—' Lord, to me who was alone, and in contemplative meditation a thought has occurred [that I

* Here the ordinances, such as the *atthasìla*, are meant.

† A religious ordinance by which the priest is bound to reside in a place during the rainy season; See *Mahà Vagga lib* iii.

‡ Contemplative meditation.

§ The appellation of the Preceptor who introduces a person for admission into the priesthood, and to whose rights the pupil ultimately succeeds.

should go and see Buddhà.] If my preceptor will permit, I will go and see the all-perfect Buddha, the lord worthy of adoration.' 'Sàdhu! Sàdhu!' (exclaimed Kachchàyana);' go thou Sona, to see the all-perfect Buddha, the lord worthy of adoration. Sona, thou wilt find Bagavà to be pleasing (to the sight) and producing delight (in the beholder)—(one moreover,) who has subdued the senses, who is of tranquil mind, who has attained to the highest self-control and tranquillity, who has self-controlled, who is [decently] covered, and who is the highest of those who had subjugated the passions. Wherefore, Sona, bow thou unto the feet of Bhagavà with thy head for me,* saying—'My preceptor the supreme Lord, Mahà Kachchàyana has desired me to bow with my head unto the feet of Bhagavà.' Say also, 'Lord there are but few bhikkhûs in Avanti, the southern country. At the expiration of three years, it was with trouble and difficulty that ten bhikkhûs were assembled from here and there for my ordination. It will (therefore) be well if Bhagavà will permit ordination in Avanti, the southern country by the introduction of a fewer number (of priests.) Since, my Lord, the ground of Avanti, the southern country, is overrun with thorns, is rough, and abounds with *gokantaka*,† it will be as well to permit the use of thicker shoes in Avanti, the southern country. Since, my Lord, the people of Avanti, the southern country prize bathing highly, and esteem purity with water (above all things), it will be as well to permit more frequent bathing in Avanti, the southern country. Since (again), my Lord, in Avanti, the southern country, skins such as sheep-skin, goat-skin and deer-skin are used for coverlets, same as eragu, moragu, majjàru and jantu‡ in the majjhima country; it will be as

* Mama vachanena—'in my words.'

† The *Ruellia Longifolio*. Rox. It is also applied by some to *Tribulus lanuginosus*. But the word here is explained by the commentators to mean 'hard dry clods of earth produced by the print of the feet of cattle.'

‡ These words are not given in our Pali glossaries; nor are they explained by the commentators.

well to permit the use of skins such as sheep skins, goat skins, and deer skins for coverlets. * * * [On the above requests being preferred, Buddha declared] Priests, in (all) foreign countries like this (Avanti) I permit ordination in an assembly of five, one being versed in the Vinaya.

IV.

Atthakathà of Sanyutta Nikàya.

Tada majjhima desato sankha vànijakà tan nagaran gantva bhandikan paṭisàmetvà ràjànan passissàmoti pannàkàra-hatthà ràja kulà'dvàran gantvà ràja uyyànan gatoti sutvà uyyànan gantvà dvàre ṭithà paṭihàrassa arochayinsu. Atha rañño nivedite ràja pakkosapetvà niyàdita-pannàkàre vanditvà ṭithe —'tàta kuto àgatatthà'ti puchchi—'Sàvatthito devà'ti. Kinti tumhàkan raṭṭhan subhikkhan dhammìko ràjà'ti. 'Àma deva'ti. Atthi pana tumhàkan desi kinchi sàsanan'ti. 'Deva na sakka uchchiṭṭha mukhehi kathetun'ti. Ràjà suvanna bhinkàrena udakan dàpesi; te mukhan vikkhàletvà darabalàbhi mukhan anjalin pagganhitvà—'deva amhàkan dese Buddha ratanan nàma uppannan'ti àhansu. Rañño Buddhoti vachane sutamatte sakala sarìran pharamànan pìti upajjì Tato 'Buddhoti tàtà vàdeta'ti—'Àma Buddho devà'—ti. Evan tikkhattun kathàpatvà Buddhoti varan aparimànan kàyan na sakkà parimànan katunti tasmin yeva pasanno sahassan datvà 'aparan kin sàsanan'ti—Puchchi 'dhamma ratanan deva uppannan'ti. Tampi sutvà tatheva tikkhattun patiññan gahetvà aparampi sahassan datvà puna 'aññan kin sàsanan'ti puchchi. 'Sangharatanan deva uppannan'ti. Tampi sutvà tatheva gahetvà aparanti sahassan datvà dinnabhàvan panne likhitv 'tàtà deviyà santikan gachchhathà'ti pesesi. Tesu gatesu amachche puchchhi; 'tàtà Buddho loke uppanno tumhe kin parissathà'ti—'Deva tumhe kin kàtukàmà'ti; 'Ahan pabbajissàmì'ti; 'mayampi pabbajissamà'ti. Te sab-

bepi gharan và kutumban và anopa-loketva-yeva asse aruyha gatà; tadaheva nikkha minsu. Vànijà Anojà-deviyà santikan gantvà pannan dassesun. Sà vàchetva rañña tumhàkan bahu katan tumhehi kin katan tàtàti puchchhi.

'At that time certain chank traders went to that city (Kukkutavati) from Majjhimadesa. Arranging their baggage, and saying 'Let us see the King,' they went with presents in hand to the palace gate. Hearing, however, that the king (Kappina) had gone to the park, they proceeded thither; and addressed the keeper at the gate. When the king was informed (of their arrival) he caused them to be summoned (before him), and inquired of those, who stood before him saluting with presents—'Sons, whence did you come?' 'Your Majesty, from *Sùratthi.*' What—is your country fertile; and your king righteous?' 'Yes, your Majesty,' replied the traders. 'What are the tidings of your country?' demanded the king. 'Your Majesty (returned the traders) it is impossible to relate them with impure mouths.' The king (thereupon) caused water to be given (to them) in a golden vase; and when they washed their mouths, and made their obeisence to the direction of Buddha, they said, 'Please your Majesty, a precious (person)* called Buddhà, has appeared in our country.' The moment he heard the word "Buddha" joy pervaded every part of his body. Again, said the king, 'Sons, is he called *Buddha*?' 'Yes, your Majesty,' replied the traders. The king having thus caused them to repeat (the word) three times—and, unable to define the supreme unaccountable wight called *Buddha*, and being (moreover) pleased with the word itself; gave them a thousand (pieces); and asked them 'What other news?' 'Please your Majesty (replied the traders) a precious thing called the *dhamma* has appeared.' When he had heard this also, he got their assurance thrice as before, and gave them another

---

* A ratana—'jewel of a person.'

thousand pieces. He again asked them 'What other news?' They again replied, that 'a precious thing called the *Sangha* had arisen.' When he had heard this also, he likewise received (their assurances) and gave them yet a thousand (pieces); and writing the fact of the gift in a leaf,* sent them saying, 'Sons, go (with this) to the Queen-Consort.' After they had left him, the king said to the Ministers, 'Sons, Buddha has appeared in the world; what will ye do?' 'Please your Majesty,' returned the Ministers, '(we will) whatever it shall please you to do?' 'I shall be a recluse,' rejoined the king. 'We too (shall) enter the priesthood,' added the Ministers. Thereupon all of them, without so much as caring for their homes or families, got upon their horses and went away on that very day. The traders, who went to Queen *Anàjà*, presented the letter to her; and when she had read it, she said to them, 'The king has done much for you; what have ye done?'

V.

Sumangala Vilāsini.

Pubbe kira Vajji ràjàno ayan choroti ànetvà dassìti ganhatha ran choranti avatvà vinichchhaya mahà-mattànan denti. Te vinichchhinitvà sache achorohoti vissajjanti sache choro hoti attanà kinchi akatvà vohàrikànan denti. Tepi vinichchhinitvà achoro che vissajjenti, choro che Suttadarà nàma honti, tesan denti. Tepi vinichchhanitvà achoro che vissajjenti, choro che A*tt*hakulikànan denti. Tepi tatheva tatvà Senàpatissa, Senàpati uparàjassa, Uparàja rañño. Rajà vinichchhinitvà achoro che vìssajjeti sache pana choro hoti *Paveni Potthakan* vàchàpeti.⁋ Tattha yena idan nàma katan tassa ayan nàma dandoti *likhitan.* ⁋Ràjà tassa kiriyan tena samànetvà tadonuchchhavikan dandan karoti.

* Panna 'leaf.'

'In aforetimes the Vajjian princes, on a person being brought and presented 'as a thief,' surrendered him to the *Vinichchhaya Mahamattà*,* without saying 'take this thief (into custody).' They, upon investigation release him, if innocent; but, if he be (found) a thief, surrender him to the *Vohàrikà*† without doing anything themselves. They (the Vohàrikà) too, upon investigation release him, if innocent; but, if otherwise, transfer him to those who are called *Suttadarà*.‡ They likewise inquire (into the matter) and discharge him, if innocent; but, if otherwise, assign him to the *Atthakulakà*.§ They also, going through the same process (surrender him) to the *Senàpati* (or Commander of the forces)—the Senàpati to the *Uparàja* (or Sub-king),—and the Uparàja to the King. The Sovereign, after inquiring into the matter discharges him, if innocent; but, if otherwise causes the *Paveni Putthakan*, or the book of Precedents'¶ to be consulted. There it is *written*, such is the punishment to him who has committed such (a crime.) The king upon comparing with that the conduct of the culprit, inflicts a suitable punishment.'

VI.

Maha Vagga.

Tena kho pana samayena Ràjagahe sattàrasavaggiyà dàrakà sahàyakà honti * * * * * * Attha kho Upalissa màtà pitunnan etadahosi—' Sache kho Upàli *lekhan* sikkheyya * * * 'Sache kho upàli lekhan sikkhissati angulio dukkha bhavissanti.' 'Sache kho upàli gananan sikkheyya' * * * * 'Sache kho Upàli gananan sikkhissati urassa

---

* 'The chief Ministers.'

† *Vohàra*—'usage,' 'customs'—'laws;' and *Vohàrikà* 'the lawyers.'

‡ *Suttadarà*—'The principal officers who mantained the rules or axioms.'

§ *Atthakulikà*—probably a Council of judges. The term is not explained.

¶ Here is an undoubted reference to a 'book.' It is the book of customs; *paveni*, that which is perpetuated from ancient times.

dukkho bhavissanti.' 'Sache kho Upàli rùpan sikkheyya * * * * Sache kho Upàli rùpan sikkhissati akkhini dukkhà bhavissanti.' * * * * 'Sache kho Upàli samanesu Sakkaputtiyesu pabbajjeyya; evan kho Upàli amhàkan achchayena sukhan jìveyya, na cha kilameyyà-ti.'

'At that time there were in Ràjagaha seventeen children who were companions. Upàli was the chief amongst them. ....Afterwards, Upàli's parents pondered: 'It may be desirable that Upàli should learn *writing*.........But, if he learn to write, his fingers may suffer pain. It is desirable that Upàli should learn *Arithmetic**.........Should he learn computation, he would suffer in his mind. It may be desirable that Upàli should learn *drawing*.........Should he learn drawing, his eyes might suffer.........Should Upàli however, become an *Ascetic* in the Sâkya fraternity, he would be enabled to live well after our deaths, and would not be distressed.'

VII.

Atthakathâ to the Dhammapada.

In the story of Kosambi Se*tt*hi, who resorted to various attempts to kill his natural son, *Ghosika*, it is stated:—

* * * Evan sante pana tan se*tt*hì ujukan oleketun nasakkoti; kinti nan màreyyantì chintento mama gàmasate àyuttakassa santikan pesetvà màràpessànìti upàyan disvà 'ayan me avajàtaputto,† iman màretvà vachchakùpe khipatù, evan kate ahan màtulassa kattabbayuttakan jànissàmì'ti'— tassa pannan likhitvà, 'tàta Ghosaka amhâkan gàma-sate àyuttako atthì, iman pannan haritvà tassa dehì'ti vatvà pannan tassa dasante bandhi. So pana akkharasamayan najànàti. ....Sà (setthi-dìta) kin pana nukho etanti tasmin niddà-

* *Ganana*—Mathematical or Astrological calculations; Arithmetic, Algebra, &c.

† A son born inferior to the father. i. e. of a mother lower in caste than the father.

yante màtà pitunnan aññav'hitatàya apassantanam otaritvà tan pannan mochetvà àdàya attanogabbhan pavisitvà dvàran pidhàya vàtapànan vivaritvà akkharasamaya kusalatàya pannan vàchetvà, 'aho andhabàlo attano marana pannan dasante bandhitvà charati sache mayà nadi*tt*hà assa natthi jìvitan'tì, tan pannan phàletvà se*tt*hissa vachanena aparan pannan likhi.

'Such being the case, the Se*tt*hi could not see him full (in the face).* Pondering how he might cause his death, and devising a means, viz. 'that he would kill him by sending him to the superintendent of his Hundred Estates'—wrote to him a *leaf* as follows—'This is my unfortunate son. Kill him, and put him into the cess-pool. When that shall have been effected, I shall know how to recompense my *Uncle*;'†—and said, 'Son, Ghosika, there is a superintendent in our Hundred Estates; take this letter, and give it to him.' So saying, he tied the letter to the end of his (son's) garments. He was illiterate. * * * [The story then proceeds to narrate that Ghosika, on his way to the Estates, took lodgings at the house of another *Setthi*; and that his daughter, who heard that the stranger had something tied to his garments], thinking what it could be, came down whilst Ghosika was asleep, and unperceived by her parents, who were elsewhere engaged. Having untied (the knot), and secured the *leaf*, she entered her own room; where, after closing the door, and opening the window, she, who was clever in letters, read the epistle. [That done], she exclaimed 'Alas! this blind idiot goes about with his own death warrant‡ tied to his garments. If it had not been seen by me, he would (surely) forfeit his life!' So saying, she destroyed that letter, and substituted (wrote) another, as if it had come from the Se*tt*hi.'§

---

* *Ujuka* 'straight.'

† A term of respect even to an underling, e. g. 'Uncle dhoby.' See C. B. A. S. Journal for 1856-8. p. 238.

‡ Lit. *panna* 'leaf.'

§ Lit. 'in the language of the Se*tt*hi.'

VIII.

SAMANTAPĀSĀDIKA

'Anujànàmi bhikkave salàkàya và pa*tt*ikàya và upanibandhitvà opunjitvà uddisitun'—iti vachanato rukkha sàramayàya *salàkàyavà* vìluvilìvatàlapannàdi-mayàya *pattikàya* và asukassa nàma salàka-bhattan'ti evan akkaràni *upanibandhitvà*, pachchhiyan và chìvara bhoge và sabba salàkàyo *opunjitvà*, punappuna he*tt*hup pariya vasena àlolàpetvà, panchanga samannàgatena bhattuddesakena sache'pi *t*hitikà atthe *t*hitikato pa*tt*hàya no che atthì teràsanato patthàya salàkà dàtabbà.

'Whereas it is said: "I permit you, priests, to ascertain (this) by writing on a thin *slip* (ticket) or upon *bark*, and by mixing (the same);"—letters should be formed* either upon a slip made of the *woody-part of a tree*, or upon a strip of the *Bambu-bark*, the *Talipot-leaf, et cetera*, to the effect that '(this is) the Food-Ticket answering to such person's name.' [This done], all the tickets should be collected into a basket, or the fold of a robe; and, having repeatedly shaken them together so that they may be [moved up-side down] mixed, they should be distributed by the *Bhattudesaka*† of five qualifications,‡ commencing according to the standing orders, if any; or, otherwise, with the seat of the eldest priest.'

KACHCHÀYANA BHEDA TÌKÀ.

(Note p. lxxii.)

The following extract, which we make from the Kachchàyana Bheda Tìkà, contains the Tradition as to who were the authors of the Supplementary Notes, and examples in Kachchàyana's Grammar.

---

* This is a past participle in the original.

† The person whose business it is to appoint the meals.

‡ The five qualifications are; 1. a knowledge of the affairs regarding the distribution of food; 2 a sense of justice; 3 freedom from ignorance; 4 absence of fear; and 5 exemption from anger.

Tenà'ha Kachchàyana Dìpaniyan.

Sandhimhi eka paññàsan
nàmamhi dvi satan bhave,
A*tt*hà rasàdhi kanchena
kàrake pancha tàlisan;
Samàse a*tt*ha vìsan'cha
dvàsa*tt*hi Taddhite matan,
A*tt*hà rasa satàkkhyàte
kite sutta satan bhave;
Unnàdimhi cha paññàsan
ñeyyan sutta pabhedato;—
Sabban sampin*d*a mànantu
cha sata sattati dvecha'...ti.

Imàni sutta sankhyàni ñyàse àgata sutta sankhyàhi nasamenti; kasmàti che? pakkhepa suttan gahet v gananta dasàdhika satta sata suttàni honti. Imàni suttàni Mahà Kachchàyanena katàni; vutti cha Sanghanandi sankhàtena Mahà Kachchàyanen 'eva katà—payogo Brahmadattena kato.. ti. Vuttan ch'etan.

"Kachchàyana kato yogo
vuttì cha Sanghanandino,
Payogo Brahmadattena
ñyàso Vimalabuddhinà"...ti.

'It is said in the Kachchàyana Dìpanì—that the distribution of Suttàni may be regarded (as follows, viz. that) there are fifty one (Suttàni) in the (book which treats on) Combination; two hundred and eighteen on Nouns; forty-five on Syntax; twenty-eight on Compounds; sixty-two on Nominal Derivatives; one hundred and eighteen on Verbs; one hundred on Verbal Derivatives; and fifty on Unnàdi. The aggregate (number is) six hundred and seventy-two.

'These numbers of aphorisms do not correspond with the numbers appearing in the Nyàsa. To explain wherefore: By the computation of the interpolated aphorisms there are seven hundred and ten aphorisms. These aphorisms were composed by Mahà Kachchàyana. The Vutti were made by *Mahà Kachchàyana* himself, (who was also) called Sanghanandi;--and the illustrations by Brahmadatta. So it is expressly stated--that

'The aphorisms were made by Kachchàyana
The Vutti by Sanghanandi*—
The illustrations by Brahmadatta—
And the Nyàsa by Vimalabuddhi.'

Netti Pakarana.

(Note p. xxiii.)

When I noticed the arguments advanced against the belief, that Mahà Kachchàyana was the author of the Pali Grammar which is named after him, I had not seen the *Netti Pakarana*, which is also stated to have been written by him. I have since procured a copy, and give, as a specimen of its style, the following selection. From an examination of that specimen I fail to perceive anything in its style, from which it may be concluded that the two works were *not* written by one and the same person. It is, what it professes to be, a very full and complete commentary of the religious matters it treats upon. It combines a commentary with a Dictionary. It quotes passages said to have been expressed by Buddha himself. The metres of the gàthàs quoted are clearly Pràkrit. And, from the interpolations of certain notes, which make reference to some of the distinguished members of the Buddhist Convocations, and which are also to be found in the originals, which I have consulted, I am the more fortified in the belief expressed in the Introduction.

* It will be observed, that the writer's statement, that Sanghanandi was identical with Mahà Kachchàyana, is not borne out by the authority quoted. From the distinct mention of different names for the authors of different parts, viz., the Grammar, its Supplements, its notes, and its principal comment, the Nyàsa; it would seem that Sanghanandi (also called Sankhanandi) was a person different from Mahà Kachchàyana.

Tattha katamo vichayohàro? 'yan puchchhitancha vissajjitancha' àdi gàthà. Ayan vichayohàro kin vichinati? Padan vichinati, pañhan vichinati, vissajjanan vichinati, pubbàparan vichinati, assàdan vichinati, àdìnavan vichinati, nissaranan vichinati, phalan vichinati, upàyan vichinati, ànattin vichinati, anugìtin vichinati, sabbe nava suttante vichinati. Yatà kin bhave? Yatà àyasmà Ajito Pàràyane bhagavantan pañhan puchchhati—

"Kenassu nivuto loko [ichchà yasma Ajito]*
Kenassu nappakàsati
Kissàbhilepanan brùsi
Kinsutassa mahabbhayan..." ti

Imàni chattàri padàni puchchhi tàni. Socha kho eko pañho, kasmà? eka vatthupariggaho. Evanhi àha—'kenassu nivuto loko'-ti—lokàdhi*tth*ànan puchchhati: 'kenassu nappakàsatì' ti—lokassa appakàsanan puchchhati: 'kissàbhi lepanan brùsi' ti—lokassa abhilepanan puchchhati: 'kinsutassa mahabbhayan'ti—tasseva lokassa mahabbhayan puchchhati. Loko tividho,—kilesa loko, bhava loko, indriya loko. Tattha vissajjanà

"Avijjà [ya] nivuto loko [Ajitàti bhagavà]
Vivichchhà† nappakàsati
Jappàbhi lepanan brùmi
Dukkham'assa mahabbhayan..." ti

Imàni chattàri padàni imehi chatuhi padehi vissajjitàni—Pa*th*aman pa*th*amena, dutiyan dutiyena, tatiyan tatiyena, chatutthan chatutthena.

'Kenassu nivuto loko'ti—pañhe 'avijjà nivuto loko'ti—vissajjanà. Nìvaranenahi nivuto loko, avijjànìvaranàhi sabbe sattà yathàha bhagavà. "Sabba sattànan bhikkhave sabba

---

* This passage within brackets is stated by the commentator, to have been interpolated in one of of the Buddhist Convocations.

† After this word, I find "pamàdà." It is, I believe, the interpolation of a note.

pànànan sabba bhùtànan pariyàyato ekam'eva nìvaranan vadàmi, yadidan—avijjà; avijjànìvaranà hi sabbe sattà, sabba so cha bhikkhave avijjàya nirodhà chàgà pa*t*inissaggà, natthi sattànan nìvaranan ti vadàmi"—tenacha pa*t*hamassa padassa vissajjanà yuttà.

'Kenassu nappakàsatì'ti—pañhe vivichchhà,* nappakàsatì'ti vissajjanà; yo puggalo nìvaranehi nivuto so vivichchhati, vivichchhànàma vuchchati vichikichchhà—So vichikichchhanto nàbhi saddahati, anabhisaddahanto viriyan nàrabhati akusalànan dhammànan pahànàya kusalànan dhammànan sachchhi kiriyàya, so idha pamàda'manuyutto viharati; pamatto sukke dhamme na upàdiyati; tassa te anupàdiyamànà nappakàsanti,—yathà'ha bhagavà—

"Dùre santo pakàsenti
Himavanto va pabbato;
Asantettha na dissanti
Ratti khittà yathà sarà;
Te gunehi pakàsenti
Kittiyà cha yasena cha"..ti.

Tena cha dutiya padassa vissajjanà yuttà.

'Kiss'àbhi lepanan brùsi'-ti pañhe 'japp'àbhi lepanan brùmì'..ti vissajjanà; jappànàma vuchcha-ti tanhà; sà kathan abhilimpati yathà'ha bhagavà—

"Ratto atthan na jà nàti
Ratto dhamman na passati;
Andhan taman tadà hoti
Yan ràgo sahate naran"..ti

Sà'yan tanhà àsattibahulassa puggalassa evan abhijappàti karitvà; tattha loko abhilitto nàma bhavati—tena cha tatiyassa padassa vissajjanà yuttà.

'Kinsu tassa mahabbhayan'ti pañhe 'dukkham'assa mahabbhayan'ti vissajjanà. Duvidhan dukkhan kàyikan cha chetasikan cha, yan kàyikan idan dukkhan, yan chetasikan idan

* "Pamàdà" also occurs here.

domanassan, sabbe sattà hi dukkhassa ubbijjanti, natthi bhayan dukkhena sama saman kuto và pana tassa uttaritaran. Tisso dukkhatà—dukkha-dhukkhatà, vipari nàma dukkhatà sankhàra dukkha-tà ti, tattha loko odhiso kadàchi karahachi dukkha. dukkhatàya muchchati, tathà viparinàma dukkhatàya; tan kissa hetu honti loke appàbàdhà'pi dìghàyukà'pi. Sankhàra dukkha tàya pana loko anupàdisesàya nibbànadhàtuyà muchchati, tasmà sankhàra dukkhatà dukkhan lokassà ti katvà 'dukkham'assa mahabbhayan'ti—tenacha chatutthassa padassa vissajjanà yuttà. Tenà'ha bhagavà 'avijjà nivuto loko...'ti.

Of the foregoing what is *vichayahàro?* [See] the gàthà—'*Yan puchchhitan cha vissajjitan cha*' etc. What does this *vichayahàro* investigate? It investigates parts of speech [words]. It investigates questions. It investigates answers. It investigates what precedes and follows [the context]. It investigates happy [results]. It investigates ill-effects. It investigates [their] non-existence. It investigates consequences. It investigates means. It investigates canons. It investigates parallel passages. It investigates all the nine-bodied suttans. What is it? Just as in the question propounded of Bhagavà by the venerable Ajita in the section [entitled] Pàràyana—*

'Say by what has the world been shrouded?
Wherefore is it not manifested?
Whereby is its attachment?
What is its great fear?'

These four sentences were thus propounded [by Ajita]. They comprise one question. Wherefore? [Because] they take in one matter. He has stated it thus: By [the first sentence] *kenassu nivuto loko,* he investigates the abiding cause of the world [living beings]; by [the second] *kenassu nappakàsati* he investigates its non-manifestation; by [the third] *kissàbhi*

* A section of Sutta Nipàta.

lepanan brûsi, he investigates its allurements; and by [the fourth] *kinsutassa mahabbhayan*, he investigates its very dreadful horror. The [loka] world is threefold, viz., world of kilesà,* world of [bhava], or existence; and the sensible [indriya], world. The explanation of the question [is as follows:]

'I say the world is shrouded by Ignorance,
'By doubt is it not manifested;
'By desire is its attachment,
'And its horror [proceeds] from Affliction.

The four sentences [first quoted] are explained by the four sentences [last quoted]. i. e., the first [of the former] by the first [of the latter], the second by the second, the third by the third, and the fourth by the fourth.

'The world is shrouded by ignorance'—is the explanation of the question, 'by what has the world been shrouded?' Yes, it is shrouded by an obstacle; yes, all beings are clothed with the obstacle of Ignorance. So it is declared by bhagavà: 'Priests, I declare that all beings, all lives, all existences have inherently a particular obstacle, viz. Ignorance;—yes, all beings are beclouded by ignorance. Priests, I declare that by completely destroying, abandoning, (and) forsaking Ignorance, (existing) beings have no impediment.' Hence the explanation of the first sentence is satisfactory.

'By doubt is it not manifested'—is the explanation of the question, 'by what has (the world) been shrouded?' He, who is impeded with an obstacle, doubts. By the (obsolete) term *vivichchhà* (in the text) *vichikichchhà* (doubt) is expressed. [Thus] a person who doubts, is devoid of pure faith. He who is devoid of pure faith, exerts not to destroy demerit, and to acquire merit. He (thus) lives clothed with procrastination. He who procrastinates, fails to practise good deeds [religious

* Evil in thoughts, desires, or affections.

and abstract meditation.] He who does not practise them, is not manifested.* So it has been declared by Bhagavà, that "The righteous are manifested far-and-wide like the Himalaya mountain; (but) the wicked are here unperceived, like darts shot at night. The former are manifested by (their) virtues, fame and renown." Hence the explanation of the second sentence is satisfactory.

'By desire, I say, is its attachment'—is the explanation of the question, 'whereby is its attachment?' By the (obsolete) term *jappà* (in the text) *tanhà* (or) lust is conveyed. How she forms an attachment is thus stated by Bhagavà:—'He who is actuated by lust, knows not causes (of things); he who is actuated by lust perceives not what is right. Whenever lust enslaves [lit. bears] a man, then is there a thick darkness.' Thus the aforesaid lust in an inordinately lustful person becomes (as if it were) a glutinous [substance.] In it the world becomes adhesive. Hence the explanation of the third sentence is satisfactory.

'Affliction† is its dreadful horror'—is the explanation of the question, 'what is its great fear?' Affliction is two-fold; that which appertains to the body, and that which appertains to the mind. That which appertains to the body is pain, and that which appertains to the mind is sorrow. All beings dread affliction. There is no dread equal to that of Affliction (dukkha.) Where indeed is a greater than that? Affliction in the abstract is three-fold—inherent misery (dukkha-dhukkhatà), vicissitudinary misery (viparinàma dukkhatà), and all-pervading misery (sankhàra dukkhatà).‡' Hence a being, sometimes, in the course (of transmigration) becomes

---

* I have rendered this passage rather freely, without reference to words.

† In the sense of the word 'trouble' in the passage—'Man is born unto trouble.' Job v. 7.

‡ Sankhàra—appertaining to all states of existence, that which comes to existence, exist, and die away.

free from inherent misery.* So likewise, from vicissitudinary misery.† From what causes? [From] there being freedom from disease, and also from longevity. A being also becomes free from all-pervading misery by means of birth-less *nibban.* Hence, treating the affliction of a being as all-pervading misery, (the reply was), 'Its dreadful horror [proceeds] from Affliction.' Hence the explanation of the fourth sentence is satisfactory. Wherefore Bhagavà has declared:—

Avijjà nivuto loko, &c.

'I say, the world is shrouded by Ignorance;—by doubt is it not manifested;—by desire is its attachment;—and its dreadful horror [proceeds] from Affliction.'

Note to p. i.

Though at the risk of being charged with egotism, I cannot refrain from giving the following as a specimen of modern Pàli, which was presented to His Excellency, Sir Charles MacCarthy, by a large and influential, and at the same time, a very learned body of Buddhist priests, headed by the learned *Sumangala*, whom I have noticed in the Introduction.

1

Paññà-ransippabandhà budha-kumuda-vanan
bodhayanto asesan
Duppaññ'anbhoja-pantin suvipulam'api yo
dùsayanto samantà;
Loken'àchinna nànà-vidha kalusa-tamo-
sanhatim dhansayanto
CHÀRLES MAK-KÀRTHI devo jayati viya sasì
sàdhu Lank' àdhinàtho:

---

* E. g. 'Brahmans'—says the Commentator.
† 'Those who are born in the *arûpa* or the incorporeal world.'

2

So vidvà Lankikànan viya piya janako
vajjayanto anatthan
Esanto ch'àpi atthan idha sachiva-sabhà-
sangame nìtikàre;
Tesan chàritta-nìtippabhuti-hita-kathà
y'àpi chhekan pasatthan
Mantindan ichchhat'ekan gati-sati-sahitan
uchchinitvà gahetun.

3

Alan tato tassa samàja-manti-
*T*hànassa viññun suvinìta-chhekan;
Nidassayàm'-ekamanà samaggà
Mayan hi Lankàya nivàsi-bhûtà.

4

JÀMES DE ALWIS abhidhàna-nàtho
Ayan vibhàvì naya-nìti dakkho;
Sakàya bhàsày'api Sìhalàya
Susikkhito Màgadhikàya ch'àpi.

5

Satthesu nekes'vapi Sìhalesu
Chhando-Nighandu ppabhutìsu sammà;
Sevàya chhek'-à chariy'à sabhànan
Supà*t*avan ñàna-balena yàto.

6

So Lankikànam'api nìti-paveni-maggan
Sammà'va ussahati ve tathato kathetun;
Lank'àdhipo yadi tameva samuchchineyya
Appevanàma janatàya hitàya ettha.

Sumangala, and others.

Address to Sir Charles MacCarthy, Kt., Governor of Ceylon, &c. &c., by Buddhist priests of Ceylon.
[*Translated from the Pali.*]

I.

"May Sir Charles MacCarthy the moon-like illustrious Governor of Ceylon, be exalted! He who delights the lily-like-pandits with the beams of his wisdom; who in every way discourages the vast lotus-field of ignorance; and who destroys the dark-gloom of wickedness which his subjects may practise.

II.

"This learned (personage), like a generous parent, obviating the ills affecting the Ceylonese, and promoting their good in the Legislative Council of this (Island); is (we are told) desirous of selecting a Councillor, discreet, wise, and renowned; and, moreover, noted for his great tact, and his knowledge of the customs and habits of the Singhalese.

III.

"Wherefore (all) we, the (undersigned) natives of Ceylon, unanimously beg leave to nominate a fit person for the membership of the said Assembly—one who is well educated, clever, erudite; viz:

IV.

"James de Alwis. He is an accomplished scholar, highly versed in Law and Polity; and well acquainted with Pali, and most intimately, with his own language—the Singhalese.

V.

"He has attained to eminence by his natural talents; and has acquired various sciences of the Singhalese, such as

Philology, Prosody, etc., by (constantly) moving amongst the most illustrious and renowned Professors.

VI.

"And he is able well and correctly to define the ancient usages and laws of the Singhalese. Wherefore, if His Excellency the Governor will be pleased to elect this (gentleman); well will it indeed be for the prosperity of the people."

(Signed) SUMANGALA,
&c., &c.

PALI GRAMMARS.

Note page xv.

The following list is, I understand, defective; and does not include the names of many Pali Grammars extant in Burmah.

Akkhara Kosalla
Akkhara Samùha
Atthaviggahanissaya
Atthabyanjana Pakarana
Bàlappabodhana
Bàlavatàra
Chùlasaddanìti
Ganthattha
Ganthàbharana
Kachchàyana or Sandhikappa
Kachchàyana Vannanà
Kachchàyana Nàtha Pakarana
Kachchàyana Sàra
Kachchàyana Yojanà
Kachchàyana Bheda

Kachchàyana Bheda *T*ìkà.
Kàraka puppha Manjarì
Mahà Nirutti
Mahà Saddanìti
Moggallàna*
Mukhamatta Dìpanì†
Nirutti Pi*t*aka
Nirutti Yojanà
Nirutti Sàra Manjusa
Pada-sàdhana
Panchikà
Panchikà Padìpa‡
Payogasiddhi§
Rùpamàlà by Sangha Ràja
Rùpamàlà by Vagegoda
Rùpasiddhi‖
Sadda Bindu
Sadda bheda Chintà
Sadda Vàchaka
Sadda Vidhàna
Sadda Vutti
Sadda Sàrattha Jàlinì
Sadda Nìti
Samàsa Chakka.
Se*tt*hantyàdi *T*ìkà
Sutta Niddesa
Upasagga Nipàta Dìpanì
Vàchakopadesa
Vàchakadìpanì
Vibhattikathà

---

* As to the age of the writer, see Introduction, p. xi. et seq.
† Also called ñyàsa.
‡ By the author of the Selalihini sandesa. As to his age see my Sidatsangarà, p. cxcii.
§ By Vanaratana.
‖ By Buddhapiya.

CORRECTIONS.

N.B.—The figures in the first column refer to the page, and those in the second to the line reckoned from the top.

*** Regard an Italic amongst Roman characters, or a Roman amongst Italics, if a vowel, as a long letter; and, if a *t* or *d* as a lingual.

Page.	Line.	
i.	8	for 'these *several*' read '*both* these.'
"	9	dele 'both.'
"	20	for 'its *composition*' read '*composing* in it.'
"	23	for '*amongst* a host' read '*with* a host.'
"	25	for '*of* the learned' read '*among* the learned.'
iv.	30	for 'sûvattato' read 'suvuttato.'
"	31	for 'gatocha' read 'vatocha.'
"	39	for 'yattàcha' read 'yatàcha.'
"	40	for 'siyanti' read 'sìyanti.'
v.	1	for 'there' read 'theri.'
"	2	for 'three' read 'thera.'
"	22	for 'pitakan' read 'pi*t*akan.'
"	25	for 'Atuvà' read '*Atthakathà.*'
"	27	for 'satthi...sangàyetvà' read 'sa*tt*hi...sangàyitvà.'
vi.	12	for 'chita' read 'ticha.'
vii.	1	for 'Abhidanapadìpikà' read 'Abhidhànapadìpikà.'
"	9	for 'dhamama' read 'dhamma.'
"	25	Regard the initial n in 'Neyyan' as ñ.
viii.	4	Regard the initial n in 'Neyyan' as ñ.
"	7	for 'nighandu' read 'nighan*d*u.'
"	30	for 'klesa' read 'kilesa.'
x.	2	for 'gnna' read 'guna.'
"	6	for 'sammagge' read 'samagge.'
"	11	for 'sambodhi' read 'sambàdhì.'
"	17	for 'pàssàda' read 'pàsàda.'
"	27	dele y in 'yesa.'
xi.	16	for 'vohàra' read 'vihàra.'
xii.	3	for 'radient' read 'radiant.'
xiii.	24	for 'Ananda' read 'ànanda.'
xiv.	1	for 'sìladi' read 'sìlàdi.'
"	3	for 'Ananda' read 'ànanda.'
"	16	for 'scraped off' read 'erased.'
"	34	for 'sukandan' read 'sukan*d*an.'
xv.	8	for 'waragurûnan' read 'waragurunan.'
"	11	for 'yatì' read 'yati.'
"	24	for 'principal' read 'leading.'
xvi.	16	for 'abhivandi yaggan' read 'abhivandiyaggan.'
"	18	for 'subuddhan' read 'suboddhan.'
"	20	for 'buddhà' read 'budhà.'
"	22	for 'attan' read 'atthan.'
"	32	for 'situttanà' read 'sìtuttarà.'

Page.	Line.	
xvii.	18	for 'panchàso' read 'panchaso.'
„	25	for 'let the first be &c.' read 'Let the first preceding consonant be separated from [its inherent] vowel.'
„	27	for 'sententions' read 'sententious.'
xviii.	6	for 'a note' read 'notes.'
„	9	for 'Sàvatti, Patàli, Baranasì' read 'Sàvatthi, Pà*t*alí, Baràṇasì.'
„	25	for 'pa*t*hama' read 'prathama.'
„	36 & 37	for 'vohara' read 'vihàra.'
xix.	5	insert a) after 'Vedas.'
„	33	insert ‡ before 'Asvalàyana' &c.
xxi.	17	for 'machchan' read 'machchhan.'
„	18	for 'patan' read 'pa*t*an.'
„	24	for 'puràtthima' read 'puratthimà.'
xxii.	3	for 'ghate-patan' read 'gha*t*e-pa*t*an.'
„	4	for 'ghata-pato' read 'gha*t*a-pa*t*o.'
„	10	for 'Manosila' read 'Manosilà.'
„	18	for 'Kachchayana Vannana' read 'Kachchàyana vannanà.'
„	19	for 'Achariya' read 'àchariya.'
„	21	for 'àhà' read 'àha.'
xxiii.	13	for 'render' read 'afford.'
„	16	for 'may demand' read 'demands.'
xxiv.	14	for 'works of' read 'works composed in.'
„	16	for 'of which' read 'from which.'
„	21	for 'attempts' read 'attempt.'
xxv.	8	for 'Grammar' read 'Grammars.'
„	10	for 'had borrowed' read 'borrowed.'
„	12	for 'samanna' read 'samaññà.'
„	14	for 'appelations' read 'appellations.'
xxvi.	19	for 'metta' read 'mettha.'
„	24	for 'sciences' read 'science.'
„	„	dele 'when' before 'disseminated.'
xxvii.	18	for 'Buddhist Church,' here as elsewhere, read 'Buddhist religion.'
„	27	for 'Angutta' read 'Anguttara.'
xxviii.	4	for 'literary and not the' read 'literary as well as the.'
„	24	for 'vinichchaya' read 'vinichchhaya.'
xxix.	2	for 'Neruttukànan' read 'Neruttikànan.'
„	18	for 'Patàliputta' read 'Pà*t*aliputta.'
xxx.	3	for 'ecumenial' read 'ecumenical.'
„	18	for 'Paka*t*ibhàvan' read 'Pakatibhàvan.'
xxxii.	19	for 'Brahman' read 'Brahmà.'
„	27	for 'falcendi' read 'falsificandi.'
xxxiii.	31	for 'mànus' read 'mànuse.'
xxxiv.	4	for 'dibha' read 'dibba.'
„	8	for 'ñànàn idhattha' read 'ñànàni idha*tt*ha.'
„	10	for 'peta' read 'petà.'
„	30	for 'jánas' read 'jhàna.'
xxxv.	12	for 'is well' read 'are well.'
xxxvi.	13	for 'have embraced' read 'embraced.'
„	17	for 'Parasi' read 'Parasu.'
„	33	for 'its' read 'his.'
xxxix.	20	for 'Lessen' read 'Lassen.'
xlii.	7	for 'indeed' read 'entirely.'
„	29	for 'ràjà' read 'ràja.'

Page.	Line.	
xlii.	30	for 'dvedasa' read 'dvàdasa.'
"	"	for 'ràjà' read 'ràja.'
xliii.	2	(same as above)
"	2	for 'sìgataranti' read 'sìghataranti.'
"	24 & 25	for 'Alasando' read 'Alasandà.'
xliv.	24	for 'adduce' read 'cite.'
xlv.	5	for 'suttante' read 'sutante.'
"	6	for 'panchante mesu' read 'panchantimesu.'
"	15 & 16	for 'ratthan' read 'ra*tt*han.'
"	20	for 'matito' read 'màtito.'
"	21 & 22	for 'puchchchismin' read 'kuchchhismin.'
"	24	for 'dassanattan' read 'dassanatthan.'
xlvii.	29	for 'sthûpa' read 'stûpa.'
xlix.	6	for 'Brahman' read 'Brahmà.'
"	9	for 'rivalled' read 'vied.'
l.	8	dele 'is' before 'Jou-lai.'
"	22	insert 'proper' before 'occasion.'
li.	1	for 'though' read 'through.'
lii.	33	insert 'S. 367 p. 1.' after 'p. 1.'
liv.	5	for 'Chandràchar'—read 'Chandràchàr.'
"	6	for 'bhasyan' read 'bhàsyan.'
"	"	for 'krit' read 'kritan.'
"	31	for 'vyàchakshanàn' read 'vyàchakshànan.'
"	32	for 'vichcchinnan' read 'vichchhinnan.'
"	"	for 'mahabashyan' read 'mahabàshyan.'
lv.	12	for 'Bl.' read 'Bengal.'
lvii.	9	insert 'himself' after 'Muller.'
lix.	33	for 'A. D.' read 'A. B.' or 'after Buddha.'
lx.	30	for 'ceceded' read 'seceded.'
lxvi.	1	insert 'those about' before 'whom.'
lxix.	29	for 'kenachadevakaraniyena' read 'kenachidevakaranìyena.'
"	31	for 'chatuvannin' read 'chàtuvannin.'
"	34	for 'dhàro' read 'daharo.'
"	"	for 'sàlasa' read 'solasa.'
"	35	for 'sakkhara' read 'sàkkhara.'
lxx.	1	for 'pàdako' read 'padako.'
"	"	for 'veyyakarano' read 'veyyàkarano.'
lxxii.	11	for 'in one' read 'with one.'
lxxv.	10	for 'data' read 'date.'
lxxvii.	33	for 'mahàrshibih' read 'maharshibih.'
lxxviii.	11	for 'Abhiràdi' read 'àbhiràdi.'
"	13	for '*s*astresu' read '*s*àstresu.'
"	22	for 'atbhutàrtham' read 'atbhûtàrthàm.'
lxxx.	22	for 'Alpabhransa' read 'Apabhransa.'
lxxxii.	15	for 'Bàlikà' read 'Bàhlikà.'
lxxxvi.	3	for 'render' read 'afford.'
"	26	insert 'the language of,' before 'their so-called.'
xc.	21	dele s. in 'initios.'
xcv.	24	for 'of which' read 'from which.'
c.	25	for 'abaddha' read 'àbaddha.'
cii.	29	insert 'a division of' before 'night.'
ciii.	10	for 'prishtata' read 'pa*s*tatà.'
"	11	for 'charanah' read 'chàranah.'

Page.	Line.	
ciii.	30	for 'kanà' read 'khamà.'
"	"	for 'kshûra' read 'kshura.'
"	31	for 'khûra' read 'khura.'
civ.	10	for 'ktantad' read 'ktàntàd.'
"	19	for 'naso ho va dirgh'-&c., read 'ñaso ho và dìrgh-&c.
"	30	for 'adirghas' read 'adìrghas.'
cv.	1	for 'chitthasya chishthah' read 'chi*tth*asya chish*th*ah.'
"	7	for 'krinmringamam' read 'krinmringamàm.'
"	14	for 'ktvodanih' read 'ktvodànih.'
"	18	for 'sodvàgatah' read 'sodhvàgatah.'
"	21	render '*s*rigàlasya *s*iàlà *s*iàle *s*iàlakah.'
"	27	for 'many a fact' read 'from many facts.'
cvi	2	insert 'any knowledge of' before 'the Pali.'
"	16	insert 'when' before 'its.'
"	20	for 'when' read 'are.'
cvii.	7	for 'nàra yà yàdi' read 'narà yày'àdi.'
"	9	for 'bàsare' read 'bhàsare.'
"	12	for 'atthakatha' read 'atthakathà.'
"	13	for 'mande' read 'man*de*.'
"	14	for 'katemi' read 'khatemi.'
"	20	for 'nipajàjpetvà' read 'nipajjàpetvà.'
"	21	for —'pentu' read—'penti.'
"	22	for 'gachchante' read 'gachchhante.'
"	31	for 'O*tt*à' read 'O*tt*a.'
"	32	for 'Kiràthà' read 'Kirata'
"	"	for 'a*tt*harasa' read 'a*tt*hàrasa.'
cviii.	8	the word 'broomstick' should be 'stick' or 'ticket.' Se 'salàka' at p. 103.
cix.	2	for 'Brahmans' read 'Brahmas.'
cx.	12	for 'of a union' read 'arising from a union of.'
cxi.	14	for 'Sankrit' read 'Sanskrit.'
cxv.	21	for 'pasàritvà' read 'pasàretvà.'
cxvi.	3	dele ya in 'Papanchasûdanìya.'
cxvii.	23	for 'game' read 'gàme.'
cxviii.	23	for 'Buddhebi' read 'Buddhebhi.'
"	30	for 'kusmehi' read kusumehi.'
"	31	for 'kusma' read 'kusuma.'
cxix.	4	for 'dhànuyà' read 'dhenuyà.'
cxx.	14	for 'turyam' read 'tûryam.'
cxxi.	25	for 'vires' read 'vis.'
cxxii.	29	for 'Ambatta' read 'Amba*tt*ha.'
"	31	for 'Attaka' read 'A*tt*aka.'
cxxiv.	2	for 'sahà' read 'saha.'
"	3	for 'Brahmanà' read 'Bràhmanà.'
"	"	for 'panàti' read 'pànàti.'
"	4	for 'vechane' read 'vachanena.'
"	15	for 'tesu' read 'tìsu;' and for 'Attaka' read 'A*tt*aka.'
"	16	for 'kathà' read 'katà.'
"	18	for 'vàdhàdi, } read 'vadhàdi.'
"	20	for 'vadàdi' }
"	21	insert 'etc.' after 'vedesu.'
"	23	for 'Attaka' read 'A*tt*aka.'
"	31	for 'vimata vinodana' read 'vimatì vinodanì.'
4	20	insert 'the' before 'third person.'

Page.	Line.	
12	25	insert 'by that tense' before 'into English.'
14	27	for 'roars' read 'hisses.'
15	3&4	for 'chattiyati' read 'chhattìyati.'
„	14	for 'chatta' read 'chhatta.'
19	8&10	for 'bhu' read 'bhû.'
30	20	for 'gamiyati' read 'gamìyati.'
35	17	for 'ghata' read 'gha*t*a;' and observe that all examples from that root should likewise be expressed by a lingual *t*.
36	5	Likewise here.
39	27	for 'nìyanti' read 'nìyyanti.'
44	6	for 'kàrapayati' read 'kàràpayati.'
47	9	for 'obhavo' read 'abhavo.'
48	last line,	insert '1856—8. p. 247.'
54	30	for 'kàkanda' read 'kàkan*d*a.'
56	6	for 'Buddà' read 'Buddha.'
„	18	for 'Kutàgàra' read 'Ku*t*àgàra.'
58	9	insert 'version' after 'Ceylonese.'
60	13	insert 'which' before 'they.'
61	4	for 'Tuwataka' read 'Tuwa*t*aka.'
„	9	for 'Sangutta' read Sanyutta.'
„	12	for 'Pitaka' read 'Pi*t*aka.'
„	31	for 'Vedattan' read 'Vedallan.'
„	32	for 'dattan' read 'dallan.' (twice.)
„	„	for 'Sammàdhitthi' read 'Sammàdi*tt*hi.'
„	„	for 'Sankhàrabhajaniyà' read 'Sankhàrabhàjaniya.'
„	„	for 'màhàpunnâman' read 'mahàpunnamàyu.'
62	27	insert 'of' after 'words.'
63	1	for 'nikkaddhita' 'nikka*dd*hita.'
„	26	for 'gambìra' read 'gambhìra.'
64 65	2&26 20	for 'akappakaranà' read 'àkappakaranà.'
„	21	for 'vijahetvà' read 'vijahitvà.'
66	3	for 'nibbuttà' read 'nibbattà.'
72	8	for 'evam'ahansu' read 'evam'àhansu.'
„	9	for 'evanavachuttha' read 'evam'avachuttha.'
„	14	for 'khìyante' read 'khìyanti.'
„	„	for 'Abhayuvarà' read 'Abhayûvarà.'
„	16	for 'attan' read 'atthan.'
73 74	20 2	for 'puchchi' read 'puchchhi.'
75	7	for 'paripatì' read 'paripa*t*ì.'
80	13	for 'passaddiyà' read 'passaddhiyà.'
93	9	dele 'bhante.'
„	„	for 'Sadhu' read 'Sàdhu.'

CORRECTIONS OF THE TEXT.

Cap. II §. 2 for සා ඉච්ච read ස ඉච්ච.
,, §. 15 for රුධා ඝිතො read රුධාදිතො.
,, §. 17 for සංවුණෙති read සංවූණෙති.
III §. 15 for ජිගච්ඡති read ජිඝච්ඡති.
,, §. 19 for අගම read අගමා.
IV §. 12 for තාසස read ඨාසස.
,, §. 36 for ජයති read ජායති.

INDEX.

ආඛ්‍යාතකප්පො.

පඨමො

CHAPTER FIRST.

ආඛ්‍යාතසාගරමථජ්ජතනී තරඞ්ගං
ධාතුජ්ජලං විකරණාගමකාල මීනං
ලොපානුබන්ධරයමත්ථ විභාගතීරං
ධීරා තරන්ති කවිනො පුථුබුද්ධි නාවා.
විචිත්තසංඛාර පරික්ඛිතං ඉමං
ආඛ්‍යාතසද්දං විපුලං අසෙසතො
පණම්‍ය සම්බුද්ධ මනන්තගොචරං
සුගොචරං යං වදතො සුණාථ මෙ.

1. අථ * පුබ්බානි විභත්තීනං ඡ පරස්සපදානි.

a අථ සබ්බාසං විභත්තීනං යානි යානි පුබ්බානි ඡ පදානි තානි තානි පරස්සපදසඤ්ඤානි හොන්ති—තංයථා—ති, අන්ති; සි, ථ; මි, ම.

පරස්සපදමිච්චනෙන ක්වත්ථො? 'කත්තරිපරස්සපදං.'

2. පරාණ්‍යත්තනොපදානි.

a සබ්බාසංවිභත්තීනං යානියානි පරානි ඡ පදානි තානිතානි අත්තනොපදසඤ්ඤානි හොන්ති—තං යථා තෙ, අන්තෙ; සෙ, ව්හෙ; එ, ම්හෙ.

අත්තනොපදමිච්චනෙන ක්වත්ථො? 'අත්තනොපදානිභාවෙච කම්මණි.'

3. ද්වෙ ද්වෙ පඨම මජ්ඣිමුත්තමපුරිසා.

a තාසංසබ්බාසං විභත්තීනං පරස්සපදානමත්තනොපදානඤ්ච ද්වෙද්වෙපදානි පඨම මජ්ඣිම උත්තම පුරිසසඤ්ඤානිහොන්ති—තං යථා ති, අන්ති, ඉති පඨමපුරිසා; සි, ථ, ඉති මජ්ඣිමපුරිසා;

---

* අධිකාරෙමඞ්ගලෙචෙව, නිප්ඵන්නෙච අවධාරණෙ:
අනන්තරෙ'පාදානෙ, අථසද්දො පවත්තති.

මි, ම, ඉති උත්තමපුරිසා; අත්තනොපදානිපි තෙ, අන්තෙ, ඉති පඨමපුරිසා; සෙ, ව්හෙ, ඉති මජ්ඣිමපුරිසා; එ, ම්හෙ, ඉති උත්තමපුරිසා—එවංසබ්බත්ථ.

පඨම මජ්ඣිමුත්තමපුරිස ඉච්චනෙන ක්වත්ථො? 'නාමම්හි පයුජ්ජමානෙපි තුල්‍යාධිකරණෙපඨමො'; 'තුම්හෙ, මජ්ඣිමො'; 'අම්හෙ, උත්තමො.'

4. සබ්බෙසමෙකාභිධානෙ පරොපුරිසො.

a සබ්බෙසං තිණ්ණං පඨම මජ්ඣිමුත්තම පුරිසානං එකාභිධානෙ පරොපුරිසො ගහෙතබ්බො—සො ච පඨති, තෙ ච පඨන්ති, ත්වං ච පඨසි, තුම්හෙ ච පඨථ, අහං ච පඨාමි=මයං පඨාම; සො පචති, තෙ පචන්ති, ත්වං පචසි, තුම්හෙ පචථ, අහං පචාමි=මයංපචාම: එවංසෙසාසු විභත්තීසු පරොපුරිසො යොජෙතබ්බො.

5. නාමම්හි පයුජ්ජමානෙපි තුල්‍යාධිකරණෙ පඨමො.

a නාමම්හි පයුජ්ජමානෙපි අප්පයුජ්ජමානෙපි තුල්‍යාධිකරණෙ පඨමොපුරිසොහොති—සොගච්ඡති, තෙගච්ඡන්ති; අප්පයුජ්ජමානෙපි ගච්ඡති, ගච්ඡන්ති.

තුල්‍යාධිකරණෙති කිමත්ථං? 'තෙන හඤ්ඤසෙ ත්වං දෙවදත්තෙන.'

6. තුම්හෙ මජ්ඣිමො.

a තුම්හෙ පයුජ්ජමානෙපි අප්පයුජ්ජමානෙපි තුල්‍යාධිකරණෙ මජ්ඣිමොපුරිසොහොති—ත්වංයාසි, තුම්හෙයාථ; අප්පයුජ්ජමානෙපි යාසි, යාථ.

තුල්‍යාධිකරණෙති කිමත්ථං? 'තයා පච්චතෙ ඔදනො.'

7. අම්හෙ උත්තමො.

a අම්හෙපයුජ්ජමානෙපි අප්පයුජ්ජමානෙපි තුල්‍යාධිකරණෙ උත්තමො පුරිසොහොති—අහංයජාමි, මයංයජාම; අප්පයුජ්ජමානෙපි යජාමි, යජාම.

තුල්‍යාධිකරණෙති කිමත්ථං? 'මයාඉජ්ජතෙබුද්ධො.'

8. කාලෙ.

a කාලෙ ඉච්චෙතං අධිකාරත්ථං වෙදිතබ්බං.

9. වත්තමානාපච්චුප්පන්නෙ.

a පච්චුප්පන්නෙකාලෙ වත්තමානාවිභත්තිහොති—'පාටලිපුත්තං ගච්ඡති;' 'සාවත්ථිංපවිසති;' 'විහරතිජෙතවනෙ'.

10. ආණත්‍යාසිට්ඨෙනුත්තකාලෙ පඤ්චමී.

a ආණත්‍යත්ථෙච ආසිට්ඨත්ථෙච අනුත්තකාලෙ පඤ්චමීවිභත්තිහොති—'කරොතුකුසලං;' 'සුඛංතෙහොතු.'

11. අනුමතිපරිකප්පත්ථෙසු සත්තමී.

a අනුමත්‍යත්ථෙච පරිකප්පත්ථෙච අනාගතකාලෙ සත්තමීවිභත්තිහොති— 'ත්වංගච්ඡෙය්‍යාසි;' 'කිමහංකරෙය්‍යාමි.'

12. අපච්චක්ඛපරොක්ඛාතීතෙ.

a අපච්චක්ඛෙ අතීතෙකාලෙ පරොක්ඛාවිභත්තිහොති— 'සුපිනෙකිලඑවමාහ;' 'එවංකිලපොරාණා ආහු.'

13. හීය්‍යොප්පභුතිපච්චක්ඛෙ හීය්‍යත්තනී.

a හිය්‍යොප්පභුති අතීතෙකාලෙ පච්චක්ඛෙවා අපච්චක්ඛෙවා හිය්‍යත්තනී විභත්තිහොති—'සොමග්ගංඅගමා;' 'තෙ අගමූ මග්ගං'.

14. සමීපෙජ්ජතනී.

a අජ්ජප්පභුති අතීතෙකාලෙ පච්චක්ඛෙවා අපච්චක්ඛෙවා සමීපෙජ්ජතනීවිභත්තිහොති—'සොමග්ගංඅගමි;' 'තෙමග්ගංඅගමුං.'

15. මායොගෙසබ්බකාලෙච.

a හිය්‍යත්තනී අජ්ජතනී ඉච්චෙතා විභත්තියො යදාමායොගො තදාසබ්බකාලෙචහොන්ති— මා ගමා, මා වචා; මා ගමී, මා වචී—චසද්දග්ගහණෙන පඤ්චමීවිභත්තිහොති: මාගච්ඡාහි.

16. අනාගතෙ භවිස්සන්ති.

a අනාගතෙකාලෙ භවිස්සන්ති විභත්තිහොති—සොගච්ඡිස්සති, සොකරිස්සති; තෙගච්ඡිස්සන්ති, තෙකරිස්සන්ති.

17. කිරියාතිපන්නෙතීතෙකාලාතිපත්ති.

a ක්‍රියාතිපන්නමත්තෙ අතීතෙකාලෙ කාලාතිපත්තිහොති— 'සොචෙ තං යානං අලභිස්සා අගච්ඡිස්සා'; 'තෙ චෙ තං යානං අලභිස්සංසු අගච්ඡිස්සංසු.'

18. වත්තමානා තිඅන්ති සිථ මිම තෙඅන්තෙ සෙව්හෙ එම්හෙ.

a වත්තමානා ඉච්චෙසාසඤ්ඤාහොති—ති, අන්ති; සි, ථ; මි, ම: තෙ, අන්තෙ; සෙ, ව්හෙ; එ, ම්හෙ—ඉච්චෙතෙසං ද්වාදසන්නං පදානං.
වත්තමානාඉච්චනෙනක්වත්ථො? 'වත්තමානා පච්චුප්පන්නෙ.'

19. පඤ්චමී තුඅන්තු හිථ මිම තං අන්තංස්සුව්හො එආමසෙ.

a පඤ්චමීඉච්චෙසාසඤ්ඤාහොති—තු, අන්තු; හි, ථ; මි, ම: තං, අන්තං; ස්සු, ව්හො; එ, ආමසෙ—ඉච්චෙතෙසංද්වාදසන්නංපදානං.
පඤ්චමීඉච්චනෙනක්වත්ථො? 'ආණත්‍යාසිට්ඨෙනුත්තකාලෙ පඤ්චමී.'

20. සත්තමී එය්‍ය එය්‍යුං එය්‍යාසි එය්‍යාථ එය්‍යාමි එය්‍යාම
එථ එරං එථො එය්‍යව්හො එය්‍යං එය්‍යාම්හෙ.

a සත්තමීඉච්චෙසා සඤ්ඤා හොති—එය්‍ය, එය්‍යුං; එය්‍යාසි, එය්‍යාථ; එය්‍යාමි, එය්‍යාම: එථ, එරං; එථො, එය්‍යව්හො; එය්‍යං, එය්‍යාම්හෙ—ඉච්චෙතෙසං ද්වාදසන්නං පදානං.

සත්තමීඉච්චනෙන ක්වත්ථො? 'අනුමතිපරිකප්පත්ථෙසු සත්තමී.'

21. පරොක්ඛා අ උ එ ත්ථ අ ම්හ ත්ථ රෙ ත්ථො ව්හො ඉ ම්හෙ.

a පරොක්ඛාඉච්චෙසා සඤ්ඤා හොති—අ, උ; එ, ත්ථ; අ, ම්හ: ත්ථ, රෙ; ත්ථො, ව්හො; ඉ, ම්හෙ—ඉච්චෙතෙසං ද්වාදසන්නං පදානං.
පරොක්ඛාඉච්චනෙන ක්වත්ථො? 'අපච්චක්ඛෙ පරොක්ඛාතීතෙ.'

22. හීයත්තනී ආ ඌ ඔ ත්ථ අ ම්හා ත්ථ ත්ථුං සෙ ව්හං ඉං ම්හසෙ.

a හීයත්තනීඉච්චෙසා සඤ්ඤා හොති—ආ, ඌ; ඔ, ත්ථ; අ, ම්හා: ත්ථ, ත්ථුං; සෙ, ව්හං; ඉං, ම්හසෙ—ඉච්චෙතෙසං ද්වාදසන්නං පදානං.
හීයත්තනීඉච්චනෙන ක්වත්ථො? 'හීයොප්පභුති පච්චක්ඛෙ හීයත්තනී.'

23. අජ්ජතනී ඊ උං ඔ ත්ථ ඉං ම්හා ආ ඌ සෙ ව්හං අ ම්හෙ.

a අජ්ජතනීඉච්චෙසා සඤ්ඤා හොති—ඊ, උං; ඔ, ත්ථ; ඉං, ම්හා; ආ, ඌ; සෙ, ව්හං; අ, ම්හෙ—ඉච්චෙතෙසං ද්වාදසන්නං පදානං.
අජ්ජතනී ඉච්චනෙන ක්වත්ථො? 'සමීපෙජ්ජතනී.'

24. භවිස්සන්ති ස්සති ස්සන්ති ස්සසි ස්සථ ස්සාමි ස්සාම
ස්සතෙ ස්සන්තෙ ස්සසෙ ස්සව්හෙ ස්සං ස්සාම්හෙ.

a භවිස්සන්තීඉච්චෙසා සඤ්ඤා හොති—ස්සති, ස්සන්ති; ස්සසි, ස්සථ; ස්සාමි, ස්සාම: ස්සතෙ, ස්සන්තෙ; ස්සසෙ, ස්සව්හෙ; ස්සං, ස්සාම්හෙ—ඉච්චෙතෙසං ද්වාදසන්නං පදානං.
භවිස්සන්තී ඉච්චනෙන ක්වත්ථො? 'අනාගතෙ භවිස්සන්ති.'

25. කාලාතිපත්ති ස්සා ස්සංසු ස්සෙ ස්සථ ස්සං ස්සම්හා
ස්සථ ස්සිංසු ස්සසෙ ස්සව්හෙ ස්සං ස්සාම්හසෙ.

a කාලාතිපත්තීඉච්චෙසා සඤ්ඤා හොති—ස්සා, ස්සංසු; ස්සෙ, ස්සථ; ස්සං, ස්සම්හා: ස්සථ, ස්සිංසු; ස්සසෙ, ස්සව්හෙ; ස්සං, ස්සාම්හසෙ—ඉච්චෙතෙසං ද්වාදසන්නං පදානං.
කාලාතිපත්තිඉච්චනෙන ක්වත්ථො? 'කිරියාතිපන්නෙ තීතෙ කාලාතිපත්ති.'

26. හීයත්තනී සත්තමී පඤ්චමී වත්තමානා සබ්බධාතුකං.

a හීයත්තනාදයො චතස්සො සබ්බධාතුක සඤ්ඤා හොති—ආගමා, ගච්ඡෙය්‍ය, ගච්ඡතු, ගච්ඡති.
සබ්බධාතුක ඉච්චනෙන ක්වත්ථො? 'ඉකාරාගමො අසබ්බධාතුකම්හි.'

ඉති ආඛ්‍යාතකප්පෙ පඨමො කණ්ඩො.

CHAPTER SECOND.

1. ධාතුලිඞ්ගෙහි පරාප්පච්චයා.

a ධාතුලිඞ්ගඉච්චෙතෙහි පරාප්පච්චයා හොන්ති—කාරෙති, ගච්ඡති; යො කොචි කරොති තං කුබ්බන්තමඤ්ඤො 'කරොහි' ඉච්චෙවං බ්‍රවීති='කාරෙති'; අථවා කරොන්තං පයොජයති='කාරෙති'; සංඝො පබ්බතමිව අත්තානමාචරති=පබ්බතායති; සමුද්දමිවඅත්තානමාචරති=සමුද්දායති; එවං සමුද්දො චිච්චිටමිව අත්තානමාචරති=චිච්චිටායති; වසිට්ඨස්ස අපච්චං=වාසිට්ඨො—එවමඤ්ඤෙපි යොජෙතබ්බා.

2. තිජගුපකිතමානෙහි ඛඡසා වා.

a තිජ, ගුප, කිත, මාන, ඉච්චෙතෙහි ධාතූහි, ඛඡසා ඉච්චෙතෙ පච්චයා හොන්ති වා—තිතික්ඛති, ජිගුච්ඡති, තිකිච්ඡති, වීමංසති.
වාති කිමත්ථං? 'තෙජති, ගොපති, මානෙති.'

3. භුජඝසහරසුපාදීහි තුමිච්ඡත්ථෙසු ච.

a භුජ, ඝස, හර, සුප, ඉච්චෙවමාදීහි ධාතූහි තුමිච්ඡත්ථෙසු ඛ, ඡ, ස, ඉච්චෙතෙ පච්චයා හොන්ති—භොත්තුමිච්ඡති=බුභුක්ඛති; ඝසිතුමිච්ඡති=ජිඝච්ඡති; හරිතුමිච්ඡති=ජිගිංසති; සුපිතුමිච්ඡති=සුසුසති; පාතුමිච්ඡති=පිවාසති.
වාති කිමත්ථං? 'භොත්තුමිච්ඡති.'
තුමිච්ඡත්ථෙසූති කිමත්ථං? 'භුජති.'

4. ආය නාමතො කත්තූපමානාදාචාරෙ.

a නාමතො කත්තූපමානා ඉච්චෙතස්මා ආචාරත්ථෙ ආය පච්චයො හොති—පබ්බතායති, චිච්චිටායති—එවමඤ්ඤෙපි යොජෙතබ්බා.

5. ඊ යූපමානා ච.

a නාමතො උපමානා ආචාරත්ථෙච ඊයපච්චයො හොති—අඡත්තං ඡත්තමිව ආචරති=ඡත්තීයති; අපුත්තං පුත්තමිව ආචරති=පුත්තීයති.

උපමානාති කිමත්ථං? 'ධම්මමාචරති.' ආචාරෙත්ති කිමත්ථං? 'ජනන මිව රක්ඛති'—එවමඤ්ඤෙපි යොජෙතබ්බා.

6. නාමම්හාත්තිච්ඡත්ථෙ.

a නාමම්හා අත්තනො ඉච්ඡත්ථෙ ඊයප්පච්චයො හොති—අත්තනො පත්තමිච්ඡතීති=පත්තීයති; එවං වත්ථීයති, පරික්ඛාරීයති, චීවරීයති, ධනීයති, පටීයති.

අත්තිච්ඡත්ථෙති කිමත්ථං? 'අඤ්ඤස්ස පත්තමිච්ඡති'—එවමඤ්ඤෙපි යොජෙතබ්බා.

7. ධාතූහි ණෙ ණය ණාපෙ ණාපයා කාරිතානි හෙත්වත්ථෙ.

a සබ්බෙහි ධාතූහි ණෙ, ණය, ණාපෙ, ණාපයා ඉච්චෙතෙ පච්චයා හොන්ති කාරිතසඤ්ඤා ච හෙත්වත්ථෙ—යො කොචි කරොති 'තං අඤ්ඤො කරොහි' ඉච්චෙවං බ්‍රවීති, අථ වා කරොන්තං පයොජෙති=කාරෙති, කාරයති, කාරාපෙති; කාරාපයති, යෙ කෙචි කරොන්ති තෙ අඤ්ඤෙ 'කරොථ කරොථ' ඉච්චෙවං බ්‍රුවන්ති=කාරෙන්ති, කාරයන්ති, කාරාපෙන්ති, කාරාපයන්ති; යො කොචි පචති තමඤ්ඤො 'පචාහි' ඉච්චෙවං බ්‍රවීති අථ වා පචන්තං පයොජෙති=පාචෙති, පාචයති, පාචාපෙති, පාචාපයති; යෙ කෙචි පචන්ති තෙ පචන්තෙ අඤ්ඤෙ 'පචථ පචථ' ඉච්චෙවං බ්‍රුවන්ති=පාචෙන්ති, පාචයන්ති, පාචාපෙන්ති, පාචාපයන්ති; එවං ගණෙති, ගණයති, ගණාපෙති, ගණාපයති; භාණෙති, භාණයති, භාණාපෙති, භාණාපයති: තථරිව අඤ්ඤෙපි යොජෙතබ්බා.

හෙත්වත්ථෙති කිමත්ථං? 'කරොති; පචති'—අත්ථග්ගහණෙන ලප්පච්චයො හොති 'ජොතලති.'

8. ධාතුරූපෙ නාමස්මා ණයො ච.

a තස්මා නාමස්මා ණයප්පච්චයො හොති කාරිතසඤ්ඤා ච ධාතුරූපෙ—හත්ථිනා අතික්කමති මග්ගං=අතිහත්ථයති; වීණාය උපගායති=උපවීණයති; දළ්හං කරොති විනයං=දළ්හයති; විසුද්ධා හොති රත්ති=විසුද්ධයති.

චසද්දග්ගහණෙන ආර, ආල, ඉච්චෙතෙ පච්චයා හොන්ති; 'අන්තරරති' 'උපක්කමාලති.'

9. භාවකම්මෙසු යො.

a සබ්බෙහි ධාතූහි භාවකම්මෙසු යප්පච්චයො හොති—ඨීයතෙ, බුජ්ඣීයතෙ, පච්චතෙ, ලබ්භතෙ, කරීයතෙ, ඉජ්ජතෙ, උච්චතෙ.

භාවකම්මෙසූති කිමත්ථං? කරොති, පචති, පඨති.

යොග්ගහණෙන අභාවකම්මෙසුපි යප්පච්චයො හොති; 'දිබ්බති.'

10. තස්ස චවග්ග යකාර වකාරත්තං සධාත්වන්තස්ස.

a තස්ස යප්පච්චයස්ස චවග්ග යකාර වකාරත්තං හොති ධාත්වන්තෙන සහ යථාසම්භවං — වුච්චතෙ, වුච්චන්තෙ; උච්චතෙ, උච්චන්තෙ; මජ්ජතෙ, මජ්ජන්තෙ; පච්චතෙ, පච්චන්තෙ; බුජ්ඣතෙ, බුජ්ඣන්තෙ; යුජ්ඣතෙ, යුජ්ඣන්තෙ; කුජ්ඣතෙ, කුජ්ඣන්තෙ; උජ්ඣතෙ, උජ්ඣන්තෙ; හඤ්ඤතෙ, හඤ්ඤන්තෙ; කය්‍යතෙ, කය්‍යන්තෙ; දිබ්බතෙ, දිබ්බන්තෙ.

11. ඉ ච ණ්ණා ගමො වා.

a සබ්බෙහි ධාතූහි යම්හි පච්චයෙ පරෙ ඉවණ්ණාගමො හොති වා — කරිය්‍යතෙ, කරීයන්ති; ගච්ඡීයතෙ, ගච්ඡිය්‍යන්ති.
වාතිකිමත්ථං ? 'කය්‍යතෙ.'

12. පුබ්බරූපඤ්ච.

a සබ්බෙහි ධාතූහි යප්පච්චයො පුබ්බරූපමාපජ්ජතෙ වා — වුඩ්ඪතෙ, ඵල්ලතෙ, දම්මතෙ, ලබ්භතෙ, සක්කතෙ, දිස්සතෙ.
වාතිකිමත්ථං ? 'දම්‍යතෙ.'

13. යථාකත්තරිච.

a යථා භාවකම්මසු යප්පච්චයස්සා දෙසො හොති තථා කත්තරි යප්පච්චයස්සා දෙසො කාතබ්බො — බුජ්ඣති, විජ්ඣති, මඤ්ඤති, සිබ්බති.

14. භූවාදිතො අ.

a භූ ඉච්චෙවමාදිතො ධාතුගණතො අප්පච්චයො හොති කත්තරි — භවති, පඨති, පචති, යජති.

15. රුධාදිතො නිග්ගහීතපුබ්බඤ්ච.

a රුධ ඉච්චෙවමාදිතො ධාතුගණතො අප්පච්චයො හොති කත්තරි පුබ්බෙ නිග්ගහීතාගමො හොති; රුන්ධති, භින්දති, ඡින්දති. චසද්දග්ගහණෙන ඉ, ඊ, එ, ඔ, ඉච්චෙතෙ පච්චයා හොන්ති නිග්ගහීතපුබ්බඤ්ච; රුන්ධිති, රුන්ධීති, රුන්ධෙති, සුම්භොති.

16. දිවාදිතො යො.

a දිවාදිතො ධාතුගණතො යප්පච්චයො හොති කත්තරි — දිබ්බති, සිබ්බති, යුජ්ඣති, විජ්ඣති, බුජ්ඣති.

17. ස්වාදිතො ණු ණා උණා ච.

a සු ඉච්චෙවමාදිතො ධාතුගණතො ණු ණා උණා ඉච්චෙතෙ

පච්චයා හොන්ති කත්තරි — අභිසුණොති, අභිසුණාති; සංවුණොති, සංවුණාති; ආවුණොති, ආවුණාති; පාපුණොති, පාපුණාති.

18. කියාදිතො ණා.

a කී ඉච්චෙවමාදිතො ධාතුගණතො ණාප්පච්චයො හොති කත්තරි — කිණාති, ජිනාති, ධුනාති, ලුණාති, පුණාති.

19. ගහාදිතොප්පණ්හාච.

a ගහ ඉච්චෙවමාදිතො ධාතුගණතො ප්ප, ණ්හා, ඉච්චෙතෙ පච්චයා හොන්ති කත්තරි — ඝෙප්පති, ගණ්හාති.

20. තනාදිතො ඔ යිර.

a තනු ඉච්චෙවමාදිතො ධාතුගණතො ඔ, යිර, ඉච්චෙතෙ පච්චයා හොන්ති කත්තරි — තනොති, තනොන්ති, කරොති, කරොන්ති, කයිරති, කයිරන්ති.

21. චුරාදිතො ණෙ ණයා.

a චුර ඉච්චෙවමාදිතො ධාතුගණතො ණෙ, ණය, ඉච්චෙතෙ පච්චයා හොන්ති කත්තරි — චොරෙති, චොරයන්ති; චින්තෙති, චින්තයන්ති; මන්තෙති, මන්තයන්ති.

22. අත්තනොපදානි භාවෙ ච කම්මණි.

a භාවෙ කම්මණි ච අත්තනොපදානි හොන්ති — උච්චතෙ, උච්චන්තෙ; ලබ්භතෙ, ලබ්භන්තෙ; මජ්ජතෙ, මජ්ජන්තෙ; සුජ්ඣතෙ, සුජ්ඣන්තෙ; කය්‍යතෙ, කය්‍යන්තෙ.

23. කත්තරි ච.

a කත්තරි ච අත්තනොපදානි හොන්ති — මඤ්ඤතෙ, රොචතෙ, සොචතෙ, සොභතෙ, බුජ්ඣතෙ, ජයතෙ.

24. ධාතුප්පච්චයෙහි විභත්තියො.

a ධාතුනිද්දිට්ඨෙහි පච්චයෙහි ඛාදිකාරිතන්තෙහි විභත්තියො හොන්ති — තිතික්ඛති, ජිගුච්ඡති, වීමංසති: තථාකං සමුද්දමිව අත්තානමාචරති = සමුද්දායති; පුත්තීයති, පාචයති.

25. කත්තරි පරස්සපදං.

a කත්තරි පරස්සපදං හොති — කරොති, පචති, පඨති, ගච්ඡති.

26. භූවාදයො ධාතවො.

a භූ ඉච්චෙවමාදයො යෙ සද්දගණා තෙ ධාතු සඤ්ඤා හොන්ති — භවති, භවන්ති; පචති, පචන්ති; චරති; චින්තයති; ගච්ඡති.

ඉති ආඛ්‍යාතකප්පෙ දුතියො කණ්ඩො.

CHAPTER THIRD.

1. ඛඡසාදිවණ්ණාන මෙකස්සරාණං ද්වෙභාවො.

a ආදිභූතානං වණ්ණානං එකස්සරාණං ඛඡසෙ ද්වෙභාවො හොති — තිතික්ඛති, ජිගුච්ඡති, තිකිච්ඡති, වීමංසති, බුභුක්ඛති, පිවාසති, දද්දල්ලති, ජහාති, චංකමති.

ඛඡිති කිමත්ථං? 'කමති, චලති.'

2. පුබ්බො බ්භාසො.

a ද්වෙභූතස්ස ධාතුස්ස යො පුබ්බො සො අබ්භාස සඤ්ඤො හොති — දධාති, දදාති, බභූව.

3. රස්සො.

a අබ්භාසෙ වත්තමානස්ස සරස්ස රස්සො හොති — දදාති, දධාති; ජහාති.

4. දුතිය චතුත්ථානං පඨම තතියා.

a අබ්භාසගතානං දුතිය චතුත්ථානං පඨම තතියා හොන්ති — චිච්ඡෙද, බුභුක්ඛති, බභූව, දධාති.

5. කවග්ගස්ස චවග්ගො.

a අබ්භාසෙ වත්තමානස්ස කවග්ගස්ස චවග්ගො හොති — චිකිච්ඡති, ජිගුච්ඡති, ජිඝච්ඡති, චංකමති, ජිගිංසති, ජංගමති.

6. මානකිතානං වතතත්තං වා.

a මානකිත ඉච්චෙතෙසං ධාතූනං අබ්භාසගතානං වකාර තකාරත්තං හොති වා යථාසංඛ්‍යං — වීමංසති, තිකිච්ඡති.

වාති කිමත්ථං? 'චිකිච්ඡති.'

7. හස්සජො.

a හකාරස්ස අබ්භාසෙ වත්තමානස්ස ජො හොති — ජහාති, ජුහති, ජුහොති, ජහාර.

8. අන්තස්සිවණ්ණාකාරො වා.

a අබ්භාසස්ස අන්තස්ස ඉවණ්ණො හොති අකාරො වා — ජිගුච්ඡති, පිවාසති, වීමංසති, ජිඝච්ඡති, බභූව, දධාති.

වාති කිමත්ථං? 'බුභුක්ඛති.'

9. නිග්ගහීතංච.

a අබ්භාසස්සඅන්තෙ නිග්ගහීතාගමොහොතිවා — චංකමති, චඤ්චලති, ජංගමති.

වාතිකිමත්ථං ? 'පිවාසති, දද්දල්ලති.'

10. තතොපාමානානං වාමංසෙසු.

a තතො අබ්භාසතො පාමානං ධාතූනං වාමං ඉච්චෙතෙ ආදෙසාහොන්තිවා යථාසංඛ්‍යං සෙපච්චයෙපරෙ — පිවාසති, වීමංසති.

11. ඨා තිට්ඨො.

a ඨා ඉච්චෙතස්ස ධාතුස්ස තිට්ඨාදෙසොහොතිවා — තිට්ඨති, තිට්ඨතු; තිට්ඨෙය්‍ය, තිට්ඨෙය්‍යුං.

වාති කිමත්ථං ? 'ඨාති.'

12. පා පිබො.

a පාඉච්චෙතස්ස ධාතුස්ස පිබාදෙසොහොතිවා — පිබති, පිබතු, පිබෙය්‍ය.

වාතිකිමත්ථං ? 'පාති.'

13. ඤාස්ස ජා ජන් නා.

a ඤාඉච්චෙතස්ස ධාතුස්ස ජා, ජන්, නා දෙසාහොන්තිවා — ජානාති, ජානෙය්‍ය, ජානියා, ජඤ්ඤා, නායති.

වාතිකිමත්ථං ? 'විඤ්ඤායති.'

14. දිසස්සපස්සදිස්සදක්ඛාවා.

a දිසඉච්චෙතස්ස ධාතුස්ස පස්ස, දිස්ස, දක්ඛ ඉච්චෙතෙ ආදෙසා හොන්තිවා — පස්සති, දිස්සති, දක්ඛති.

වාතිකිමත්ථං ? 'අද්දස.'

15. ව්‍යඤ්ජනන්තස්සචො ඡප්පච්චයෙසුච.

a ව්‍යඤ්ජනන්තස්ස ධාතුස්සචොහොති ඡප්පච්චයෙපරෙ — ජිගුච්ඡති, තිකිච්ඡති, ජිඝච්ඡති.

16. කොඛෙච.

ව්‍යඤ්ජනන්තස්ස ධාතුස්ස කොහොති ඛප්පච්චයෙපරෙ — තිතික්ඛති, බුභුක්ඛති.

17. හරස්සගිංසෙ.

a හරඉච්චෙතස්ස ධාතුස්ස සබ්බස්සෙව ගිං ආදෙසොහොති සෙප්පච්චයෙපරෙ — ජිගිංසති.

18. බ්‍රූභූනමාහ භූවාපරොක්ඛායං.

a බ්‍රූභූ ඉච්චෙතෙසංධාතූනං ආහ, භූව, ඉච්චෙතෙ ආදෙසා හොන්ති පරොක්ඛායං විභත්තියං — ආහ, ආහු, බභූව, බභූවු.

පරොක්ඛායන්ති කිමත්ථං ? 'අබ්‍රවුං'.

19. ගමිස්සන්තො ච්ඡො වා සබ්බාසු.

a ගමුඉච්චෙතස්ස ධාතුස්ස අන්තොමකාරස්ස ච්ඡො හොති වා ස බ්බාසු පච්චයවිභත්තීසු —— ගච්ඡමානො, ගච්ඡන්තො ; ගච්ඡති, ගමෙති ; ගච්ඡතු, ගමෙතු ; ගච්ඡෙය්‍ය, ගමෙය්‍ය ; අගච්ඡ, අගම ; අගච්ඡි, අගමි ; ගච්ඡිස්සති, ගමිස්සති ; අගච්ඡිස්සා, අගමිස්සා ; අගච්ඡීයති, අගමීයති.

ගමිස්සෙති කිමත්ථං? 'ඉච්ඡති.'

20. වචස්සජ්ජතනියම්හි අකාරො ඔ.

a වචඉච්චෙතස්සධාතුස්ස අකාරො ඔත්තමාපජ්ජතෙ අජ්ජතනිම්හි —— අවොච, අවොචුං.

අජ්ජතනිම්හීති කිමත්ථං ? 'අවච, අවචු.'

21. අකාරො දීඝං හිමිමෙසු.

a අකාරො දීඝමාපජ්ජතෙ, හි, මි, ම, ඉච්චෙතාසු විභත්තීසු —— ගච්ඡාහි, ගච්ඡාමි, ගච්ඡාම, ගච්ඡාමසෙ—මිකාරග්ගහණෙන හිවි භත්තිම්හි අකාරස්සවිදීඝං නාපජ්ජතෙ—ගච්ඡ හි.

22. හිලොපං වා.

a හිවිභත්තිලොපමාපජ්ජතෙ වා —— ගච්ඡ, ගච්ඡාහි ; ගම, ගමෙහි ; ගමය, ගමයාහි.

හීති කිමත්ථං ? 'ගච්ඡති, ගමීයති.'

23. හොතිස්සරෙහො හෙහ භවිස්සන්තිම්හි ස්සස්ස ච.

a හූ ඉච්චෙතස්ස ධාතුස්ස සරෙ, එහ, ඔහ, එත්තමාපජ්ජතෙ භවිස්සන්තිම්හි විභත්තිම්හි, ස්සස්ස ච ලොපො හොති වා —— හෙහිති, හෙහින්ති ; හොහිති, හොහින්ති ; හෙති, හෙන්ති ; හෙහිස්සති, හෙහිස්සන්ති ; හොහිස්සති, හොහිස්සන්ති ; හෙස්සති, හෙස්සන්ති.

හූති කිමත්ථං ? 'භවිස්සති, භවිස්සන්ති.' භවිස්සන්තිම්හීති කිමත්ථං ? 'හොති, හොන්ති.'

24. කරස්සසප්පච්චයස්සකාහො.

a කරඉච්චෙතස්සධාතුස්ස සප්පච්චයස්සකාහ ආදෙසොහොති වා භවිස්සන්තිවිභත්තිම්හි ස්සස්සනිච්චං ලොපොහොති —— කාහති, කාහිති ; කාහසි, කාහිසි ; කාහාමි, කාහාම.

වාති කිමත්ථං ? 'කරිස්සති, කරිස්සන්ති'—සප්පච්චයග්ගහණෙන අඤ්ඤෙසුපි භවිස්සන්තියා විභත්තියා—ඛාමි, ඛාම ; ඡාමි, ඡාම ; ඉච්චාදෙසා හොන්ති. 'වක්ඛාමි, වක්ඛාම'-වචධාතු, 'වච්ඡාමි' 'වච්ඡාම-වසධාතු.'

ඉති ආඛ්‍යාතකප්පෙ තතියො කණ්ඩො.

CHAPTER FOURTH.

1. දන්තස්සංමිමෙසු.

a දම්ඉච්චෙතස්ස ධාතුස්ස අන්තස්ස අංහොති මිමඉච්චෙතෙසු — දම්මි, දම්ම.

2. අසංයොගන්තස්සවුද්ධිකාරිතෙ.

a අසංයොගන්තස්ස ධාතුස්ස කාරිතෙවුද්ධිහොති — කාරෙති, කාරෙන්ති; කාරයති, කාරයන්ති; කාරාපෙති, කාරාපෙන්ති; කාරාපයති, කාරාපයන්ති.

අසංයොගන්තස්සෙතිකිමත්ථං? 'චින්තයති, මන්තයති.'

3. ඝටාදීනංවා.

a ඝටාදීනං ධාතූනං අසංයොගන්තානං වුද්ධිහොතිවා කාරිතෙ — ඝාටෙති, ඝටෙති, ඝාටයති, ඝාටාපෙති, ඝටාපයති, ඝටාපයති; ගාමෙති, ගමෙති, ගාමයති, ගමයති.

ඝටාදීනමිතිකිමත්ථං? 'කාරෙති.'

4. අඤ්ඤෙසුච.

a අඤ්ඤෙසුච පච්චයෙසු සබ්බෙසංධාතූනං අසංයොගන්තානං වුද්ධිහොති — ජයති, භවති, හොති — චසද්දග්ගහණෙන ණුපච්චයස්සාපි වුද්ධිහොති, අභිසුණොති, සංවුණොති.

5. ගුහදුසානංදීඝං.

a ගුහදුසඉච්චෙතෙසං ධාතූනං සරෙ දීඝමාපජ්ජතෙ කාරිතෙ — ගූහයති, දූසයති.

6. වච වස වහා දීනමුකාරොවස්සයෙ.

a වච වස වහ ඉච්චෙවමාදීනං ධාතූනං වකාරස්ස උකාරො හොති යෙපච්චයෙපරෙ — උච්චතෙ, වුච්චති, වුස්සති, වුය්හති.

7. හවිපරියයොලොවා.

a හකාරස්සවිපරියයොහොති යපච්චයෙපරෙ යපච්චයස්සච ලොහොතිවා — වුය්හති, වුළ්හති.

8. ගහස්සඝෙප්පෙ.

a ගහඉච්චෙතස්සධාතුස්ස සබ්බස්සෙව ඝෙකාරොහොති ප්පපච්චයෙපරෙ — ඝෙප්පති.

9. හලොපොණ්හාම්හි.

a ගහඉච්චෙතස්ස ධාතුස්ස හකාරස්ස ලොපොහොති ණ්හාම්හි පච්චයෙපරෙ — ගණ්හාති.

10. කරස්සකාසත්තමජ්ජතනිම්හි.

a කරඉච්චෙතස්සධාතුස්ස සබ්බස්සකාසත්තංහොතිවා අජ්ජතනි විභත්තිම්හි—අකාසි, අකාසුං; අකරි, අකරුං—අත්තමිති භාවනිද්දෙසෙන අඤ්ඤත්ථාපිසාගමොහොති, අහොසි, අදාසි.

11. අසස්මා මිමානං ම්හිම්හාන්තලොපොච.

a අසඉච්චෙතායධාතුයා මිම ඉච්චෙතාසං විභත්තීනං ම්හි ම්හාදෙසාහොන්තිවා ධාතුස්සන්තො ලොපොච—අම්හි, අම්හ; අස්මි, අස්ම.

12. ථස්සත්ථත්තං.

a අසඉච්චෙතස්සධාතුස්ස ථස්සවිභත්තිස්ස ත්ථත්තංහොති ධාත්වන්තස්සලොපොච—අත්ථ.

13. තිස්ස ත්ථිත්තං.

a අසඉච්චෙතායධාතුයා තිස්සවිභත්තිස්ස ත්ථිත්තංහොති ධාත්වන්තස්සලොපොච—අත්ථි.

14. තුස්සත්ථුත්තං.

a අසඉච්චෙතායධාතුයාතුස්ස විභත්තිස්ස ත්ථුත්තංහොති ධාත්වන්තස්සලොපොච—අත්ථු.

15. සිම්හිච.

a අසස්සෙවධාතුස්ස සිම්හි විභත්තිම්හි අන්තස්සලොපොචහොති—කොනුත්වමසි.

16. ලභස්මා ඊ ඉන්නං ත්ථ ත්ථං.

a ලභඉච්චෙතායධාතුයා ඊංඉන්නං විභත්තීනං ත්ථත්ථං ආදෙසාහොන්ති ධාත්වන්තස්සලොපොච—අලත්ථ, අලත්ථං.

17. කුසස්මාදිච්ඡි.

a කුසඉච්චෙතාය ධාතුයා ඊවිභත්තිස්ස ච්ඡිහොති ධාත්වන්තස්සලොපොච—අක්කොච්ඡි.

18. දාධාතුස්සදජ්ජංවා.

a දාඉච්චෙතස්ස ධාතුස්ස සබ්බස්ස දජ්ජාදෙසොහොතිවා—දජ්ජාමි, දජ්ජෙය්‍ය, දදාමි, දදෙය්‍ය.

19. වදස්ස වජ්ජං.

a වදඉච්චෙතස්ස ධාතුස්ස සබ්බස්ස වජ්ජාදෙසොහොතිවා—වජ්ජාමි, වජ්ජෙය්‍ය, වදාමි, වදෙය්‍ය.

20. ගමුස්සඝම්මං.

a ගමුඉච්චෙතස්සධාතුස්ස සබ්බස්ස ඝම්මාදෙසො හොතිවා — ඝම්මතු, ඝම්මාහි, ඝම්මාමි.

වාතිකිමත්ථං ? 'ගච්ඡතු, ගච්ඡාහි, ගච්ඡාමි.'

21. යම්හිදා ධා මා ඨා හා පා මහ මථා දීනමී.

a යම්හි පච්චයෙපරෙ දා ධා මා ඨා හා පා මහ මථ ඉච්චෙවමාදීනං අන්තො ඊකාරමාපජ්ජතෙ — දීයති, ධීයති, මීයති, ඨීයති, හීයති, පීයති, මහීයති, මථීයති.

22. යජස්සාදිස්සි.

a යජඉච්චෙතස්ස ධාතුස්ස ආදිස්ස ඉකාරාදෙසො හොති යෙපච්චයෙපරෙ — ඉජ්ජතෙ මයාබුද්ධො.

23. සබ්බතොඋං ඉංසු.

a සබ්බෙහිධාතූහි උංවිභත්තිස්ස ඉංස්වාදෙසොහොති — උපසංකමිංසු, නිසීදිංසු.

24. ජරමරාණං ජීර ජීය්‍ය මීය්‍යාවා.

a ජරමරඉච්චෙතෙසංධාතූනං ජීරජීය්‍යමීය්‍යආදෙසාහොන්ති වා — ජීරති, ජීරන්ති ; ජීය්‍යති, ජීය්‍යන්ති ; මීයති, මිය්‍යන්ති ; මරති, මරන්ති.

25. සබ්බත්ථාසස්සාදිලොපොච.

a සබ්බත්ථවිභත්තිප්පච්චයෙසු අසඉච්චෙතස්ස ධාතුස්ස ආදිස්ස ලොපොහොතිවා — සියා, සන්ති, සන්තො, සමානො.

වාතිකිමත්ථං ? 'අසි.'

26. අසබ්බධාතුකෙ භූ.

a අසඉච්චෙවධාතුස්ස භූහොතිවා අසබ්බධාතුකෙපරෙ — භවිස්සති, භවිස්සන්ති.

වාතිකිමත්ථං ? 'ආසුං.'

27. එය්‍යස්සඤාතො ඉයාඤ්ඤාවා.

a එය්‍යවිභත්තිස්සඤා, ඉච්චෙතාය ධාතුයා පරස්ස ඉයාඤ්ඤාදෙසාහොන්තිවා — ජානියා, ජඤ්ඤා.

වාතිකිමත්ථං ? 'ජානෙය්‍ය.'

28. නාස්සලොපොයකාරත්තං.

a ඤාඉච්චෙතාය ධාතුයානාපච්චයස්ස ලොපොහොතිවා යකාරත්තඤ්ච — ජඤ්ඤා, නායති.

වාතිකිමත්ථං ? 'ජානාති.'

29. ලොපඤ්චෙත්තමකාරො.

a අකාරප්පච්චයො ලොපමාපජ්ජතෙ එත්තඤ්චහොතිවා — වජ්ජෙමි, වදෙමි; වජ්ජාමි, වදාමි.

30. උත්තමොකාරො.

a ඔකාරප්පච්චයො උත්තමාපජ්ජතෙවා — කුරුතෙ කරොති.

ඔකාරොතිකිමත්ථං? 'හොති.'

31. කරස්ස කාරොච.

a **කරඉච්චෙතස්ස ධාතුස්ස අකාරො උත්තමාපජ්ජතෙවා — කුරුතෙ, කරොති; කුබ්බතෙ, කුබ්බති, කයිරති.**

කරස්සෙතිකිමත්ථං? 'සරති, මරති.'

32. ඔ අව සරෙ.

a **ඔකාරස්සධාත්වන්තස්ස සරෙපරෙ අවහොතිවා — චවති, භවති.**

සරෙතිකිමත්ථං? 'හොති'—ඔතිකිමත්ථං? 'ජයති.'

33. එ අය.

a **එකාරස්සධාත්වන්තස්ස සරෙපරෙ අයාදෙසොහොතිවා — නයති, ජයති.**

සරෙතිකිමත්ථං? 'නෙති.'

34. තෙආවායාකාරිතෙ.

a **තෙ ඔ එ ඉච්චෙතෙ ආව ආය ආදෙසෙ පාප්පුණන්ති කාරිතෙ — ලාවෙති, නායෙති—යොගවිභාගෙන අඤ්ඤස්මිපි ආයහොති, ගායති.**

35. ඉකාරාගමො අසබ්බධාතුකම්හි.

a **සබ්බම්හි අසබ්බධාතුකම්හි ඉකාරාගමොහොති — ගමිස්සති, කරිස්සති, ලභිස්සති, පචිස්සති.**

අසබ්බධාතුකම්හීතිකිමත්ථං? 'ගච්ඡති, කරොති, ලභති, පචති.'

36. ක්වචිධාතුවිභත්තිප්පච්චයානං දීඝවිපරීතාදෙස ලොපාගමාච.

a **ඉධආඛ්‍යාතෙ අනිප්පන්නෙසු සාධනෙසු ක්වචි ධාතුවිභත්තිප්පච්චයානං දීඝවිපරීත ආදෙසලොප ආගම ඉච්චෙතානි කාරියානි ජිනවචනානුරූපානි කාතබ්බානි — ජායති, කරෙය්‍ය, ජානියා, සියා, කරෙ, ගච්ඡෙ, ජඤ්ඤා, වක්ඛෙථ, දක්ඛෙථ, දිච්ඡති, ආගච්ඡුං, අහොසි, අහෙසුං ඉච්චෙවමාදීනි අඤ්ඤානිපි සාධනානි යොජෙතබ්බානි.**

37. අත්තනොපදානි පරස්සපදත්තං.

අත්තනොපදානි ක්වචි පරස්සපදමාපජ්ජන්තෙ — වුච්චති, ලබ්භති, පච්චති, කරීයති, සිජ්ඣති.

ක්වචීතිකිමත්ථං? 'වුච්චතෙ, ලබ්භතෙ, පච්චතෙ, කරීයතෙ, සිජ්ඣතෙ.'

38. අකාරාගමො හීයත්තනජ්ජතනීකාලාතිපත්තීසු.

ක්වචි අකාරාගමො හොති හීයත්තනජ්ජතනී කාලාතිපත්ති ඉච්චෙතාසු විභත්තීසු — අගමා, අගමී, අගමිස්සා.

ක්වචීතිකිමත්ථං? 'ගමා, ගමී, ගමිස්සා.'

39. බ්‍රූතො ඊ තිම්හි.

බ්‍රූ ඉච්චෙතාය ධාතුයා ඊකාරාගමො හොති තිම්හි විභත්තිම්හි — බ්‍රවීති.

40. ධාතුස්සන්තො ලොපොනෙකසරස්ස.

ධාතුස්ස අන්තො ක්වචි ලොපො හොති අනෙකසරස්ස — ගච්ඡති, පචති, සරති, මරති, චරති.

අනෙකසරස්සෙතිකිමත්ථං? 'පාති, යාති, දාති, භාති, වාති' — ක්වචීති කිමත්ථං? 'මහීයති, මරීයති.'

41. ඉසුයමානමන්තො ච්ඡො වා.

ඉසු යම ඉච්චෙවමාදීනං ධාතූනමන්තො ච්ඡො හොති වා — ඉච්ඡති, නියච්ඡති.

වාතිකිමත්ථං? 'එසති, නියමති.'

42. කාරිතානං ණො ලොපං

කාරිත ඉච්චෙවමෙතෙසං පච්චයානං ණො ලොපමාපජ්ජතෙ — කාරෙති, කාරයති, කාරාපෙති, කාරාපයති.

සාසනත්ථං සමුද්දිට්ඨං මයාඛ්‍යාතං සමාසතො
සකබුද්ධිවිසෙසෙන චින්තයන්තු විචක්ඛණා.

ඉති ආඛ්‍යාතකප්පෙ චතුත්ථො කණ්ඩො.